14th International Joint Conference on Natural Language Processing and the 4th Conference of the Asia-Pacific Chapter of the Association for Computational Linguistics (IJCNLP-AACL 2025)

System Demonstrations

Mumbai, India
20-24 December 2025

ISBN: 979-8-3313-3245-7

Printed from e-media with permission by:

Curran Associates, Inc.
57 Morehouse Lane
Red Hook, NY 12571

Some format issues inherent in the e-media version may also appear in this print version.

Printed with permission by Curran Associates, Inc. (2026)

For permission requests, please contact the Association for Computational Linguistics at the address below.

Association for Computational Linguistics
209 N. Eighth Street
Stroudsburg, Pennsylvania 18360

Phone: 1-570-476-8006
Fax: 1-570-476-0860

acl@aclweb.org

Additional copies of this publication are available from:

Curran Associates, Inc.
57 Morehouse Lane
Red Hook, NY 12571 USA
Phone: 845-758-0400
Fax: 845-758-2633
Email: curran@proceedings.com
Web: www.proceedings.com

IJCNLP-AACL 2025

The 14th International Joint Conference on Natural Language Processing and The 4th Conference of the Asia-Pacific Chapter of the Association for Computational Linguistics: System Demonstrations

Proceedings of the System Demonstrations

December 20-24, 2025

Introduction

Welcome to the System Demonstrations of The 14th International Joint Conference on Natural Language Processing and The 4th Conference of the Asia-Pacific Chapter of the Association for Computational Linguistics (IJCNLP-AACL 2025).

System demonstrations play a vital role in bridging the gap between cutting-edge research and practical applications in natural language processing. As the field continues to evolve rapidly with large language models and multimodal systems, showcasing working prototypes has become essential for understanding real-world feasibility and impact. This demonstration track provides a unique venue for researchers to present their innovative NLP systems and engage with the community through live interactions.

This year, we received 21 demonstration submissions spanning diverse NLP applications including dialogue systems, information extraction, and responsible AI tools. After a rigorous review process, we selected 11 high-quality demonstrations that showcase both technical innovation and practical utility. Each accepted demonstration was evaluated based on system novelty, implementation robustness, and potential for real-world deployment.

We are grateful to our program committee members for their thorough evaluations and constructive feedback. We also thank all authors for their contributions and for advancing the state of the art in NLP system development.

We hope you enjoy the demonstration sessions and find inspiration for your own research and development endeavors.

Ayu Purwarianti and Xuebo Liu
IJCNLP-AACL 2025 System Demonstration Chairs

Mumbai, India December 2025

Program Committee

Demonstration Chairs

Ayu Purwarianti, Bandung Institute of Technology
Xuebo Liu, Harbin Institute of Technology, Shenzhen

Reviewers

Mariia Fedorova
Musa Izzanardi Wijanarko
Chaoqun He
Carsten Schnober
Javier García Gilabert
Linfan Zhang
Jungyeul Park
HYUNBYUNG PARK
Yasmin Moslem
Ke Lin
Joanne Boisson
Yudong Tao
Mario Ezra Aragon
Kshitij P Fadnis
Nischal Reddy Chandra
Seongbum Seo
Chuan-Ju Wang
Xiaochang Li
Zhexiong Liu
Bram Vanroy
Shuo Xing
Tianlin Zhang
Tim Schopf
Ona de Gibert
Hasan Iqbal
Dachun Sun
Aunabil Chakma
Tuan-Phong Nguyen
Marek Suppa
Qiang Sun
Christopher Klamm
John Philip McCrae
Youyang Ng
Yoshihide Kato
Luigi Di Caro
Sanjay Das
Sotaro Takeshita
Suman Adhya
Xin Xu
Pengfei Yu
Esteban Garces Arias

Ruochen Li
Shuhang Lin
Christian Heumann
Kehai Chen
Yide Ran
Liang Xie
Hao Yu
Zibu Wei
Jiahe Song
Tim Fischer
Herry Sujaini
Afiyati
Moch Arif Bijaksana
Faza Thirafi
Rifki Afina Putri
Muqtafi Akhmad
Arie Ardiyanti Suryani
Fariska Zakhralativa Ruskanda

Table of Contents

ImageTra: Real-Time Translation for Texts in Image and Video

Hour Kaing[1] **Jiannan Mao**[2] **Haiyue Song**[1]
Chenchen Ding[1] **Hideki Tanaka**[1] **Masao Utiyama**[1]
[1]ASTREC, UCRI, NICT, Japan [2]Gifu University, Gifu, Japan
[1]{hour_kaing, haiyue.song, chenchen.ding, hideki.tanaka, mutiyama}@nict.go.jp
[2]mao@mat.info.gifu-u.ac.jp

Abstract

There has been a growing research interest in in-image machine translation, which involves translating texts in images from one language to another. Recent studies continue to explore pipeline-based systems due to its straightforward construction and the consistent improvement of its underlined components. However, the existing implementation for such pipeline often lack extensibility, composability, and support for real-time translation. Therefore, this work introduces *ImageTra*—an open-source toolkit designed to facilitate the development of the pipeline-based system of in-image machine translation. The toolkit integrates state-of-the-art open-source models and tools, and is designed with a focus on modularity and efficiency, making it particularly well-suited for real-time translation. The toolkit is released at `https://github.com/hour/imagetra`.

1 Introduction

In-image machine translation (IIMT) refers to the task of translating texts in an image from one language to another, and generating a new image that embeds the translations (Mansimov et al., 2020; Tian et al., 2023, 2025). Ultimately, the background and text style of the translations inherit the characteristics of the original texts, as illustrated in Figure 1. Such systems have a significant value for research and a wide range of applications, including platform-independent automatic subtitle translation, manga translation, and real-time translation from camera input. Although commercial products like Google Translate offer real-time translation features, their underlying technical solutions are not transparent and difficult to customize for other purposes or downstream applications.

Recent studies continue to explore pipeline-based systems due to their straightforward construction (Qian et al., 2024; Vaidya et al., 2025; Kaing et al., 2025). These systems typically consist of three main components: optical character recognition (OCR), machine translation (MT), and scene text editing (STE). The pipeline-based systems remain the state-of-the-art compared to end-to-end solutions (Salesky et al., 2024), primarily because of the task difficulty and data bottlenecks where the models training rely heavily on synthetic data in end-to-end approaches (Li et al., 2025). In contrast, the data available for each component of the pipeline-based systems is richer and multilingual (Long et al., 2022; Bañón et al., 2020), making it easier to enhance individual components and, in turn, improve the overall performance of the pipeline-based systems.

Figure 1: A translation example using ImageTra.

Although open-source tools are available for each component thanks to active research communities, they were developed and improved independently, without consideration for compatibility with other components when building a pipeline-based system. While assembling these tools into an IIMT pipeline may seem straightforward, researchers and practitioners still need to invest a significant amount of effort in implementation. Although several studies have released code to reproduce their pipelines (Qian et al., 2024; Vaidya et al., 2025), existing implementations often lack extensibility and composability, and they do not support real-time translation.

This work aims to reduce that burden by introducing `ImageTra`—an open-source toolkit designed to facilitate the development of IIMT systems. For composibility, our toolkit enable researchers and practitioners to plug and play various state-of-the-art open-source models and tools to

Proceedings of The 14th International Joint Conference on Natural Language Processing and The 4th Conference of the Asia-Pacific Chapter of the Association for Computational Linguistics: System Demonstrations, pages 1–8

build IIMT systems capable of translating text in images, videos, or a live camera video (real-time translation)[1]. For extensibility, the toolkit is feasible to customize each component to support other tools or models, which is beneficial for both academic and industrial research. Both composibility and extensibility of our toolkit are demonstrated in Section 3.3. Additionally, for real-time translation, our toolkit has features to enhance efficiency such as translation caching, text tracking, and API hosting. For accessibility, our toolkit is implemented in Python and is pip-installable, and is released under the MIT license, permitting unrestricted use, modification, and redistribution.

For evaluation, we assess the efficiency and quality of various pipeline configurations, with particular focus on OCR, and analyze the impact of the translation caching and text tracking features on efficiency in Section 4. The experimental results demonstrate that both features significantly reduce the pipeline's inference time.

2 Related Works

In-Image Machine Translation. This task is recently getting many attentions due to the advancement of machine learning techniques. Many works have explored the end-to-end approaches (Mansimov et al., 2020; Salesky et al., 2021; Ma et al., 2023; Lan et al., 2024; Tian et al., 2023, 2025), which are not generalized yet particularly on the scene text scenario. Meanwhile, the pipeline-based systems have been explored as well by integrating OCR, MT, and STE systems into a pipeline (Qian et al., 2024; Vaidya et al., 2025; Kaing et al., 2025). The implementation of these works are mostly opened mainly to reproduce their results, which are not easy to be adapted especially to support real-time translation.

Optical Character Recognition. This task is a long-standing task in computer vision, and modern OCR systems face increasingly complex challenges, such as handling document-level and scene text images. These tasks are typically divided into two subtasks: text detection (Zhou et al., 2017; Baek et al., 2019; Liao et al., 2020) and text recognition (Shi et al., 2016; Bautista and Atienza, 2022; Du et al., 2025). A wide range of open-source OCR tools are available, many of which continue to improve in terms of accuracy, efficiency, and language coverage. For example, but not limited to, DocTR supports multiple model architectures, allowing users to choose specific models for detection and recognition. Similarly, OpenOCR supports several detection and recognition models including its own state-of-the-art models (Du et al., 2025). On the other hand, tools like EasyOCR and PaddleOCR emphasize support for diverse languages, with PaddleOCR also being recognized for its computational efficiency (Cui et al., 2025).

Machine Translation. Text-based machine translation provides an efficient way to transform information from one language into another (Bahdanau et al., 2014; Vaswani et al., 2017). Many effective techniques have been introduced for improving translation quality of low-resource languages such as data augmentation (Sennrich et al., 2016; Kaing et al., 2024), multilingual training (Dabre et al., 2020; Costa-Jussà et al., 2022), and multimodal training (Elliott et al., 2016; Hirasawa et al., 2020; Gu et al., 2021), among others. Multilingual models offer other advantages especially their efficiency, as they can handle diverse languages within a single model. Therefore, our toolkit begins with support for the NLLB200 model family (Costa-Jussà et al., 2022), which is considered the state-of-the-art in multilingual machine translation.

Scene Text Editing. This task involves modifying texts within natural scene images while preserving the visual consistency and contextual integrity of surrounding elements. SRNet was the first model introduced for this purpose, explicitly separating foreground and background components (Wu et al., 2019). Subsequent works extended this approach to better handle irregular or curved text (Yang et al., 2020), enable character-level editing (Roy et al., 2020; Qu et al., 2023), and incorporate diffusion-based frameworks (Zeng et al., 2024; Fang et al., 2025). Subramanian et al. (2021) extended SRNet to edit videos and incorporated additional techniques to make the edited text in videos smoother. It is worth noting that these studies primarily focus on model architecture and are restricted to editing English text. Besides the fact that SRNet remains impressive and has consistently been used as a baseline, it has recently been adapted to perform cross-lingual editing, particularly within the IIMT pipeline, including English↔Hindi (Vaidya et al., 2025) and English→Japanese (Kaing et al., 2025). Hence, our toolkit begins with SRNet support in this version.

[1]A video is technically a set of images and the IIMT task can be generalized to a video as well as a live camera video.

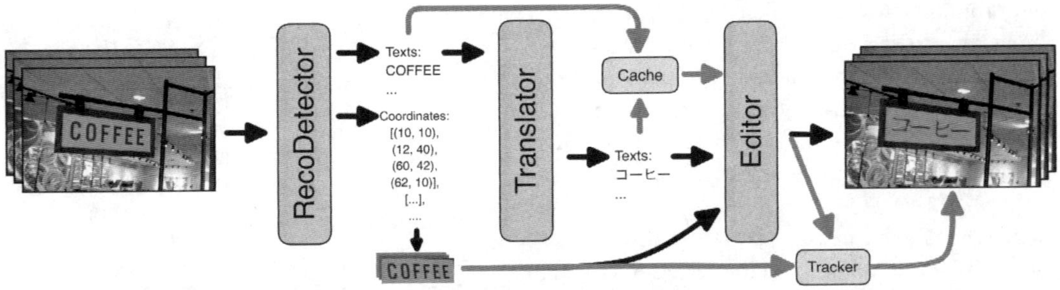

Figure 2: Overview of a pipline in ImageTra. Green indicate proposed features to enhance real-time translation.

3 The Toolkit: ImageTra

ImageTra is a playground where researchers and practitioners can quickly build an IIMT pipeline using the existing tools and models. The pipeline in ImageTra is composed of three main components: `RecoDetector`, `Translator`, and `Editor`. The composed pipeline can then be applied to an image, a video, or a live stream video. Additional features include translation caching, text tracking, and API hosting for server-client use cases, as illustrated in Figure 2.

3.1 Main Components

RecoDetector. This component takes an image as input, detects text regions, recognizes the texts inside the regions, and returns the coordinates of the regions and the recognized texts. Currently, our toolkit wraps four popular open-source OCR tools under this component: DocTR[2], OpenOCR[3], EasyOCR[4], and PaddleOCR[5].

Translator. This component takes recognized texts from `RecoDetector` and translates them into a specific language. We wrap the family of NLLB models (Costa-Jussà et al., 2022) and the TexTra API service[6] under this component.

Editor. This component aims to convert the translated texts from `Translator` into pieces of images and embed them into the whole scene image. The component takes several inputs, including the coordinates of detected texts and the translations. Two types of editors can be created in this component. The first one is a renderer that outputs a rendered translation. To fit the translation into the region of its original text, the font size is estimated based on the character length of the translations and the width and height of the region. It's worth noting that the lengths of the translation and its original text are often different, which may not fit the translation nicely. The second type of editor returns a fused translation that shares the same background and text style as its original text. For the second type of editor, we wrap the conventional SRNet model (Wu et al., 2019), which also leverages the rendered translation as part of its generation.

3.2 Real-Time Video Translation

To improve the efficiency of real-time translation, we introduce three additional features: translation caching, text tracking, and an API-based service.

Translation Caching. When translating texts in video, texts repetition across video frames is inevitable and using a translator to translate them all the time is not efficient especially when the translator model is large and the inference speed is slower. This could make the pipeline slow and less practical for real-time translation. We address this by introducing a simple solution by caching the already translated sentence using a dictionary that maps a source text with a target text.

Text Tracking. Translation caching eliminates redundant translator calls by reusing previously processed texts. To further improve efficiency, we apply text tracking to match detected regions across consecutive frames, allowing translated text from the prior frame to be directly reused in the current frame. This reduces computation for both the translator and the editor, thereby accelerating the pipeline. Specifically, the tracker identifies text regions matched between the previous and current frames. If a matched region in the previous frame has a score greater than or equal to that of its counterpart in the current frame, the region in the current frame is directly replaced with the translated text

[2]`https://github.com/mindee/doctr`
[3]`https://github.com/Topdu/OpenOCR`
[4]`https://github.com/JaidedAI/EasyOCR`
[5]`https://github.com/PaddlePaddle/PaddleOCR`
[6]`https://mt-auto-minhon-mlt.ucri.jgn-x.jp`

image from the previous frame. For tracking, we leverage the existing multi-object tracking library—boxmot[7], which supports a variety of algorithms, including botsort (Aharon et al., 2022), strongsort (Du et al., 2023), deepocsort (Maggiolino et al., 2023), bytetrack (Zhang et al., 2022), and ocsort (Cao et al., 2023).

API. The pipeline can also be served as an API, which allows us to run the pipeline on a server and call the pipeline from a local machine. This will enable broader application especially for real-time translation scenario where a local machine has a camera but no GPU.

3.3 Usage Examples

Here we present a basic example for building an IIMT pipeline and how to use it to translate texts in an image and a video with a few lines of code. Specifically, we first create the three components and then integrate them into the pipeline named `Image2Image`. Since this pipeline can take multiple images as input, we can use it to translate a video frame-by-frame. Lastly, the translated image and video are saved simply using a `save` function.

```
from imagetra.detector.paddleocr import PaddleOCRRecoDetector
from imagetra.translator.nllb import NLLBTranslator
from imagetra.editor.render import RenderEditor
from imagetra.pipeline.img2img import Image2Image

recodetector = PaddleOCRRecoDetector(lang='en')
translator = NLLBTranslator(
    'facebook/nllb-200-distilled-600M',
    trg_lang='jpn_Jpan',
    cache=True, # translation cache
)
editor = RenderEditor('<font_path>')

pipeline = Image2Image(
    recodetector=recodetector,
    editor=editor,
    translator=translator,
)

from imagetra.common.media import Image
img = Image.load('image.jpeg')
result = pipeline([img])[0]
result.img.save('result.jpeg')

from imagetra.common.media import Video
video = Video.load('video.mp4')
results = pipeline(video.frames)
for i, result in enumerate(results):
    video.replace(result.img, i)
video.save('result.mp4')
```

You may have noticed that the translation caching is activated when the `Translator` component is created with `cache=True`. We can further speed up the pipeline on the video translation using a tracker. To do that, we just need to replace `Image2Image` with `Video2Vdieo` and specify the tracker type during inference, e.g, `bytetrack`. The rest of the codes are the same.

[7] `https://github.com/mikel-brostrom/boxmot`

```
pipeline = Video2Video(...)
results = pipeline(video.frames, tracker_type='bytetrack')
```

As there are plenty of other tools and models that are not directly supported yet, we can also integrate them into the pipeline by simply inheriting the base class and overriding the main function of each component as follows.

```
from imagetra.detector.base import BaseRecoDetector
from imagetra.translator.base import BaseTranslator
from imagetra.editor.base import BaseEditor

class CustomRecoDetector(BaseRecoDetector):
    def recodetect(self, imgs):
        # code here
        return bboxs, det_scores, texts, reco_scores

class CustomTranslator(BaseTranslator):
    def translate(self, texts, src_lang, trg_lang):
        # code here
        return translations

class CustomEditor(BaseEditor):
    def edit(self, texts, imgs):
        # code here
        return edited_imgs
```

The above example are explained in python code to show how a pipeline can be constructed and customized. Beside this, we can quickly run the pipeline using a command line interface, of which details can be found in our project homepage.

4 Evaluation

We assume that the overall quality of the pipeline primarily depends on the intrinsic quality of its underlying components, which we expect will continue to be actively improved and domain-generalized by their respective communities. Therefore, our evaluation focuses on the pipeline's efficiency and its trade-off with quality, particularly in the context of real-time translation. We analyze the impact of both translation caching and text tracking features, while also examining optimal configurations, with particular attention to the OCR component. To simulate a realistic real-time translation scenario, our evaluation is conducted on the DSText video dataset from ICDAR2023 (Wu et al., 2023), which provides ground-truth coordinates of English text and their transcriptions. Furthermore, the pipeline is constrained to translating only one frame at a time.

4.1 Impact of Translation Caching

Figure 3 compares the latency of the NLLB model family with 600M, 1.3B, and 3.3B parameters. The models translate the DSText dataset transcriptions into German, one frame at a time. Latency is measured as the average time per frame (in seconds)

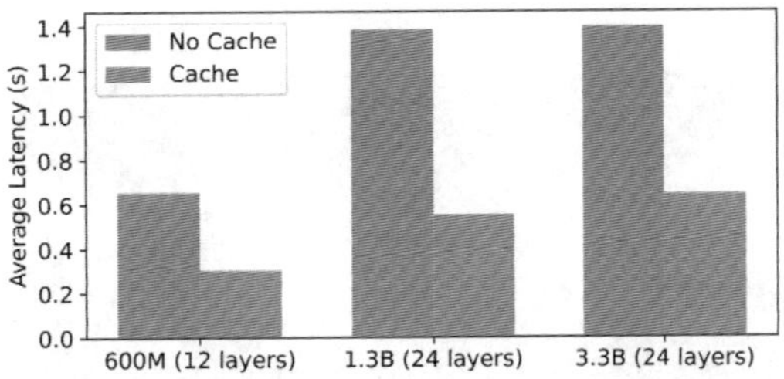

Figure 3: Translation latency of NLLB models across different sizes, with and without translation cache. The y-axis is the latency per frame in seconds.

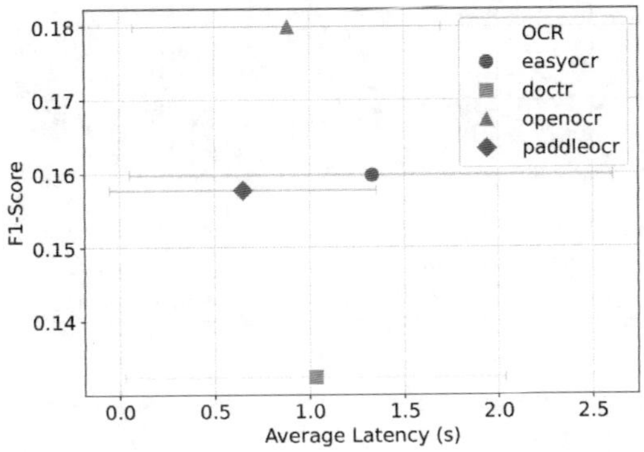

Figure 4: F1-score and average latency of the pipeline with different OCRs.

for each MT model. The results show that larger models tend to have slower inference speeds, as expected, and that model depth significantly contributes to higher latency. Our translation caching substantially improves inference speed, achieving a twofold increase in this experiment.

4.2 Performance of OCRs

Figure 4 compares four OCR tools in terms of latency and accuracy. For latency, we measure the inference time of the pipeline using different OCRs, while keeping the MT model (NLLB-600M) and the editor (RenderEditor) fixed. For accuracy, we compute F1-scores on the OCR outputs following the evaluation protocol of the end-to-end text detection and recognition task in ICDAR2019 (Nayef et al., 2019). Specifically, we first observed that the DSText dataset contains labels marked as "##DONT#CARE##", which are typically used when text in the image is unreadable by annotators due to low resolution or other distortions. Following the ICDAR2019 protocol, both ground-truth regions labeled as "##DONT#CARE##" and predicted regions overlapping with them are excluded

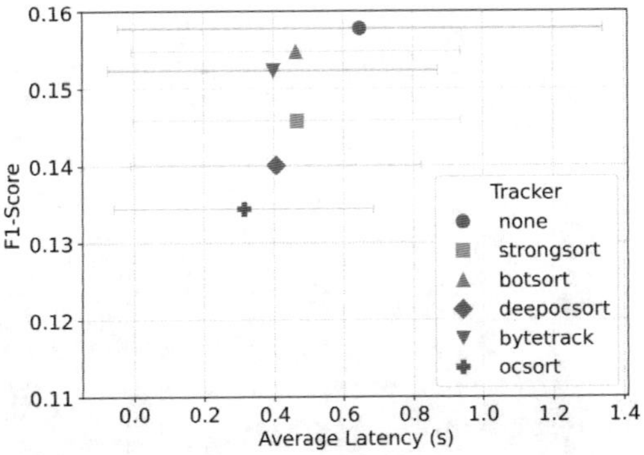

Figure 5: F1-score and average latency of the pipeline using different trackers.

from evaluation (Nayef et al., 2019). After this filtering, true positives are defined as the number of matched texts between the ground truth and predictions, denoted $|M|$. Two texts are considered matched if (i) the intersection-over-union (IoU) of their regions exceeds 0.5, and (ii) their surface forms are exactly identical. Precision P and recall R are then computed as $\frac{|M|}{|T|}$ and $\frac{|M|}{|G|}$, respectively, where $|T|$ is the number of predicted texts and $|G|$ is the number of ground-truth texts. The F1-score is calculated as $\frac{2 \cdot P \cdot R}{P+R}$.

The results show that OpenOCR achieve the best accuracy while PaddleOCR has the best inference speed. This findings is equivalent what is claimed by these tools, for instance, in each of their home page, the OpenOCR teams claims that their tool outperform PaddleOCR and the PaddleOCR teams present their tool as a lightweight OCR system. On another hand, EasyOCR maintains similar performance with PaddleOCR but has the worst inference time. The performance of DocTR is the worst but maintains similar inference speed with OpenOCR. To this end, this result suggest OpenOCR for accurracy and PaddleOCR for inference speed.

4.3 Impact of Text Tracking

Since PaddleOCR is the most efficient system among the four OCRs, we use it to establish a baseline performance and evaluate the impact of trackers on pipeline translation, as shown in Figure 5. The results demonstrate the efficiency gains from using trackers, which reduce the average latency per frame by up to 0.34 seconds. However, a trade-off between accuracy and efficiency is observed; for example, the fastest tracker, `ocsort`, achieves a 0.02 lower F1-score compared with the

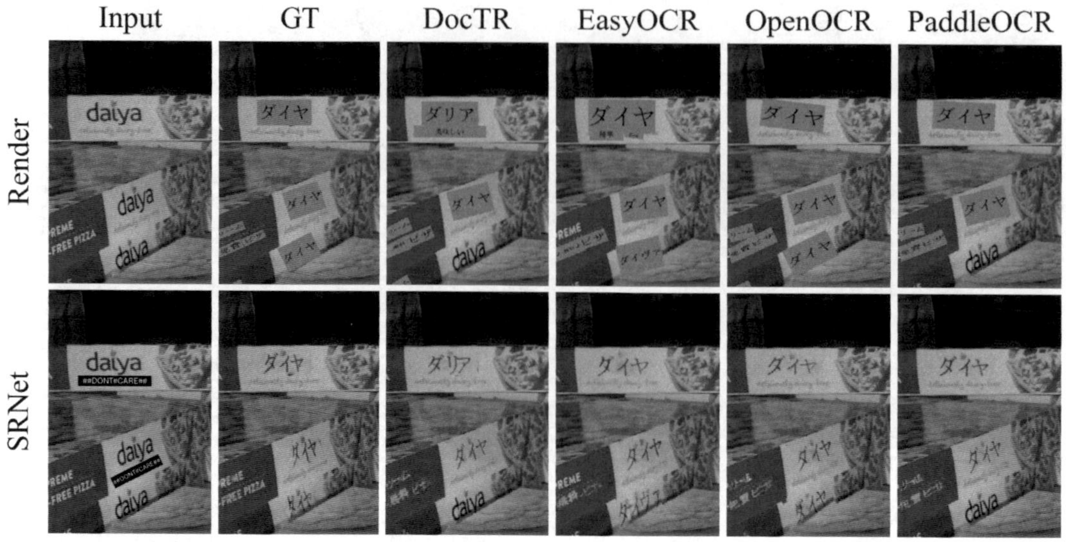

Figure 6: Comparison of outputs generated by pipelines using various OCRs (columns) and editors (rows). GT refers to ground truth where both coordinates and texts are provided in the dataset. The image in the second row under "Input" is used to highlight the "##DONT#CARE##" regions since it is identical with the image above it.

baseline. To this end, the results suggest employing `bytetrack` or `botsort` in the pipeline, as they achieve performance comparable to the baseline while reducing latency.

4.4 Qualitative Analysis

Figure 6 presents an output example translated from English to Japanese using pipelines that integrate different OCR systems and editors. For comparison, we also include the output generated from ground-truth detection and recognition (GT), excluding the "##DONT#CARE##" regions. The editors compared are Render and SRNet; for the latter, we retrained an English-to-Japanese SRNet model on synthetic data following the same settings as Kaing et al. (2025). The example shown is a cropped frame from a video in the DSText dataset. We selected a slow-motion video and chose a relatively sharp frame, further cropping it to enhance readability in the illustration.

Overall, the pipeline produces reasonable results across different OCRs. The outputs are generally consistent, with only minor variations in handling off-angle or blurry text and in the detected coordinates. Among them, OpenOCR achieves results most closely aligned with the ground truth (GT), consistent with the findings in Figure 4. When SRNet is used, the translations of the word "daiya" are clearly readable, and the original text is cleanly erased—except for the small green dot above the letter i, which is preserved. These results are notable given that the model was trained solely on synthetic data. Nevertheless, the model continues to face challenges with more complex cases, such as text over colorful backgrounds or characters with higher visual complexity (e.g., Kanji). We believe that integrating state-of-the-art scene text editors could substantially enhance the quality of the pipeline's outputs.

5 Conclusion

This work introduces ImageTra—an open-source toolkit for building pipeline-based IIMT systems that leverage state-of-the-art models and tools. The toolkit supports real-time translation and integrates two key features to enhance efficiency: translation caching and text tracking. Our evaluation demonstrates that these features significantly reduce inference latency without compromising accuracy.

While the current implementation yields promising results, there remains considerable room for improvement in both efficiency and accuracy. For instance, real-time translation could be enhanced by adopting lightweight, unified models that operate in a more end-to-end manner. Furthermore, translation quality could be improved by leveraging contextual information rather than translating words or phrases in isolation. Pursuing these directions is a core part of our development roadmap as we work toward practical, real-world applications.

References

Nir Aharon, Roy Orfaig, and Ben-Zion Bobrovsky. 2022. Bot-sort: Robust associations multi-pedestrian tracking. *arXiv preprint arXiv:2206.14651*.

Youngmin Baek, Bado Lee, Dongyoon Han, Sangdoo Yun, and Hwalsuk Lee. 2019. Character region awareness for text detection. In *Proceedings of the IEEE/CVF conference on computer vision and pattern recognition*, pages 9365–9374.

Dzmitry Bahdanau, Kyunghyun Cho, and Yoshua Bengio. 2014. Neural machine translation by jointly learning to align and translate.

Marta Bañón, Pinzhen Chen, Barry Haddow, Kenneth Heafield, Hieu Hoang, Miquel Esplà-Gomis, Mikel L. Forcada, Amir Kamran, Faheem Kirefu, Philipp Koehn, Sergio Ortiz Rojas, Leopoldo Pla Sempere, Gema Ramírez-Sánchez, Elsa Sarrías, Marek Strelec, Brian Thompson, William Waites, Dion Wiggins, and Jaume Zaragoza. 2020. ParaCrawl: Web-scale acquisition of parallel corpora. In *Proceedings of the 58th Annual Meeting of the Association for Computational Linguistics*, pages 4555–4567.

Darwin Bautista and Rowel Atienza. 2022. Scene text recognition with permuted autoregressive sequence models. In *European conference on computer vision*, pages 178–196.

Jinkun Cao, Jiangmiao Pang, Xinshuo Weng, Rawal Khirodkar, and Kris Kitani. 2023. Observation-centric sort: Rethinking sort for robust multi-object tracking. In *Proceedings of the IEEE/CVF conference on computer vision and pattern recognition*, pages 9686–9696.

Marta R Costa-Jussà, James Cross, Onur Çelebi, Maha Elbayad, Kenneth Heafield, Kevin Heffernan, Elahe Kalbassi, Janice Lam, Daniel Licht, Jean Maillard, and 1 others. 2022. No language left behind: Scaling human-centered machine translation. *arXiv preprint arXiv:2207.04672*.

Cheng Cui, Ting Sun, Manhui Lin, Tingquan Gao, Yubo Zhang, Jiaxuan Liu, Xueqing Wang, Zelun Zhang, Changda Zhou, Hongen Liu, Yue Zhang, Wenyu Lv, Kui Huang, Yichao Zhang, Jing Zhang, Jun Zhang, Yi Liu, Dianhai Yu, and Yanjun Ma. 2025. Paddleocr 3.0 technical report. *Preprint*, arXiv:2507.05595.

Raj Dabre, Chenhui Chu, and Anoop Kunchukuttan. 2020. A comprehensive survey of multilingual neural machine translation. *CoRR*, abs/2001.01115.

Yongkun Du, Zhineng Chen, Hongtao Xie, Caiyan Jia, and Yu-Gang Jiang. 2025. Svtrv2: Ctc beats encoder-decoder models in scene text recognition. In *ICCV*.

Yunhao Du, Zhicheng Zhao, Yang Song, Yanyun Zhao, Fei Su, Tao Gong, and Hongying Meng. 2023. Strongsort: Make deepsort great again. *IEEE Transactions on Multimedia*, 25:8725–8737.

Desmond Elliott, Stella Frank, Khalil Sima'an, and Lucia Specia. 2016. Multi30K: Multilingual English-German image descriptions. In *Proceedings of the 5th Workshop on Vision and Language*, pages 70–74.

Zhengyao Fang, Pengyuan Lyu, Jingjing Wu, Chengquan Zhang, Jun Yu, Guangming Lu, and Wenjie Pei. 2025. Recognition-synergistic scene text editing. In *Proceedings of the Computer Vision and Pattern Recognition Conference*, pages 13104–13113.

Weiqi Gu, Haiyue Song, Chenhui Chu, and Sadao Kurohashi. 2021. Video-guided machine translation with spatial hierarchical attention network. In *Proceedings of the 59th Annual Meeting of the Association for Computational Linguistics and the 11th International Joint Conference on Natural Language Processing: Student Research Workshop*, pages 87–92.

Tosho Hirasawa, Zhishen Yang, Mamoru Komachi, and Naoaki Okazaki. 2020. Keyframe segmentation and positional encoding for video-guided machine translation challenge 2020.

Hour Kaing, Chenchen Ding, Hideki Tanaka, and Masao Utiyama. 2024. Robust neural machine translation for abugidas by glyph perturbation. In *Proceedings of the 18th Conference of the European Chapter of the Association for Computational Linguistics (Volume 2: Short Papers)*, pages 311–318.

Hour Kaing, Haiyue Song, Chenchen Ding, Jiannan Mao, Hideki Tanaka, and Masao Utiyama. 2025. Towards scene text translation for complex writing systems. In *NLP2025*, pages 234–238.

Zhibin Lan, Liqiang Niu, Fandong Meng, Jie Zhou, Min Zhang, and Jinsong Su. 2024. Translatotron-V(ison): An end-to-end model for in-image machine translation. In *Findings of the Association for Computational Linguistics: ACL 2024*, pages 5472–5485.

Bo Li, Shaolin Zhu, and Lijie Wen. 2025. MIT-10M: A large scale parallel corpus of multilingual image translation. In *Proceedings of the 31st International Conference on Computational Linguistics*, pages 5154–5167.

Minghui Liao, Zhaoyi Wan, Cong Yao, Kai Chen, and Xiang Bai. 2020. Real-time scene text detection with differentiable binarization. In *Proceedings of the AAAI conference on artificial intelligence*, volume 34, pages 11474–11481.

Shangbang Long, Siyang Qin, Dmitry Panteleev, Alessandro Bissacco, Yasuhisa Fujii, and Michalis Raptis. 2022. Towards end-to-end unified scene text detection and layout analysis. In *Proceedings of the IEEE/CVF Conference on Computer Vision and Pattern Recognition (CVPR)*, pages 1049–1059.

Cong Ma, Yaping Zhang, Mei Tu, Yang Zhao, Yu Zhou, and Chengqing Zong. 2023. E2timt: Efficient and effective modal adapter for text image machine translation. In *International Conference on Document Analysis and Recognition*, pages 70–88.

Gerard Maggiolino, Adnan Ahmad, Jinkun Cao, and Kris Kitani. 2023. Deep oc-sort: Multi-pedestrian tracking by adaptive re-identification. In *2023 IEEE International conference on image processing (ICIP)*, pages 3025–3029. IEEE.

Elman Mansimov, Mitchell Stern, Mia Chen, Orhan Firat, Jakob Uszkoreit, and Puneet Jain. 2020. Towards end-to-end in-image neural machine translation. In *Proceedings of the First International Workshop on Natural Language Processing Beyond Text*, pages 70–74.

Nibal Nayef, Yash Patel, Michal Busta, Pinaki Nath Chowdhury, Dimosthenis Karatzas, Wafa Khlif, Jiri Matas, Umapada Pal, Jean-Christophe Burie, Cheng-lin Liu, and 1 others. 2019. Icdar2019 robust reading challenge on multi-lingual scene text detection and recognition—rrc-mlt-2019. In *2019 International conference on document analysis and recognition (ICDAR)*, pages 1582–1587. IEEE.

Zhipeng Qian, Pei Zhang, Baosong Yang, Kai Fan, Yiwei Ma, Derek F. Wong, Xiaoshuai Sun, and Rongrong Ji. 2024. AnyTrans: Translate AnyText in the image with large scale models. In *Findings of the Association for Computational Linguistics: EMNLP 2024*, pages 2432–2444.

Yadong Qu, Qingfeng Tan, Hongtao Xie, Jianjun Xu, Yuxin Wang, and Yongdong Zhang. 2023. Exploring stroke-level modifications for scene text editing. In *Proceedings of the AAAI Conference on Artificial Intelligence*, volume 37, pages 2119–2127.

Prasun Roy, Saumik Bhattacharya, Subhankar Ghosh, and Umapada Pal. 2020. Stefann: scene text editor using font adaptive neural network. In *Proceedings of the IEEE/CVF Conference on Computer Vision and Pattern Recognition*, pages 13228–13237.

Elizabeth Salesky, David Etter, and Matt Post. 2021. Robust open-vocabulary translation from visual text representations. In *Proceedings of the 2021 Conference on Empirical Methods in Natural Language Processing*, pages 7235–7252.

Elizabeth Salesky, Philipp Koehn, and Matt Post. 2024. Benchmarking visually-situated translation of text in natural images. In *Proceedings of the Ninth Conference on Machine Translation*, pages 1167–1182.

Rico Sennrich, Barry Haddow, and Alexandra Birch. 2016. Improving neural machine translation models with monolingual data. In *Proceedings of the 54th Annual Meeting of the Association for Computational Linguistics (Volume 1: Long Papers)*, pages 86–96.

Baoguang Shi, Xiang Bai, and Cong Yao. 2016. An end-to-end trainable neural network for image-based sequence recognition and its application to scene text recognition. *IEEE transactions on pattern analysis and machine intelligence*, 39(11):2298–2304.

Jeyasri Subramanian, Varnith Chordia, Eugene Bart, Shaobo Fang, Kelly Guan, Raja Bala, and 1 others. 2021. Strive: Scene text replacement in videos. In *Proceedings of the IEEE/CVF International Conference on Computer Vision*, pages 14549–14558.

Yanzhi Tian, Xiang Li, Zeming Liu, Yuhang Guo, and Bin Wang. 2023. In-image neural machine translation with segmented pixel sequence-to-sequence model. In *Findings of the Association for Computational Linguistics: EMNLP 2023*, pages 15046–15057.

Yanzhi Tian, Zeming Liu, Zhengyang Liu, and Yuhang Guo. 2025. Exploring in-image machine translation with real-world background. In *Findings of the Association for Computational Linguistics: ACL 2025*, pages 124–137.

Shreyas Vaidya, Arvind Kumar Sharma, Prajwal Gatti, and Anand Mishra. 2025. Show me the world in my language: Establishing the first baseline for scene-text to scene-text translation. In *International Conference on Pattern Recognition*, pages 312–328.

Ashish Vaswani, Noam Shazeer, Niki Parmar, Jakob Uszkoreit, Llion Jones, Aidan N. Gomez, Lukasz Kaiser, and Illia Polosukhin. 2017. Attention is all you need.

Liang Wu, Chengquan Zhang, Jiaming Liu, Junyu Han, Jingtuo Liu, Errui Ding, and Xiang Bai. 2019. Editing text in the wild. In *Proceedings of the 27th ACM international conference on multimedia*, pages 1500–1508.

Weijia Wu, Yuzhong Zhao, Zhuang Li, Jiahong Li, Mike Zheng Shou, Umapada Pal, Dimosthenis Karatzas, and Xiang Bai. 2023. Icdar 2023 competition on video text reading for dense and small text. In *Document Analysis and Recognition - ICDAR 2023: 17th International Conference, San José, CA, USA, August 21–26, 2023, Proceedings, Part II*, page 405–419.

Qiangpeng Yang, Jun Huang, and Wei Lin. 2020. Swaptext: Image based texts transfer in scenes. In *Proceedings of the IEEE/CVF Conference on Computer Vision and Pattern Recognition*, pages 14700–14709.

Weichao Zeng, Yan Shu, Zhenhang Li, Dongbao Yang, and Yu Zhou. 2024. Textctrl: Diffusion-based scene text editing with prior guidance control. *Advances in Neural Information Processing Systems*, 37:138569–138594.

Yifu Zhang, Peize Sun, Yi Jiang, Dongdong Yu, Fucheng Weng, Zehuan Yuan, Ping Luo, Wenyu Liu, and Xinggang Wang. 2022. Bytetrack: Multi-object tracking by associating every detection box. In *European conference on computer vision*, pages 1–21.

Xinyu Zhou, Cong Yao, He Wen, Yuzhi Wang, Shuchang Zhou, Weiran He, and Jiajun Liang. 2017. East: an efficient and accurate scene text detector. In *Proceedings of the IEEE conference on Computer Vision and Pattern Recognition*, pages 5551–5560.

Human-in-the-Loop Generation of Adversarial Texts: A Case Study on Tibetan Script

Xi Cao[♡♠], **Yuan Sun**[♡♠✉],
Jiajun Li[◇♣], **Quzong Gesang**[◇♣], **Nuo Qun**[◇♣✉], **Tashi Nyima**[◇♣]
[♡]Institute of National Security, Minzu University of China, Beijing, China
[◇]School of Information Science and Technology, Xizang University, Lhasa, China
[♠]National Language Resource Monitoring & Research Center | Minority Languages Branch, Beijing, China
[♣]The State Key Laboratory of Tibetan Intelligence, Lhasa, China
caoxi@muc.edu.cn, sunyuan@muc.edu.cn, q_nuo@utibet.edu.cn

Abstract

DNN-based language models excel across various NLP tasks but remain highly vulnerable to textual adversarial attacks. While adversarial text generation is crucial for NLP security, explainability, evaluation, and data augmentation, related work remains overwhelmingly English-centric, leaving the problem of constructing high-quality and sustainable adversarial robustness benchmarks for lower-resourced languages both difficult and understudied. First, method customization for lower-resourced languages is complicated due to linguistic differences and limited resources. Second, automated attacks are prone to generating invalid or ambiguous adversarial texts. Last but not least, language models continuously evolve and may be immune to parts of previously generated adversarial texts. To address these challenges, we introduce HITL-GAT[1], an interactive system based on a general approach to human-in-the-loop generation of adversarial texts. Additionally, we demonstrate the utility of HITL-GAT through a case study on Tibetan script, employing three customized adversarial text generation methods and establishing its first adversarial robustness benchmark, providing a valuable reference for other lower-resourced languages.

1 Introduction

The adversarial attack refers to an attack method in which the attacker adds imperceptible perturbations to the original input, resulting in the incorrect judgment of a DNN-based model. The examples generated during textual adversarial attacks are called adversarial texts.

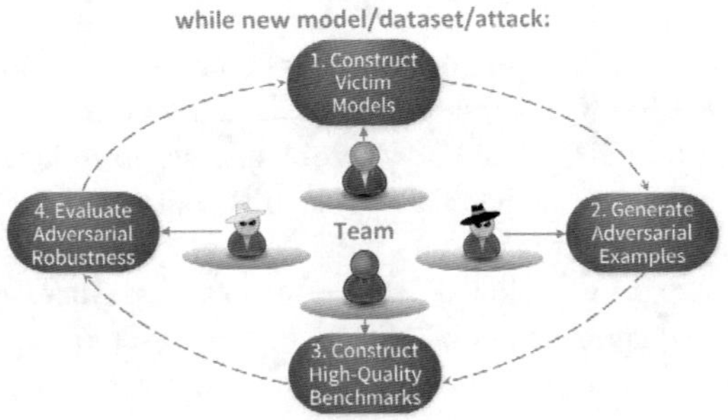

Figure 1: Workflow of HITL-GAT. While a new language model, downstream dataset, or textual adversarial attack method emerges, we can enter the loop to make the adversarial robustness benchmark evolve.

Due to the general adaptability of language models to classification tasks, adversarial robustness evaluation is mainly focused on the domain. Currently, most of the adversarial text generation methods target higher-resourced languages, especially English. Because of the differences in textual features and language resources, it is challenging to transfer these methods to other languages. **Problem 1: How do we generate adversarial texts for lower-resourced languages?**

Wang et al. (2021a) apply 14 textual adversarial attack methods to GLUE tasks (Wang et al., 2019) to construct the widely used adversarial robustness benchmark AdvGLUE. In their construction, they find that most textual adversarial attack methods are prone to generating invalid or ambiguous adversarial texts, with around 90% either changing the original semantics or hindering the annotators' unanimity. In our case study on Tibetan script, we also come to the same conclusion. **Problem 2: How do we construct high-quality adversarial robustness benchmarks?**

Wang et al. (2023) employ ANLI (Nie et al., 2020) and AdvGLUE (Wang et al., 2021a) to assess the adversarial robustness of ChatGPT and

✉ Corresponding Author
[1]Video Demonstration:
https://youtu.be/tXla4yAggwA
Code Repository:
https://github.com/CMLI-NLP/HITL-GAT
Victim Models:
https://huggingface.co/collections/UTibetNLP/tibetan-victim-language-models-669f614ecea872c7211c121c

Proceedings of The 14th International Joint Conference on Natural Language Processing and The 4th Conference of the Asia-Pacific Chapter of the Association for Computational Linguistics: System Demonstrations, pages 9–16
December 20-24, 2025 ©2025 Association for Computational Linguistics

several previous popular language models and find ChatGPT is the best. However, both ANLI and AdvGLUE are constructed using fine-tuned BERT (Devlin et al., 2019) and RoBERTa (Liu et al., 2019) as victim models. Language models are evolving, while adversarial robustness benchmarks never. We argue that new language models may be immune to part of previously generated adversarial texts. Lower-resourced languages are at a very early stage of adversarial robustness evaluation compared to higher-resourced languages, and it is essential to envisage sustainable adversarial robustness evaluation in advance. **Problem 3: How do we update adversarial robustness benchmarks?**

To address the above problems, we introduce `HITL-GAT`, an interactive system for human-in-the-loop generation of adversarial texts. Figure 1 depicts the workflow of `HITL-GAT`. In a loop where a new language model, downstream dataset, or textual adversarial attack method emerges, our team starts to construct victim models, generate adversarial examples, construct high-quality benchmarks, and evaluate adversarial robustness. The loop allows adversarial robustness benchmarks to evolve along with new models, datasets, and attacks (**Problem 3**). Figure 2 depicts the four stages in one pipeline detailedly. Firstly, we fine-tune the previous model and the new model on the same downstream datasets to construct victim models. Subsequently, we implement adversarial attacks on the victim models constructed from the previous model upon downstream datasets to generate adversarial examples. Afterward, we customize filter conditions and conduct human annotation to construct a high-quality adversarial robustness benchmark (**Problem 2**). Finally, we evaluate the adversarial robustness of the new model on the benchmark. Additionally, we make a case study on one lower-resourced language, Tibetan, based on the general human-in-the-loop approach to adversarial text generation (**Problem 1**).

The contributions of this paper are as follows:

(1) We propose a general human-in-the-loop approach to adversarial text generation. This approach can assist in constructing and updating high-quality adversarial robustness benchmarks with the emergence of new language models, downstream datasets, and textual adversarial attack methods.

(2) We develop an interactive system called `HITL-GAT` based on the general approach to human-in-the-loop generation of adversarial texts. This system is successfully applied to a case study on one lower-resourced language.

(3) We demonstrate the utility of `HITL-GAT` through a case study on Tibetan script, employing three customized adversarial text generation methods and establishing its first adversarial robustness benchmark, providing a valuable reference for other lower-resourced languages.

(4) We open-source both the system and the case study under GNU General Public License v3.0 to facilitate future explorations. Our code repository received 42 stars, and our 12 victim models were downloaded more than 5,000 times before paper submission on November 15, 2025.

2 Related Work

2.1 Textual Adversarial Attack Frameworks

TextAttack (Morris et al., 2020) and OpenAttack (Zeng et al., 2021) are two powerful and easy-to-use Python frameworks for textual adversarial attacks. They are both for text classification, supporting English and Chinese, with similar toolkit functionality and complementary attack methods. From a developer's perspective, TextAttack utilizes a relatively rigorous architecture to unify different attack methods, while OpenAttack is more flexible. SeqAttack (Simoncini and Spanakis, 2021) and RobustQA (Boreshban et al., 2023) are textual adversarial attack frameworks for named entity recognition and question answering, respectively, supporting English only. These frameworks provide an excellent platform to stress-test the adversarial robustness of models targeting higher-resourced languages. However, the weaponization of lower-resourced languages against NLP security (Lent, 2025; Yoo et al., 2025; Lent et al., 2025) highlights the urgent need for research in this area. To our knowledge, `HITL-GAT` is the first interactive system to build adversarial robustness benchmarks from scratch for a truly low-resource language.

2.2 Human-in-the-Loop Adversarial Text Generation

Wallace et al. (2019) guide human authors to keep crafting adversarial questions to break the question answering models with the aid of visual model predictions and interpretations. They conduct two rounds of adversarial writing. In the first round, human authors attack a traditional ElasticSearch model `A` to construct the adversarial set `x`. Then, they use `x` to evaluate `A`, a bidirectional recurrent neural network model `B`, and a deep averaging net-

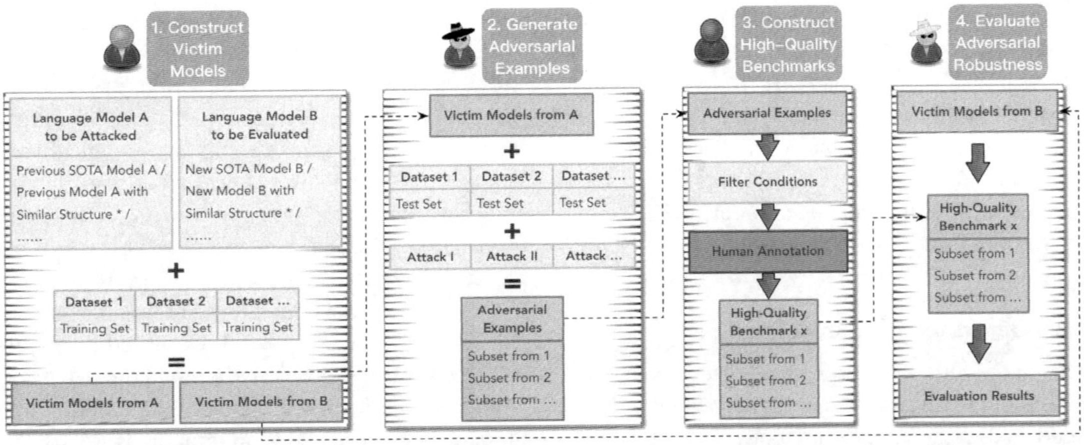

Figure 2: Flowchart of HITL-GAT. Our system contains four stages in one pipeline: **victim model construction**, **adversarial example generation**, **high-quality benchmark construction**, and **adversarial robustness evaluation**. System outputs are highlighted in purple background. Human choices are highlighted in yellow background. Human annotation is highlighted in red background.

work model C. In the second round, they train A, B, and C on a larger dataset. Human authors attack A and B to construct the adversarial set x and x'. Then, they use x and x' to evaluate A, B, and C. We see their human-in-the-loop approach as an embryo of adversarial robustness benchmark evolution, despite the high labor cost of relying on human authors to think and write adversarial texts. Most goals of using a human-in-the-loop approach in NLP tasks are to improve the model performance in various aspects (Wang et al., 2021b). With these goals, language models evolve. As continuous advancement of model capabilities, it is imperative to explore the paradigm for benchmark evolution. To our knowledge, even though our work is preliminary, we are the first to explore the evolution of adversarial robustness benchmarks.

3 Implementation

Definition Due to the general adaptability of language models to the text classification task, our work focuses on the adversarial robustness evaluation of language models on this task. The definition of textual adversarial attacks on text classification is as follows. For a text classifier F, let x ($x \in X$, X includes all possible input texts) be the original input text and y ($y \in Y$, Y includes all possible output labels) be the corresponding output label of x, denoted as $F(x) = \arg\max_{\dot{y} \in Y} P(\dot{y}|x) = y$. For a successful textual adversarial attack, let $x' = x + \delta$ be the perturbed input text, where δ is the imperceptible perturbation, denoted as $F(x') = \arg\max_{\dot{y} \in Y} P(\dot{y}|x') \neq y$.

Overview Our system for human-in-the-loop generation of adversarial texts, HITL-GAT, contains four stages in one pipeline: **victim model construction**, **adversarial example generation**, **high-quality benchmark construction**, and **adversarial robustness evaluation**. Figure 2 depicts the flowchart of HITL-GAT. These four stages will be detailed in the following four subsections respectively. Our flexible interactive system allows users to either go through the entire pipeline or directly start at any stage. Gradio (Abid et al., 2019) is an open-sourced Python package that allows developers to quickly build a web demo or application for machine learning. LlamaBoard is the user-friendly GUI (Graphical User Interface) of LlamaFactory (Zheng et al., 2024). The GUI of our system is powered by Gradio and draws inspiration from the design of LlamaBoard.

3.1 Construct Victim Models

This stage aims at constructing victim language models via a fine-tuning paradigm.

When a new language model B emerges, in order to better evaluate the adversarial robustness of B, we need to quantitatively and thoroughly perform evaluation on multiple downstream tasks. For the purpose of stress-testing the adversarial robustness of B more effectively, i.e., constructing a stronger adversarial robustness benchmark with high quality, we can choose at least one previous SOTA or similar-structured language model A to implement textual adversarial attacks on it to generate updated adversarial texts. We can also follow this stage when a new downstream dataset n is available.

In this stage, we fine-tune A and B on the training set of the same downstream datasets 1,2,...,n to construct victim language models. The victim model construction stage is depicted in the first part of Figure 2.

3.2 Generate Adversarial Examples

This stage aims at automatically generating the first-round adversarial texts with the help of various textual adversarial attack methods.

The way human authors keep thinking and writing adversarial texts (Wallace et al., 2019) is high-labor-cost. With the emergence of automated textual adversarial attacks, such as TextFooler (Jin et al., 2020), BERT-ATTACK (Li et al., 2020), SemAttack (Wang et al., 2022), and TextCheater (Peng et al., 2024), adversarial text generation has become relatively easy. We can directly enter this stage when a new textual adversarial attack N appears.

In this stage, we implement textual adversarial attacks I,II,...,N on the victim language models constructed from language model A upon the test set of downstream datasets 1,2,...,n to generate the first-round adversarial texts automatically. The adversarial example generation stage is depicted in the second part of Figure 2.

3.3 Construct High-Quality Benchmarks

This stage aims at constructing a high-quality adversarial robustness benchmark by customizing filter conditions and conducting human annotation.

The construction process of AdvGLUE (Wang et al., 2021a), a widely used adversarial robustness benchmark, tells us that most textual adversarial attack methods are prone to generating invalid or ambiguous adversarial texts, with around 90% either changing the original semantics or hindering the annotators' unanimity. Therefore, human annotation is indispensable and can make benchmarks more practical and relevant. In order to reduce the cost of human annotation, the first-round adversarial texts need to be screened automatically first using appropriate filter conditions. Due to the fact that humans perceive texts through their eyes and brains, both filter conditions and human annotation should follow the visual and semantic similarity between adversarial texts and original texts. Filter conditions can be the following metrics: Edit Distance, Normalized Cross-Correlation Coefficient (from the perspective of visual similarity); Cosine Similarity, BERTScore (Zhang et al., 2020) (from the perspective of semantic similarity); and so on. Human annotation still requires additional consideration of annotators' unanimity so that adversarial texts can be deemed human-acceptable. For example, given an original text and an adversarial text, we ask several annotators to score the human acceptance of the adversarial text based on the visual and semantic similarity between the two texts, from 1 to 5. The higher the score, the higher the human acceptance. If all annotators score the human acceptance of the adversarial text as 4 or 5, the adversarial text will be included in the adversarial robustness benchmark.

In this stage, we screen out the examples that do not satisfy the customized filter conditions from the first-round adversarial texts, and then manually annotate the remaining examples to construct the high-quality adversarial robustness benchmark x. The high-quality benchmark construction stage is depicted in the third part of Figure 2.

3.4 Evaluate Adversarial Robustness

This stage aims at quantitatively and thoroughly evaluating the adversarial robustness of new language models using the constructed high-quality adversarial robustness benchmark.

The adversarial robustness benchmark x is a collection of n subsets, each of which contains high-quality adversarial texts generated from the test set of the corresponding downstream dataset. We take the average accuracy on n subsets as the adversarial robustness ($AdvRobust$) of the new language model B on x, denoted as:

$$AdvRobust = \frac{\sum_{i=1}^{n} Accuracy_i}{n}. \quad (1)$$

In this stage, we utilize the constructed high-quality adversarial robustness benchmark x to evaluate the adversarial robustness of the language model B quantitatively and thoroughly. The adversarial robustness evaluation stage is depicted in the fourth part of Figure 2.

4 Case Study

In this section, we go through the entire pipeline under the existing conditions to construct the first adversarial robustness benchmark for Tibetan script and conduct the adversarial robustness evaluation on Tibetan language models. We will introduce the existing conditions and the whole process in the following two subsections respectively.

4.1 Existing Conditions

Below is the involved language models, downstream datasets, and attack methods.

4.1.1 Language Models

`Tibetan-BERT`[1] (Zhang et al., 2022). A BERT-based monolingual model targeting Tibetan. It is the first Tibetan BERT model and achieves a good result on the specific downstream Tibetan text classification task.

`CINO`[2] (Yang et al., 2022). A series of XLM-RoBERTa-based multilingual models including Tibetan. It is the first multilingual model for Chinese minority languages and achieves a SOTA performance on multiple downstream monolingual or multilingual text classification task.

4.1.2 Downstream Datasets

`TNCC-title`[3] (Qun et al., 2017). A Tibetan news title classification dataset. This dataset contains a total of 9,276 Tibetan news titles, which are divided into 12 classes.

`TU_SA`[4] (Zhu et al., 2023). A Tibetan sentiment analysis dataset. It is built by translating and proofreading 10,000 sentences from two public Chinese sentiment analysis datasets. In this dataset, negative or positive class each accounts for 50%.

4.1.3 Attack Methods

Over the past few years, we have developed several Tibetan textual adversarial attack methods, aiming to draw attention to the NLP security in lower-resourced languages, as listed below. Our past work (Cao et al., 2023) is the only one engaged with a truly low-resource language among the research samples in the literature *NLP Security and Ethics, in the Wild* (Lent et al., TACL 2025, page 719).

`TSAttacker` (Cao et al., 2023). An embedding-similarity-based Tibetan textual adversarial attack. It utilizes the cosine distance between static syllable embeddings to generate substitution syllables.

`TSTricker` (Cao et al., 2024). A context-aware-based Tibetan textual adversarial attack. It utilizes two BERT-based masked language models with tokenizers of two different granularities to generate substitution syllables or words respectively.

`TSCheater` (Cao et al., 2025). A visual-similarity-based Tibetan textual adversarial attack. It utilizes a self-constructed Tibetan syllable visual similarity database to generate substitution candidates.

4.2 Whole Process

Figure 2 and Section 3 introduce the four stages of `HITL-GAT`. Below we use a case study on Tibetan script to illustrate the whole process, which is also demonstrated in the video and Figure 3.

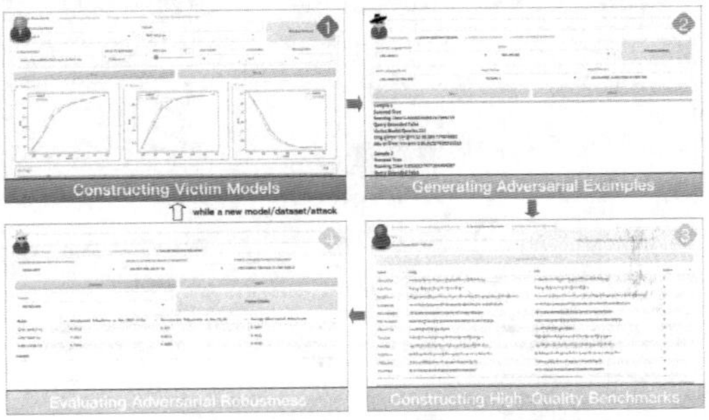

Figure 3: Screenshots of `HITL-GAT`.

In the victim model construction stage, we choose the language model and downstream dataset, and then the default fine-tuning hyperparameters will be loaded. Once the "Start" button is clicked, the fine-tuning starts and the GUI displays a progress bar, metric plots (F1/macro-F1, Accuracy, and Loss) and running logs. Here, we fine-tune `Tibetan-BERT` and `CINO` series on the training set of `TNCC-title` and `TU_SA` to construct the victim language models.

Next, in the adversarial example generation stage, we choose the language model and downstream dataset, and then the victim language model will be loaded. Once the "Start" button is clicked, the attack starts and the GUI displays generated examples. Here, we implement `TSAttacker`, `TSTricker`, and `TSCheater` on the victim language models constructed from `Tibetan-BERT` upon the test set of `TNCC-title` and `TU_SA` to generate the first-round adversarial texts.

Thereafter, in the high-quality benchmark construction stage, we screen out the examples that do not satisfy the customized filter condition $levenshtein\_distance/text\_length <= 0.1$

[1] https://huggingface.co/UTibetNLP/tibetan_bert
[2] https://huggingface.co/hfl/cino-small-v2
https://huggingface.co/hfl/cino-base-v2
https://huggingface.co/hfl/cino-large-v2
[3] https://github.com/FudanNLP/Tibetan-Classification
[4] https://github.com/UTibetNLP/TU_SA

from the first-round adversarial texts, and then manually annotate the remaining examples to construct the first Tibetan adversarial robustness benchmark called `AdvTS`. Given an original text and an adversarial text, we ask 3 annotators to score the human acceptance of the adversarial text based on the visual and semantic similarity between the two texts, from 1 to 5. The higher the score, the higher the human acceptance. If all annotators score the human acceptance of the adversarial text as 4 or 5, the adversarial text will be included in `AdvTS`. Below is the guidelines for human annotation.

Score 1: Definite Reject. Humans can intuitively perceive that the perturbations significantly alter the appearance or semantics of the original text.

Score 2: Reject. Humans can intuitively perceive that the perturbations do alter the appearance or semantics of the original text.

Score 3: Marginal Reject or Accept. Humans can intuitively perceive that the perturbations alter the appearance or semantics of the original text not too much.

Score 4: Accept. After careful observation or thought for 5 seconds, humans find that perturbations only slightly alter the appearance or semantics of the original text.

Score 5: Definite Accept. After careful observation for 5 seconds, humans can not find that perturbations alter the appearance of the original text. Or, after careful thought for 5 seconds, humans find that perturbations do not alter the semantics of the original text.

Finally, in the adversarial robustness evaluation stage, we utilize `AdvTS` to evaluate the adversarial robustness of `CINO` series with Equation 1. The *AdvRobust* of `CINO-small-v2`, `CINO-base-v2`, and `CINO-large-v2` is 0.5609, 0.5572, and 0.5726 respectively.

While a new language model, downstream dataset, or textual adversarial attack method emerges, we can enter the loop again to make the adversarial robustness benchmark evolve.

5 Discussion

Due to the fact that humans perceive texts through their eyes and brains, when the perturbed text tends to the original text in visual or semantic similarity, we consider such perturbations to be imperceptible. To construct imperceptible perturbations, we can start from the following three aspects.

Transplanting existing general methods. From the perspective of semantic approximation, using synonyms for substitution is a general method. Sources of synonyms can be static word embeddings (Alzantot et al., 2018), dictionaries (Ren et al., 2019), and predictions of masked language models (Li et al., 2020).

Using intrinsic textual features. Different languages have different features inherent in their texts. For example, in abugidas (Tibetan script, Devanagari script, etc.), many pairs of confusable letters result in visually similar syllables (Kaing et al., 2024; Cao et al., 2025).

Using extrinsic encoding features. In the process of historical development, there are many cases of "same language with different encodings". For example, due to the technical problems in history, there are two Tibetan coded character sets in national standards of P.R.C (basic set: GB 16959-1997 and extension set: GB/T 20542-2006, GB/T 22238-2008); due to the simplification of Chinese characters, simplified and traditional Chinese exist. Encoding issues between different languages also deserve attention. For example, the Latin letter `x` (U+0078) and the Cyrillic letter `х` (U+0445) look the same; ZWNJ (zero width non-joiner, U+200C) is used extensively for certain prefixes, suffixes and compound words in Persian, but it is invisible and useless in most other languages.

6 Conclusion

This paper introduces `HITL-GAT`, an interactive system for human-in-the-loop generation of adversarial texts. Our approach employs a four-stage iterative loop: victim model construction, adversarial example generation, high-quality benchmark construction, and adversarial robustness evaluation. The loop ensures adversarial robustness benchmarks to co-evolve with advancements in language models, downstream datasets, and textual adversarial attack methods. Additionally, we demonstrate the utility of `HITL-GAT` through a case study on Tibetan script, employing three customized adversarial text generation methods and establishing its first adversarial robustness benchmark. Our work provides a valuable reference for other lower-resourced languages, especially languages in the Asia-Pacific that use abugidas as their writing system. The weaponization of lower-resourced languages against NLP security highlights the critical gap and the urgent need for research in this area.

Limitations

The system and the case study presented in this paper are the crystallization of our research on the adversarial robustness of Tibetan language models over the past few years. The summarized approach is only applicable to classification tasks. Given the heightened sensitivity necessary for working with lower-resourced languages, our case study is conducted on insensitive tasks with ethical best practices in mind. Due to the existing conditions of lower-resourced languages, our case study can only be conducted this far. However, this does not prevent it from serving as an early paradigm for researching the evolution of adversarial robustness benchmarks. We will continue to develop `HITL-GAT` and conduct more case studies on other minority languages.

Ethical Considerations

Our work adheres to the ACM Code of Ethics. The purpose of this paper is to promote research on NLP security, especially for lower-resourced languages. The textual adversarial attack methods mentioned in this paper must be used positively, thus preventing any malicious misuse. Additionally, adherence to the model or dataset license is mandatory when using our system or fork versions, thus preventing any potential misuse.

Acknowledgments

This work benefited greatly from the encouragement, advice, and help of others. Thank you to Heather Lent at Aalborg University for her encouragement and detailed feedback on our manuscript. Thank you to Chen Zhang at Peking University and Andong Chen at Harbin Institute of Technology for their early advice. We also thank the anonymous reviewers of *ACL for their insightful comments.

Finally, thanks to the following open-sourced projects: OpenAttack (Zeng et al., 2021), Gradio (Abid et al., 2019), LlamaFactory (Zheng et al., 2024), Transformers (Wolf et al., 2020), Datasets (Lhoest et al., 2021), etc.

This work is supported by the Science and Technology Strategic Consulting Project of the Chinese Academy of Engineering (2025-XZ-16-06), the Key Project of Xizang Natural Science Foundation (XZ202401ZR0040), the National Social Science Foundation of China (22&ZD035), the National Natural Science Foundation of China (61972436), and the MUC (Minzu University of China) Foundation (2025XYCM39).

References

Abubakar Abid, Ali Abdalla, and 4 others. 2019. Gradio: Hassle-free sharing and testing of ML models in the wild. *Preprint*, arXiv:1906.02569.

Moustafa Alzantot, Yash Sharma, and 4 others. 2018. Generating natural language adversarial examples. In *Proceedings of the 2018 Conference on Empirical Methods in Natural Language Processing*.

Yasaman Boreshban, Seyed Morteza Mirbostani, and 5 others. 2023. RobustQA: A framework for adversarial text generation analysis on question answering systems. In *Proceedings of the 2023 Conference on Empirical Methods in Natural Language Processing: System Demonstrations*.

Xi Cao, Dolma Dawa, and 2 others. 2023. Pay attention to the robustness of Chinese minority language models! Syllable-level textual adversarial attack on Tibetan script. In *Proceedings of the 3rd Workshop on Trustworthy Natural Language Processing*.

Xi Cao, Quzong Gesang, and 3 others. 2025. TSCheater: Generating high-quality Tibetan adversarial texts via visual similarity. In *ICASSP 2025 - 2025 IEEE International Conference on Acoustics, Speech and Signal Processing*.

Xi Cao, Nuo Qun, and 3 others. 2024. Multi-granularity Tibetan textual adversarial attack method based on masked language model. In *Companion Proceedings of the ACM Web Conference 2024*.

Jacob Devlin, Ming-Wei Chang, and 2 others. 2019. BERT: Pre-training of deep bidirectional Transformers for language understanding. In *Proceedings of the 2019 Conference of the North American Chapter of the Association for Computational Linguistics: Human Language Technologies, Volume 1 (Long and Short Papers)*.

Di Jin, Zhijing Jin, and 2 others. 2020. Is BERT really robust? A strong baseline for natural language attack on text classification and entailment. In *34th AAAI Conference on Artificial Intelligence, AAAI 2020*.

Hour Kaing, Chenchen Ding, and 2 others. 2024. Robust neural machine translation for abugidas by glyph perturbation. In *Proceedings of the 18th Conference of the European Chapter of the Association for Computational Linguistics (Volume 2: Short Papers)*.

Heather Lent. 2025. Beyond Weaponization: NLP security for medium and lower-resourced languages in their own right. *Preprint*, arXiv:2507.03473.

Heather Lent, Erick Galinkin, and 4 others. 2025. NLP security and ethics, in the wild. *Transactions of the Association for Computational Linguistics*, 13:709–743.

Quentin Lhoest, Albert Villanova del Moral, and 30 others. 2021. Datasets: A community library for natural language processing. In *Proceedings of the 2021 Conference on Empirical Methods in Natural Language Processing: System Demonstrations*.

Linyang Li, Ruotian Ma, and 3 others. 2020. BERT-ATTACK: Adversarial attack against BERT using BERT. In *Proceedings of the 2020 Conference on Empirical Methods in Natural Language Processing*.

Yinhan Liu, Myle Ott, and 8 others. 2019. RoBERTa: A robustly optimized BERT pretraining approach. *Preprint*, arXiv:1907.11692.

John Morris, Eli Lifland, and 4 others. 2020. TextAttack: A framework for adversarial attacks, data augmentation, and adversarial training in NLP. In *Proceedings of the 2020 Conference on Empirical Methods in Natural Language Processing: System Demonstrations*.

Yixin Nie, Adina Williams, and 4 others. 2020. Adversarial NLI: A new benchmark for natural language understanding. In *Proceedings of the 58th Annual Meeting of the Association for Computational Linguistics*.

Hao Peng, Shixin Guo, and 6 others. 2024. TextCheater: A query-efficient textual adversarial attack in the hard-label setting. *IEEE Transactions on Dependable and Secure Computing*, 21(4):3901–3916.

Nuo Qun, Xing Li, and 2 others. 2017. End-to-end neural text classification for Tibetan. In *Proceedings of the 16th Chinese National Conference on Computational Linguistics*.

Shuhuai Ren, Yihe Deng, and 2 others. 2019. Generating natural language adversarial examples through probability weighted word saliency. In *Proceedings of the 57th Annual Meeting of the Association for Computational Linguistics*.

Walter Simoncini and Gerasimos Spanakis. 2021. SeqAttack: On adversarial attacks for named entity recognition. In *Proceedings of the 2021 Conference on Empirical Methods in Natural Language Processing: System Demonstrations*.

Eric Wallace, Pedro Rodriguez, and 3 others. 2019. Trick me if you can: Human-in-the-loop generation of adversarial examples for question answering. *Transactions of the Association for Computational Linguistics*, 7:387–401.

Alex Wang, Amanpreet Singh, and 4 others. 2019. GLUE: A multi-task benchmark and analysis platform for natural language understanding. In *7th International Conference on Learning Representations, ICLR 2019*.

Boxin Wang, Chejian Xu, and 3 others. 2022. SemAttack: Natural textual attacks via different semantic spaces. In *Findings of the Association for Computational Linguistics: NAACL 2022*.

Boxin Wang, Chejian Xu, and 6 others. 2021a. Adversarial GLUE: A multi-task benchmark for robustness evaluation of language models. In *Proceedings of the Neural Information Processing Systems Track on Datasets and Benchmarks 2021*.

Jindong Wang, Xixu Hu, and 11 others. 2023. On the robustness of ChatGPT: An adversarial and out-of-distribution perspective. In *ICLR 2023 Workshop on Trustworthy and Reliable Large-Scale Machine Learning Models*.

Zijie J. Wang, Dongjin Choi, and 2 others. 2021b. Putting humans in the natural language processing loop: A survey. In *Proceedings of the First Workshop on Bridging Human–Computer Interaction and Natural Language Processing*.

Thomas Wolf, Lysandre Debut, and 20 others. 2020. Transformers: State-of-the-art natural language processing. In *Proceedings of the 2020 Conference on Empirical Methods in Natural Language Processing: System Demonstrations*.

Ziqing Yang, Zihang Xu, and 5 others. 2022. CINO: A Chinese minority pre-trained language model. In *Proceedings of the 29th International Conference on Computational Linguistics*.

Haneul Yoo, Yongjin Yang, and Hwaran Lee. 2025. Code-switching red-teaming: LLM evaluation for safety and multilingual understanding. In *Proceedings of the 63rd Annual Meeting of the Association for Computational Linguistics (Volume 1: Long Papers)*.

Guoyang Zeng, Fanchao Qi, and 7 others. 2021. OpenAttack: An open-source textual adversarial attack toolkit. In *Proceedings of the 59th Annual Meeting of the Association for Computational Linguistics and the 11th International Joint Conference on Natural Language Processing: System Demonstrations*.

Jiangyan Zhang, Kazhuo Deji, and 3 others. 2022. Research and application of Tibetan pre-training language model based on BERT. In *Proceedings of the 2022 2nd International Conference on Control and Intelligent Robotics*.

Tianyi Zhang, Varsha Kishore, and 3 others. 2020. BERTScore: Evaluating text generation with BERT. In *8th International Conference on Learning Representations, ICLR 2020*.

Yaowei Zheng, Richong Zhang, and 3 others. 2024. LlamaFactory: Unified efficient fine-tuning of 100+ language models. In *Proceedings of the 62nd Annual Meeting of the Association for Computational Linguistics (Volume 3: System Demonstrations)*.

Yulei Zhu, Kazhuo Deji, and 2 others. 2023. Sentiment analysis of Tibetan short texts based on graphical neural networks and pre-training models. *Journal of Chinese Information Processing*, 37(2):71–79.

Real-time Commentator Assistant for Photo Editing Live Streaming

Matīss Rikters and Goran Topić
National Institute of Advanced Industrial Science and Technology
{firstname.lastname}@aist.go.jp

Abstract

Live commentary has the potential of making specific broadcasts such as sports or video games more engaging and interesting to watch for spectators. With the recent popularity rise of online live streaming many new categories have entered the space, like art in its many forms or even software development, however, not all live streamers have the capability to be naturally engaging with the audience. We introduce a live commentator assistant system that can discuss what is visible on screen in real time. Our experimental setting is focused on the use-case of a photo editing live stream. We compare several recent vision language models for commentary generation and text to speech models for spoken output, all on relatively modest consumer hardware configurations.

1 Introduction

Introducing live commentary to a broadcast can meaningfully impact the enjoyment of its viewers, but being a fun and engaging commentator is a skill that many people simply do not possess. Existing systems can sometimes require a significant amount of compute and often cannot function in real-time on consumer hardware. Our goal is to build a virtual commentator assistant system that would be capable of functioning on a consumer-level laptop or desktop while also performing other resource-intensive tasks in the background or foreground such as photo editing and live streaming software.

We choose the domain of photo editing live streaming for its simplicity and somewhat slow nature. This allows us to sample the screen with a far lower frequency, enabling all necessary computation to run on-device in adequate time. Aside from photo editing, there are many other slow-paced categories for live streaming, such as making miniature models, software and game development, or even cooking. Additionally, the popularity of VTubers has tremendously grown in the live streaming space, which are online entertainers who use virtual avatars instead of showing themselves directly live on camera. This inspires us to also create a visual animated character who would be personified to speak out the generated comments.

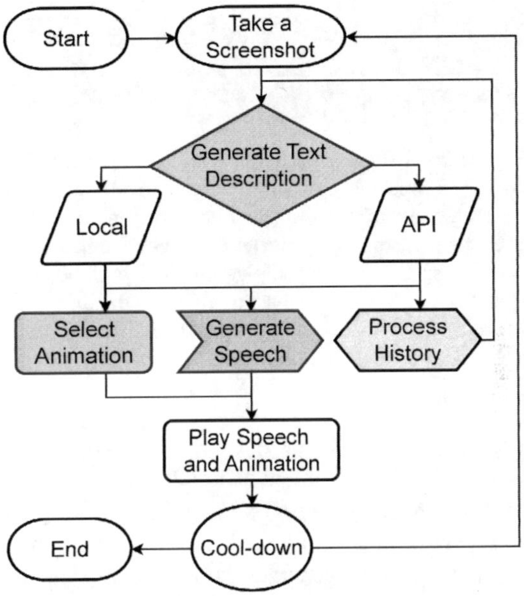

Figure 1: Live commentary system overview flowchart.

2 Related Work

Previous work (Ishigaki et al., 2023) has focused on generating audio commentary from game telemetry data, specifically – a racing game which allows such data collection. Unlike our work, their method does not consider what is actually shown on the screen. They also use a separate server for calculations and only produce audio output.

Yamazaki et al. (2023) propose an open-domain avatar chatbot in a virtual reality environment, which incorporates speech recognition, modules for spoken text processing and refinement, avatar

Proceedings of The 14th International Joint Conference on Natural Language Processing and The 4th Conference of the Asia-Pacific Chapter of the Association for Computational Linguistics: System Demonstrations, pages 17–24

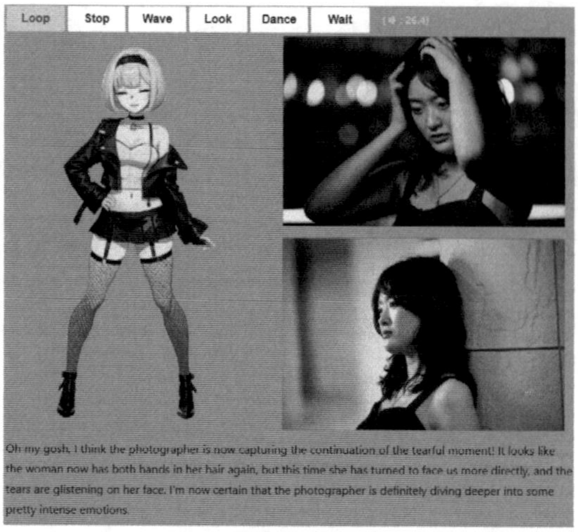

Figure 2: A screenshot of the user interface for control. The first row shows the main control buttons for character animations, a status timer showing how many seconds it takes to generate text, speech, and how long until all speech is finished playing back, and the cool-down timer, if enabled. Further down is the animated character, current and previous photo (screenshot), and the generated text comment to be spoken out.

expression generation, text to speech (TTS), as well as use of an LLM for text comprehension and generation. While the authors mention that using an 82B parameter LLM and an in-house TTS solution is challenging for generation speed, there is no detail on what hardware is used or processing time for each component.

Marrese-Taylor et al. (2022) sample suitable utterances from open-domain input videos and generate textual commentary to enhance the viewing experience. However, their approach is not real-time and the nature of open-domain videos makes the task much more difficult to tackle.

3 Architecture

The system consists of three main components as highlighted in Figure 1 - text generation from the screenshot, speech generation from the text and visual expression animation based on the text contents. After clicking the 'Loop' button (top-left in Figure 2), the process begins and keeps running until the 'Stop' button is pressed. A screenshot is automatically taken, a text description is generated based on the screenshot, and speech is generated based on the text, along with selecting an appropriate animation for the assistant character to display while the speech is being played.

After a configurable cool-down period, the process starts again; however, in subsequent iterations, the model is also supplied with the last screenshot and previously generated comments, to contextualise the current screenshot. To avoid the history becoming too large and overburdening the model, a history compaction process is also implemented, to summarise history and compact it to a predefined size. Figure 3 shows the system at work with the animated avatar overlay on top of the photo editing view, as well as the current screenshot on the bottom left and the previous screenshot on the bottom right side.

3.1 Spoken Text Generation

For the task of generating spoken text based on the screenshot of the photo currently being edited, we use a smaller-sized multimodal large language model (LLM) on device to accommodate a good balance of memory usage and relative performance. By default we choose *Phi-3.5-vision-instruct* (Abdin et al., 2024), but the model parameter is configurable with support for several other similar models, which are loaded from the Hugging Face model library[1]. Model performance is compared in the Experiments and Results sections. We also enable the use of online API versions of multimodal LLMs such as *Gemini-2.5-flash* by Google or *GPT 4o* by OpenAI to offload this more intensive task in GPU-poor scenarios.

The comments get generated from the first screenshot based on the default prompt (listed in the Appendix), and then from a combination of the most recent current screenshot and the one prior. Previous generated comments are maintained as context, and optionally summarised in a compact history representation after a certain configurable threshold.

3.2 History Compacting

By default, all the comments generated by the model are kept in the memory, and provided to the model as context for the user's current activity. If left unchecked, after a while this will result in more time spent in comment generation, as well as incur larger fees if a paid remote API is used. To control this, a history size range can be specified. If a maximum size is set, then the history will be compacted when this size (in number of comments) is reached. The most recent comments, up

[1]https://huggingface.co/models

Figure 3: A screenshot of the live-stream view with the assistant character and current/previous photos overlay.

to the minimum size setting, will be retained as-is, while the older comments will be summarised into a single comment representing old history.

3.3 Speech Generation

When searching for a viable approach for speech generation, we set a criterion that the speech generated by the model should sound more like a fictional character than an actual person, along with having capabilities to generate speech with emotion instead of being monotone. However, the main criterion was model size and generation speed, while maintaining reasonable output quality.

We found that the *Kokoro-82M* model[2] performs amazingly well for its size and also allows for some customisation of the generated voice. We compare it with several other text to speech (TTS) models in sizes up to 350M parameters in the Experiments and Results sections.

3.4 Visual Character and Animation

To generate the visual character, we used the AI Anime Generator[3] on Perchance (a platform for creating and sharing random generators) using Stable Diffusion (Rombach et al., 2022) as a backend. The character was generated based on a prompt describing a selection of unique visual features and a simple uniform background for easy removal.

Next, we used the *Wan2.1-I2V-14B-720P* model (Wang et al., 2025) to generate short animations for various situations. We generated several variations of the character talking calmly to enrich the diversity of expressions shown. We also prompted the model to generate specific animations for occasions when the character would express particular interest, happiness, fear, affection and other emotions. In addition, we prepared animation versions for the character to enter the screen from the side; leave the screen; wave hello or good bye; wait patiently for the next time to start speaking; look around to both sides pretending to be bored; and slowly dance while nothing interesting is happening.

Running specific animations can be controlled through the user interface (UI). However most are selected automatically, depending on the contents of the generated text. The selection of specific animations expressing interest, happiness, fear, affection and other emotions is based on pre-defined regular expressions. For example, the regular expression to trigger the animation showing the character being scared is “*\b(?:scar\w+|creep\w*|fright\w*|spook\w*)\b*".

[2]`https://huggingface.co/hexgrad/Kokoro-82M`
[3]`https://perchance.org/ai-anime-generator`

Model	Size	R3090	G1650L	R3070L	R4070L	R4090L	M3 Pro	Average
Phi-3.5	4.2B	9.8	111.0	11.0	13.6	10.0	103.4	43.1
Phi-4	5.6B	14.2	-	1360.6	1270.2	11.0	-	664.0
Gemma 3	4B	25.9	548.3	25.5	34.6	25.1	38.3	116.3
	12B	31.4	-	421.0	510.2	32.2	-	248.7
Qwen 2.5-VL	3B	9.9	247.2	12.4	19.3	11.1	20.7	53.4
	7B	10.2	-	12.4	32.9	10.6	-	16.5
FastVLM	0.5B	9.1	13.7	6.7	11.0	8.7	7.3	9.4
	1.5B	11.3	-	8.4	16.0	11.6	12.9	12.0
	7B	12.1	-	12.9	25.8	11.9	-	15.7
	Average	14.9	230.0	207.9	214.8	14.7	36.5	

Table 1: Results on text description generation in seconds on select consumer hardware. We abbreviate RTX and GTX to R and G, and Laptop to L for the NVIDIA GPU models. All results are averages over 30 runs. A dash represents unsuccessful runs for the specific model-hardware combination.

		1 Image	2 Images
Phi-3.5	4.2B	363.1	632.5
Phi-4	5.6B	385.4	682.7
Gemma	4B	534.8	727.1
	12B	429.8	505.1
Qwen2.5-VL	3B	458.1	582.0
	7B	395.3	615.6
FastVLM	0.5B	690.9	779.0
	1.5B	706.1	891.5
	7B	816.3	823.7
	Average	531.1	693.2

Table 2: Average text length in characters with one or two images as inputs. All averages over 30 runs.

4 Experiments

We experiment with testing the system on four consumer-grade gaming laptops with NVIDIA GTX 1650 4GB, RTX 3070 8GB, RTX 4070 8GB and RTX 4090 16GB GPUs, one desktop with RTX 3090 24GB, and a Macbook with M3 Pro and 18GB of memory. We run the experiments in two different settings - 1) running all models locally; and 2) running speech generation locally, but relying on Google Gemini[4] or OpenAI GPT[5] for text generation.

For text generation, we compare four different multimodal language model families and test model sizes from 0.5B to 12B parameters. The models are compared on generation speed, length of the generated comments, and also how much do newly generated comments overlap with previously generated comments in the same session.

Meanwhile in terms of speech models, we only consider models up to 350M parameters in size, as anything larger takes too much time and GPU memory to feasibly be part of our system. TTS models are mainly compared in terms of generation speed.

Flash attention (Dao, 2024) is used on compatible hardware (everything except M3 Pro and GTX 1650). All models are loaded with 4-bit precision (Dettmers et al., 2023) if compatible (everything except M3 Pro and the Phi-4 model).

A short demonstration video recording is available on YouTube[6]. We also release our source code in a public GitHub repository under a permissive license[7].

5 Results

The experiment results maily help us validate model compatibility with reasonable consumer hardware, as well as validate our choices of default models and other supported models. We consider the laptop with the RTX 4090 Laptop GPU as our main baseline hardware configuration, the GTX 1650 Laptop GPU – our minimum configuration, and the M3 Pro – our alternative configuration.

5.1 Text Generation

For the task of comment generation, we compare the following versions of recent multimodal LLMs – Phi 3.5 Vision Instruct (Abdin et al., 2024), Phi

[4]Gemini 2.5 Flash-Lite (August 2025) - https://ai.google.dev/gemini-api/docs/models#gemini-2.5-flash-lite

[5]GPT-4o mini (August 2025) https://platform.openai.com/docs/models/gpt-4o-mini

[6]https://www.youtube.com/watch?v=LuPcfsqPSso

[7]https://github.com/M4t1ss/live-photo-commentary

Model	Size	History 0 tok	History 0 chr	History 1 tok	History 1 chr	History 5 tok	History 5 chr	Average tok	Average chr
Phi-3.5	4.2B	53.1%	8.3%	55.8%	8.2%	80.4%	19.7%	63.1%	12.1%
Phi-4	5.6B	56.9%	7.2%	70.2%	6.5%	91.6%	53.2%	72.9%	22.3%
Gemma	4B	55.6%	12.4%	51.1%	8.3%	59.0%	9.5%	55.2%	10.1%
	12B	50.4%	11.8%	46.8%	9.5%	49.1%	9.6%	48.8%	10.3%
Qwen2.5-VL	3B	52.8%	6.9%	46.0%	7.4%	71.3%	22.5%	56.7%	12.3%
	7B	50.4%	8.1%	48.7%	7.7%	45.4%	9.0%	48.2%	**8.3%**
FastVLM	0.5B	56.0%	10.1%	93.2%	53.5%	99.3%	82.3%	82.9%	48.7%
	1.5B	59.4%	9.2%	90.1%	24.4%	98.5%	47.0%	82.7%	26.9%
	7B	57.3%	8.1%	79.0%	7.9%	87.5%	35.8%	74.6%	17.3%
Gemini	2.5-flash	43.2%	8.5%	39.8%	8.0%	43.6%	7.6%	**42.2%**	**8.0%**
GPT	4o-mini	52.1%	12.9%	51.4%	11.0%	48.1%	12.9%	50.5%	12.3%
	Average	54.7%	9.1%	64.5%	14.8%	75.8%	32.1%		

Table 3: Average text overlap between the last two generated comments with different history compacting thresholds in terms of overlapping tokens (tok) and character substring overlap (chr).

4 Multimodal Instruct (Abouelenin et al., 2025), Gemma 3 (Kamath et al., 2025) in 4B and 12B sizes, Qwen 2.5-VL (Bai et al., 2025) in 3B and 7B sizes, and FastVLM (Vasu et al., 2025) in 0.5B, 1.5B and 7B sizes.

As can be seen in table 1, all tested models run smoothly on the baseline configuration and generate comments within 10-11 seconds, aside from the two Gemma 3 models, which overall seem to be among the slowest on all tested hardware. However, both on the minimum and the alternative configurations Phi 4, Gemma 3 12B, Qwen 2.5-VL 7B and FastVLM 7B are entirely unable to run. Out of all models tested, Phi 4 has the least compatibility – unable to run on two GPUs and on two others taking over 20 minutes to produce a result.

Table 2 shows that the FastVLM models tend to generate longer outputs regardless whether the input is one image or two. The other models generate comments with an average length of 446 characters while the average for FastVLM models is 686 characters. Comparing two image inputs to one image input, the increase in average generated characters is around 160, with outliers like Phi 3.5 almost doubling the amount compared to single image, and Gemma 3 12B only generating around 40 characters more for dual image inputs.

Upon manual inspection of the generated comments, we noticed that at times there is substantial overlap between the current and previous comments generated by some models, or even a 1:1 copy – not based on the input images at all. Therefore, we evaluated handling of our history feature

Model	Size	Time, s
Bark	300M	48.8
Bark-small	80M	27.5
Kokoro-82M	82M	**0.5**
OuteTTS-0.1	350M	87.6
MMS-TTS-ENG	36M	5.8
SpeechT5	145M	7.5

Table 4: Comparison of several smaller text to speech models, showing model size and average generation time over 10 runs. Input text was on average 555 characters long ranging between 347 and 828 characters.

by the LLMs using a set of 10 consecutive photos from the same photo shoot as inputs. In table 3 we look at how the multimodal LLMs handle our history compacting approach, by comparing passing history lengths of 0 (history turned off), 1, and 5 previously generated comments along with the prompt. We measure the percentage of overlapping tokens (words) between two consecutive outputs, as well as the percentage of overleaping characters. The FastVLM models are overall worst in terms ov both overlap metrics, while Gemma 3 and Qwen 2.5-VL models along with Gemini and GPT APIs perform best here. Some models like both Phi models, Qwen 2.5-VL 3B, and FastVLM 7B only suffer from the overlapping output issue with the longer history of 5 comments.

5.2 Speech Generation

Most modern TTS models have at least 0.5B parameters, which can hinder efficient execution on consumer hardware. We test base and small versions of the Bark model from Suno[8], Kokoro-82M, OuteTTs-0.1[9], MMS-TTS-ENG (Pratap et al., 2024), and SpeechT5 (Ao et al., 2022). As these models are quite small in terms of parameters, we only consider testing on our baseline hardware configuration. All tests were performed on 10 previously generated comments from Phi 4, ranging between 347 and 828 characters in length.

Table 4 shows that the Kokoro-82M is by far the overall fastest TTS model, taking on average only 0.5 seconds to generate speech for the previously generated comments from the multimodal LLMs, which is over 10 times faster than the next fastest – MMS-TTS. Based on these results, we select Kokoro-82M as the default model and add MMS-TTS-ENG and SpeechT5 as alternative options to select in our system.

6 Conclusion

In this paper, we introduce a live commentator assistant system for the use case of photo editing online live streaming, which generates real-time commentary based on what is visible on-screen. It is capable of fully functioning locally alongside live streaming and photo editing software with moderate consumer hardware requirements, as well as utilising multimodal LLM APIs to offload a major part of the required computation supporting even lower-grade hardware.

For future work we consider a wide range of potential improvements and expansions of our proposed task. In terms of expanding the scope of the task, we plan on utilising dialogue-styled commentary based on either user input or live-stream chat to make the interaction even more engaging. Other avenues of expanding the scope include enhancing live streams with additional explanatory graphics as on-screen overlays, and exploring the applicability of short video capture commentary. As for the actual quality of the generated text, we plan on performing a small-scaled human evaluation study to obtain a broader insight on the quality of the generated text beyond token and character overlap. Further improvements of output quality may also be achieved by implementing output filtering based on heuristics (Rikters, 2018) or the model attention mechanism output (Rikters and Fishel, 2017).

[8]https://github.com/suno-ai/bark

[9]https://github.com/edwko/OuteTTS

Limitations

In this work, we only considered using models that are publicly available at no cost to enable reproducibility. The computation setup for our experiments is relatively modest and well within reach for most who would be willing to reproduce our experiments.

Our proposed system is easily reproducible with publicly available model checkpoints and open-source tools which are cited in this paper. Our full workflow shall be released on GitHub. For the blind submission, we prepared an anonymised version as an attachment. Our system is also not limited to the specific model families cited in the paper, so one could simply swap out the text or speech models for others compatible with the Hugging Face Transformers workflow.

Ethical Considerations

Our work is fully in accordance with the ACL Code of Ethics[10]. We use only publicly available open-weight models and relatively low compute amounts while conducting our experiments to enable reproducibility. We do not conduct studies on other humans or animals in this research.

References

Marah Abdin, Jyoti Aneja, Hany Awadalla, Ahmed Awadallah, Ammar Ahmad Awan, Nguyen Bach, Amit Bahree, Arash Bakhtiari, Jianmin Bao, Harkirat Behl, Alon Benhaim, Misha Bilenko, Johan Bjorck, Sébastien Bubeck, Martin Cai, Qin Cai, Vishrav Chaudhary, Dong Chen, Dongdong Chen, and 110 others. 2024. Phi-3 technical report: A highly capable language model locally on your phone. *Preprint*, arXiv:2404.14219.

Abdelrahman Abouelenin, Atabak Ashfaq, Adam Atkinson, Hany Awadalla, Nguyen Bach, Jianmin Bao, Alon Benhaim, Martin Cai, Vishrav Chaudhary, Congcong Chen, Dong Chen, Dongdong Chen, Junkun Chen, Weizhu Chen, Yen-Chun Chen, Yi ling Chen, Qi Dai, Xiyang Dai, Ruchao Fan, and 55 others. 2025. Phi-4-mini technical report: Compact yet powerful multimodal language models via mixture-of-loras. *Preprint*, arXiv:2503.01743.

Junyi Ao, Rui Wang, Long Zhou, Chengyi Wang, Shuo Ren, Yu Wu, Shujie Liu, Tom Ko, Qing Li, Yu Zhang, Zhihua Wei, Yao Qian, Jinyu Li, and Furu Wei. 2022. SpeechT5: Unified-modal encoder-decoder

[10]https://www.aclweb.org/portal/content/acl-code-ethics

pre-training for spoken language processing. In *Proceedings of the 60th Annual Meeting of the Association for Computational Linguistics (Volume 1: Long Papers)*, pages 5723–5738, Dublin, Ireland. Association for Computational Linguistics.

Shuai Bai, Keqin Chen, Xuejing Liu, Jialin Wang, Wenbin Ge, Sibo Song, Kai Dang, Peng Wang, Shijie Wang, Jun Tang, Humen Zhong, Yuanzhi Zhu, Mingkun Yang, Zhaohai Li, Jianqiang Wan, Pengfei Wang, Wei Ding, Zheren Fu, Yiheng Xu, and 8 others. 2025. Qwen2.5-vl technical report. *Preprint*, arXiv:2502.13923.

Tri Dao. 2024. FlashAttention-2: Faster attention with better parallelism and work partitioning. In *International Conference on Learning Representations (ICLR)*.

Tim Dettmers, Artidoro Pagnoni, Ari Holtzman, and Luke Zettlemoyer. 2023. Qlora: Efficient finetuning of quantized llms. In *Advances in Neural Information Processing Systems*, volume 36, pages 10088–10115. Curran Associates, Inc.

Tatsuya Ishigaki, Goran Topić, Yumi Hamazono, Ichiro Kobayashi, Yusuke Miyao, and Hiroya Takamura. 2023. Audio commentary system for real-time racing game play. In *Proceedings of the 16th International Natural Language Generation Conference: System Demonstrations*, pages 9–10, Prague, Czechia. Association for Computational Linguistics.

Aishwarya Kamath, Johan Ferret, Shreya Pathak, Nino Vieillard, Ramona Merhej, Sarah Perrin, Tatiana Matejovicova, Alexandre Ramé, Morgane Rivière, Louis Rouillard, Thomas Mesnard, Geoffrey Cideron, Jean bastien Grill, Sabela Ramos, Edouard Yvinec, Michelle Casbon, Etienne Pot, Ivo Penchev, Gaël Liu, and 196 others. 2025. Gemma 3 technical report. *Preprint*, arXiv:2503.19786.

Edison Marrese-Taylor, Yumi Hamazono, Tatsuya Ishigaki, Goran Topić, Yusuke Miyao, Ichiro Kobayashi, and Hiroya Takamura. 2022. Open-domain video commentary generation. In *Proceedings of the 2022 Conference on Empirical Methods in Natural Language Processing*, pages 7326–7339, Abu Dhabi, United Arab Emirates. Association for Computational Linguistics.

Vineel Pratap, Andros Tjandra, Bowen Shi, Paden Tomasello, Arun Babu, Sayani Kundu, Ali Elkahky, Zhaoheng Ni, Apoorv Vyas, Maryam Fazel-Zarandi, Alexei Baevski, Yossi Adi, Xiaohui Zhang, Wei-Ning Hsu, Alexis Conneau, and Michael Auli. 2024. Scaling speech technology to 1,000+ languages. *J. Mach. Learn. Res.*, 25(1).

Matīss Rikters. 2018. Impact of Corpora Quality on Neural Machine Translation. In *Proceedings of the 8th Conference Human Language Technologies - The Baltic Perspective (Baltic HLT 2018)*, Tartu, Estonia.

Matīss Rikters and Mark Fishel. 2017. Confidence Through Attention. In *Proceedings of the 16th Machine Translation Summit (MT Summit 2017)*, Nagoya, Japan.

Robin Rombach, Andreas Blattmann, Dominik Lorenz, Patrick Esser, and Björn Ommer. 2022. High-resolution image synthesis with latent diffusion models. In *Proceedings of the IEEE/CVF Conference on Computer Vision and Pattern Recognition (CVPR)*, pages 10684–10695.

Pavan Kumar Anasosalu Vasu, Fartash Faghri, Chun-Liang Li, Cem Koc, Nate True, Albert Antony, Gokul Santhanam, James Gabriel, Peter Grasch, Oncel Tuzel, and Hadi Pouransari. 2025. Fastvlm: Efficient vision encoding for vision language models. In *Proceedings of the IEEE/CVF Conference on Computer Vision and Pattern Recognition (CVPR)*.

Ang Wang, Baole Ai, Bin Wen, Chaojie Mao, Chen-Wei Xie, Di Chen, Feiwu Yu, Haiming Zhao, Jianxiao Yang, Jianyuan Zeng, Jiayu Wang, Jingfeng Zhang, Jingren Zhou, Jinkai Wang, Jixuan Chen, Kai Zhu, Kang Zhao, Keyu Yan, Lianghua Huang, and 42 others. 2025. Wan: Open and advanced large-scale video generative models. *arXiv preprint arXiv:2503.20314*.

Takato Yamazaki, Tomoya Mizumoto, Katsumasa Yoshikawa, Masaya Ohagi, Toshiki Kawamoto, and Toshinori Sato. 2023. An open-domain avatar chatbot by exploiting a large language model. In *Proceedings of the 24th Annual Meeting of the Special Interest Group on Discourse and Dialogue*, pages 428–432, Prague, Czechia. Association for Computational Linguistics.

A Prompt Format

Table 5 shows examples of prompts used for generating comments. We use the exact same prompts for all models without fine-tuning them to each model individually. The default example prompts are formed in a way that works best with our proposed use-case of editing photography (e.g. mentioning gridlines, sliders, addressing the photographer). For other use-cases these prompts can be updated as needed.

<table>
<tr><th>Prompt</th><th>Text</th><th>Addition</th></tr>
<tr><td>SYSTEM</td><td>You are a friendly chatty commentator who likes to casually describe work done by a photographer in various details, even by pondering the implications on work, or leisure, being performed, etc. Write your response in a very personal way using personal pronouns and explaining what you see, perhaps also adding how it makes you feel. Do your best to not be repetitive in your choice of words. You MUST keep the response length to no more than three sentences. You MUST NOT mention any specific layout elements or tools that may be visible on the screen, such as gridlines or sliders.</td><td></td></tr>
<tr><td>MAIN</td><td>Summarize what is visible in the current photo, <|image_1|>. How is it different from the previous photo, <|image_2|>? There may be some subtle differences as well. Do not describe the previous photo; assume you have described it already. It is only there for context, so you can notice the new things in the current photo. Do not mention photos explicitly; use words like ‘I can see...’ or ‘The photographer is now...’ and similar. Use the comment history for context and continuity, but the utmost priority should be on describing the current activity, as reflected in the current photo. DO NOT repeat comments from the history.</td><td>+ ENDING</td></tr>
<tr><td>FIRST</td><td>Summarize what is visible in this image: <|image_1|></td><td>+ ENDING</td></tr>
<tr><td>ENDING</td><td>Do not at all mention any specific layout elements or tools that may be visible on the screen, such as overlays, gridlines or sliders. To adjust intonation, please add dedicated punctuation like ; : , . ! ? ... ( ) “ ” For example, to emphasize a word or a phrase, surround it with "quotation marks". However, since the text will undergo speech synthesis, do not use anything unpronounceable, like emojis.</td><td></td></tr>
<tr><td>COMPACT</td><td>Summarize in one short paragraph your (the assistant’s) comments so far on the current activity; i.e. compact it into a single comment of comparable size to one individual original comment, that encapsulates the essence of the current activity’s past. If some older comments pertain to a different activity, you can ignore them; focus only on the current activity. This is what you (the assistant) commented before:</td><td></td></tr>
<tr><td>HISTORY</td><td>This is what you (the assistant) commented before:</td><td></td></tr>
</table>

Table 5: Examples of prompts used for comment text generation. The FIRST prompt is used only at the beginning when there is just one screenshot, after which the MAIN prompt is used. The HISTORY prompt is used to maintain recent context, and COMPACT – for consolidating older history into a short summary.

Supporting Plain Language Summarization of Psychological Meta-Analyses with Large Language Models

Yarik Menchaca Resendiz[1,2], **Martin Kerwer**[1], **Anita Chasiotis**[1], **Marlene Bodemer**[1], **Kai Sassenberg**[1] and **Roman Klinger**[2]
[1]Leibniz-Institut für Psychologie (ZPID), Trier, Germany
[2]Fundamentals of Natural Language Processing, University of Bamberg, Germany
{ymr,mk,ac,mabo,ksa}@leibniz-pyschology.org, roman.klinger@uni-bamberg.de

Abstract

Communicating complex scientific findings to non-experts remains a major challenge in fields like psychology, where research is often presented in highly technical language. One effective way to improve accessibility, for non-experts, is through plain language summaries, which summarize key insights into simple and understandable terms. However, the limited number of institutions that produce lay summaries typically relies on psychology experts to create them manually – an approach that ensures high quality but requires significant expertise, time, and effort. In this paper, we introduce the KLARpsy App, a system designed to support psychology experts in creating plain language summaries of psychological meta-analyses using Large Language Models (LLM). Our system generates initial draft summaries based on a 37-criterion guideline developed to ensure clarity for non-experts. All summaries produced through the system are manually validated and edited by KLARpsy authors to ensure factual correctness and readability. We demonstrate how the system integrates LLM-generated content into an expert-in-the-loop workflow. The automatic evaluation showed a mean semantic-similarity score of 0.73 against expert-written summaries, and human evaluation on a 5-point Likert scale averaged above 3 (higher is better), indicate that the generated drafts are of high quality. The application and code are open source.

1 Introduction

Plain language summaries play an important role in making scientific findings accessible to broader audiences. In psychology and other disciplines, research findings are often communicated in technical language that can be difficult for non-experts to understand. This becomes especially challenging in the context of meta-analyses, where findings from multiple studies are summarized using specialized terminology and statistical information.

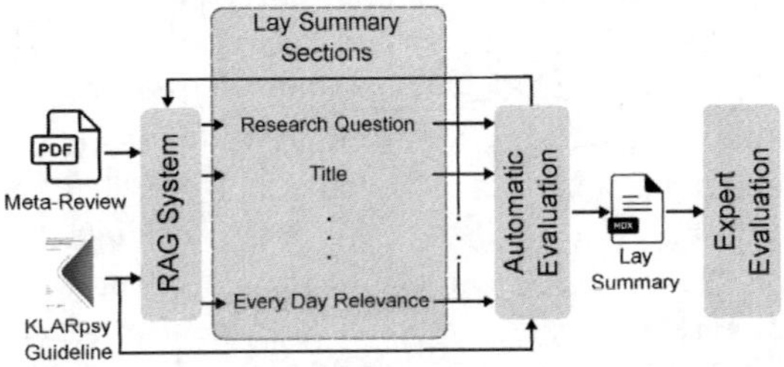

Figure 1: Workflow overview of the KLARpsy App, which follows the KLARpsy guidelines for summarizing psychological texts.

In recent years, there has been a growing initiative both in policy and practice – to promote more accessible scientific communication. For example, plain language summaries are now required for clinical trials in the European Union (under Regulation EU No. 536/2014; European Commission, 2023; Center for Drug Evaluation and Research et al., 2017; European Medicines Agency, 2022). These efforts aim to help non-experts understand and engage with research evidence.

Despite these developments, creating plain language summaries remains a time-consuming and expert-driven task. Summaries need to be both clear and accurate – especially in fields like psychology, where findings often inform health decisions or clinical practice. At the same time, new tools based on large language models offer promising support for generating initial drafts. These models are capable of producing fluent text (Shaib et al., 2023; Turbitt et al., 2023), but their reliability, particularly when it comes to factual accuracy, remains limited (Tomlin et al., 2024).

In this paper, we present KLARpsy App (Figure 1), a system developed to support psychology experts in creating plain language summaries of psychological meta-analyses[1]. Rather than re-

[1]We refer to scientific publications that include at least one meta-analysis as "meta-analyses".

Proceedings of The 14th International Joint Conference on Natural Language Processing and The 4th Conference of the Asia-Pacific Chapter of the Association for Computational Linguistics: System Demonstrations, pages 25–35
December 20-24, 2025 ©2025 Association for Computational Linguistics

placing human expertise, the system is designed to work alongside it. It generates initial drafts based on a structured 37-point guideline to produce summaries for lay readers (Chasiotis et al., 2023). These drafts are then reviewed, edited, and finalized by domain experts, as ensuring factual accuracy and accessible language is essential. Even in full expert workflows, lay summaries are often checked by other experts or by laypersons.

Our approach highlights the potential of human-AI collaboration in scientific communication. By combining the efficiency of LLMs with expert oversight, KLARpsy App aims to reduce the load of producing summaries while maintaining high standards of quality. We also provide an evaluation, both automatic and human, of the system's outputs to better understand its strengths and limitations in practice. The code and an installable executable are available at `https://github.com/leibniz-psychology/klarpsy-summarization-assistant`.

2 Related Work

Automatic plain-text generation has been a long-standing area of research in natural language processing. Early work in this space focused on rule-based and statistical methods. Classical approaches include template-based generation and extractive summarization techniques that rely on word-frequency and cue-phrase detection (Tas and Kiyani, 2017; Reiter and Dale, 1997; El-Kassas et al., 2021; Kloehn et al., 2018).

In recent years, the field has increasingly shifted toward the use of large language models – such as GPT-Family (OpenAI, 2022, 2023), LLaMA-Family (Touvron et al., 2023; Grattafiori et al., 2024), and Mixtral (Jiang et al., 2024) – due to their ability to generate fluent, coherent text. This transition has significantly influenced the development of plain language summaries, especially in the scientific and biomedical domains. Recent work has evaluated LLMs in generating lay summaries of complex biomedical content, often highlighting their strengths in readability and fluency (Shaib et al., 2023; Turbitt et al., 2023; Tailor et al., 2024).

However, a limitation in LLM-based applications – not only summarization – is the risk of hallucination (i.e., the generation of inaccurate or fabricated information), which is particularly problematic in medical and scientific contexts where factual accuracy is critical (Tomlin et al., 2024). For instance, Fang et al. (2024) introduced the FAREBIO benchmark to evaluate factual consistency in biomedical lay summaries, showing that high fluency often correlates with diminished factual reliability.

To address this limitation, recent studies have explored human-in-the-loop frameworks where LLMs serve as assistive tools rather than standalone applications (Ovelman et al., 2024; Salazar-Lara et al., 2024; Tomlin et al., 2024; Chamberlain James, 2024). For example, Shyr et al. (2024) used engineered prompts with ChatGPT-4 to generate layperson-level summaries of clinical research abstracts. They validated performance using participant feedback from the ResearchMatch platform. Srivastava et al. (2024) introduced PIECE, a system that improves mental health dialogue summarization by first selecting important parts of the conversation using counseling knowledge. It then guides a language model with a structured plan to generate clearer and more accurate summaries. Showing the importance of humans in the loop, which is especially relevant in health care systems.

Our work builds on previous research by guiding LLM-based generation using a 37-point psychological guideline to produce lay summaries (Chasiotis et al., 2023). Rather than aiming to fully automate the process, our application is designed to function as a tool within a human-in-the-loop framework. The generated summaries are reviewed and validated by psychological experts to ensure accuracy and clarity.

3 KLARpsy App

This section introduces KLARpsy App, a system designed to assist psychology experts in generating plain language summaries of psychological meta-analyses. The tool uses a retrieval-augmented generation (RAG) system to produce initial summary drafts (in an MDX format, similar to a Markdown file), which are then reviewed and refined by domain experts and published[2]. The draft is guided by a 37-point criterion developed specifically for generating lay psychological summaries. Rather than replacing expert judgment, KLARpsy App supports a human-in-the-loop workflow that ensures both clarity and factual correctness. Section 3.1 provides a detailed overview of the system's architecture and workflow, while Section 3.2 outlines the psychological guideline that guides the system.

[2]`https://klarpsy.de/klarpsytexte/`

3.1 System Description

KLARpsy App is implemented as a retrieval-augmented generation system (Figure 1) using a client/server architecture. The client provides an easy-to-use interface for non-computer-science experts (e.g., psychologists), while the server performs the computationally intensive model inference. In this paper, we use OpenAI's GPT family as the backend because it eliminates the need for local GPU resources, enabling distribution as a standalone executable (e.g., a Windows .exe or a macOS .dmg) for non-technical users. The system can be easily updated to run local language models.

The application accepts as input one or more PDF files (meta-analyses), and optionally, a configuration file that specifies parameters such as the underlying model, API credentials, section lengths, and custom prompts.

The system is designed to generate 16 distinct sections that together form a plain language summary of a psychological meta-analysis. These sections include, for example, the Title, Background, and Research Question, and are structured according to the criteria defined in the KLARpsy guideline. Each section is generated independently, based on relevant content extracted from the meta-analysis. However, to maintain coherence and consistency across the full summary, the system models interdependencies between sections. For instance, the generation of the Title and Main Message depends on the content of the Research Question section. To handle these dependencies, KLARpsy App employs a chain-of-thought prompting strategy, where the content from earlier sections is explicitly passed as input into the generation of subsequent sections. For example, when generating the Title, the system first extracts the original scientific title from the meta-analysis and then paraphrases it to align with the identified research question.

The KLARpsy guideline defines two types of sections in the lay summary, each requiring a different generation strategy: (1) Free-text generation sections (e.g., Background, Interpretation of Results) are generated using zero-shot and few-shot prompting, guided by open-ended natural language instructions that incorporate the KLARpsy criteria (e.g., "Explain this in simple terms for a general audience."). (2) Information extraction and template filling sections follow fixed structures (e.g., Study Objective, Participant Information) that are generated using structured extraction and output generation techniques (Willard and Louf, 2023; OpenAI, 2024). Prompts for these sections include explicit output schemas to ensure the model adheres to predefined formats such as bullet points, labeled fields, or fixed templates (e.g., "The researchers searched for studies [topic_of_the_meta-analysis]. [Description_of_selection criteria]").

To further ensure the quality of the generated content, each section undergoes an automatic evaluation and optimization loop, which includes Structural checks (e.g., section length, formatting completeness) and readability assessments using established metrics such as Flesch Reading Ease (Flesch, 1948), Gunning Fog Index (Gunning, 1952), and SMOG Index (Mc Laughlin, 1969), to verify that the language is accessible to non-experts.

3.2 KLARpsy Guideline

The KLARpsy guideline (Chasiotis et al., 2023) provides a structured framework for writing lay summaries of psychological meta-analyses. Developed at the Leibniz Institute of Psychology (ZPID)[3], it aims to make complex research findings transparent and accessible to a non-specialist audience while maintaining neutrality and scientific accuracy.

Each KLARpsy text consists of 16 standardized content sections: Title, Key message, Authors and Affiliations, Background, Research Question, Study Selection, Study Selection Criteria, Study Approach, Study Variables, Key Results, Result Interpretation, Result Bias, Results Reliability, Every Day Relevance, and Funding and Conflicts of Interest (See Appendix A for an example). The guideline includes 37 criteria, organized into six categories: (1) *General content* ensures alignment with the original meta-analysis; (2) *Contextual attributes* address target audience and publication process; (3) *Linguistic attributes* cover tone, choice of words (e.g., handling of jargon and technical terms); (4) *Formal attributes* relate to structure, standardized formulation, and word limits, etc.; (5) *Presentation of results* guides the reporting of statistical findings; and (6) *Presentation of evidence quality* covers reliability of the evidence, such as reporting ratings or disclosing authors' conflicts of interest.

[3] https://leibniz-psychology.org/

4 Evaluation

We evaluate the initial drafts produced by KLARpsy App, which are intended to be refined through human-in-the-loop editing, using both automatic (Section 4.1) and human (Section 4.2) evaluations. In addition, in Section 4.3, we compare KLARpsy App against FlexRAG (Zhuocheng et al., 2025), an out-of-the-box RAG system.

4.1 Automatic Evaluation

The automatic evaluation consists of two parts: (1) assessing how well the KLARpsy App replicates expert-written summaries; and (2) evaluating the application's ability to generate lay summaries.

For the first part, we use 99 expert-written lay summaries as gold standards.[4] We then compare the model-generated summaries at the section level using two methods: BLEU scores and semantic similarity (we prompt GPT-4 to rate the similarity between corresponding sentences on a 5-level scale). BLEU provides a standard measure of word-level overlap, while the semantic-similarity score captures the overall idea even when phrasing differs. Table 1 reports the performance of the KLARpsy App replicating KLARpsy texts (expert-written). As expected, BLEU scores are generally low, since the same information can be phrased in many different ways. The exception is the *Authors* section, where BLEU scores are higher because author names must be directly extracted from the paper, leaving little room for paraphrasing. Semantic similarity (S. sim.), however, provides a more informative signal, showing stronger alignment between generated and human-written text. Sections involving information extraction (e.g., Authors, Conflict of Interest, Study Selection) achieve the highest similarity scores. In contrast, sections requiring more open-ended generation have a slightly lower performance (e.g., Research question, Background). Notably, the Results Reason section shows one of the lowest scores (0.56), likely reflecting the tendency of LLMs to generate assertive rather than uncertain statements – a limitation we discuss further in Section 4.2.

We evaluate readability using three standard indices: (1) Flesch Reading Ease (FRE), which ranges from 0–100 with higher values indicating easier text, (2) Gunning Fog Index, and (3) SMOG Index, both of which estimate the years of education required for comprehension (lower scores indicate simpler text). Table 2 reports scores for generated text, with expert-written references shown in parentheses. On average, KLARpsy App achieves a Gunning Fog score of 15.1 and a SMOG score of 13.8 – similar to expert-written texts – corresponding to a high school to early college reading level. This aligns with FRE values and suggests that readers do not need specialized training or professional expertise to understand the generated summaries.

Section	**KLARpsy**		**FlexRAG**	
	BLEU	**S. sim.**	**BLEU**	**S. sim.**
Title	0.02	0.70	0.01	0.13
Key message	0.03	0.62	0.01	0.10
First author	0.22	0.67	0.04	0.33
Affiliation	0.06	0.49	0.03	0.14
Authors	0.68	0.80	0.00	0.08
Background	0.02	0.62	0.01	0.13
Research Question	0.09	0.75	0.01	0.13
Selection criteria	0.04	0.65	0.00	0.18
Study selection	0.10	0.63	0.01	0.17
Study approach	0.04	0.62	0.01	0.15
Study variables	0.02	0.63	0.00	0.11
Key results	0.03	0.66	0.00	0.12
Results reason	0.07	0.53	0.00	0.14
Results bais	0.33	0.85	0.08	0.80
R. reliability	0.02	0.45	0.01	0.17
Everyday relevance	0.02	0.56	0.01	0.12
Funding	0.11	0.58	0.00	0.05
Conflict of interest	0.45	0.80	0.01	0.13
Average	0.15	0.73	0.01	0.20

Table 1: Evaluation of KLARpsy App and FlexRAG against 99 human-written texts across the KLARpsy sections.

4.2 Human Evaluation

For the human evaluation, three psychological experts evaluate the 10 generated lay summaries using a five-point Likert scale (Not at all, Slightly, Somewhat, Moderately, Extremely) across six statements: (1) the information in this slot correctly reflects the content/title; (2) the text avoids irrelevant information; (3) the language is understandable for laypeople; (4) the uncertainty in existing scientific findings is adequately reflected in the choice of words (or the language too assertive); (5) the text is neutral (i.e., without judgemental or advice); and (6) I would not recognize that the text has been written by an AI. These aspects were chosen based on the requirements of the KLARpsy guideline. Lay summaries are expected to use a neutral and non-directive tone to ensure that they are not mis-

[4] The 99 lay summaries were written by an expert and reviewed by another expert and a layperson to guarantee factual accuracy and accessible language, following the KLARpsy guideline. The summaries are available at https://klarpsy.de/klarpsytexte/)

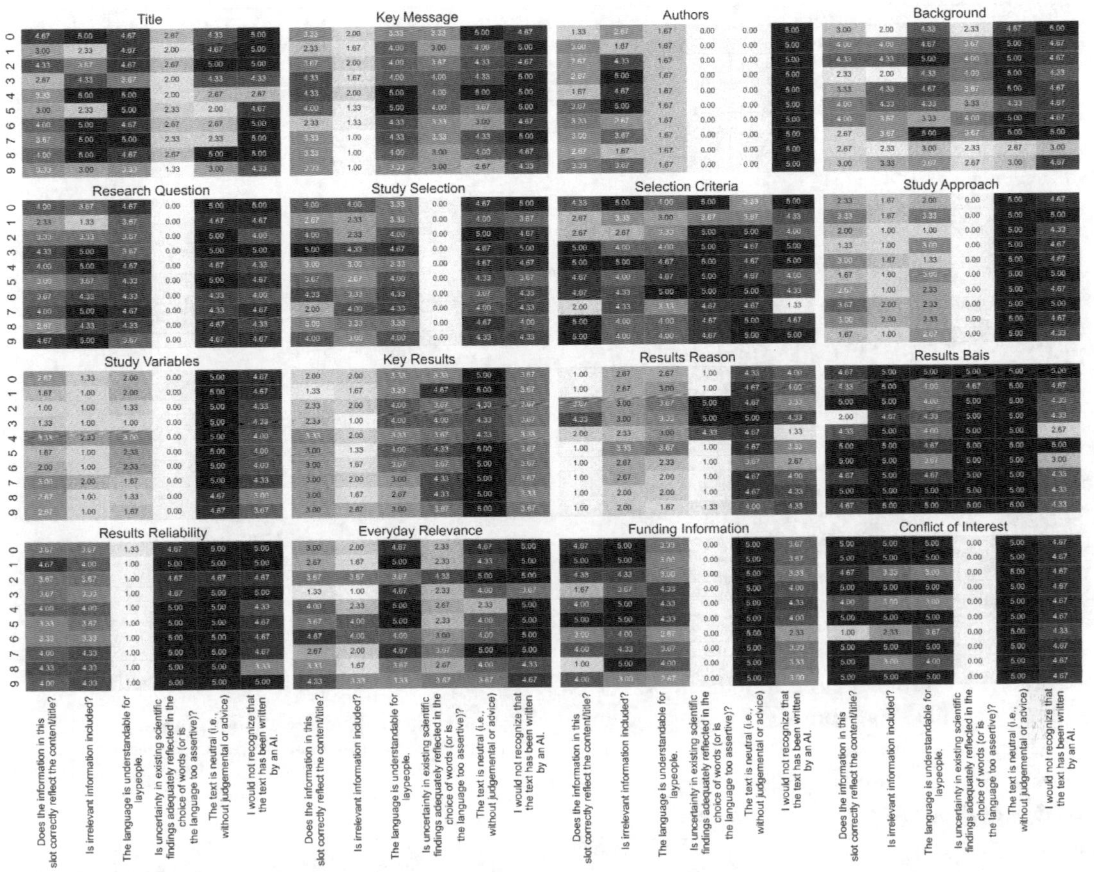

Figure 2: Section-level human evaluation results. Each heatmap shows the distribution of scores (1–5; higher/darker is better) across six evaluation criteria (x-axis) for the 10 papers (y-axis). Columns with a value of zero indicate that the criterion was not applicable (e.g., uncertainty does not apply to author names).

understood as guidelines or directions, but instead as evidence-based information. Table 3 reports the inter-annotator agreement among the three experts, with an average across the 16 sections of 0.60, indicating a high level of agreement.

Figure 2 presents heatmaps of section-level scores across the six criteria. Information extraction sections (e.g., Selection Criteria, Authors, and Funding Information) scored consistently high–predominantly dark green cells. In contrast, sections involving the presentation and interpretation of results (e.g., Study Variables, Research Question, and Results Reason) showed lower scores – primarily due to Criterion 4 (Is uncertainty in existing findings adequately reflected . . . ?) and Criterion 2 (Is irrelevant information included?). These results show that while LLMs handle information extraction reliably, they tend to produce verbose formulations and overstated claims about findings (e.g., "Treatment X helped patients" instead of "Treatment X benefited N out of 100 patients").

Table 4 shows the average score for each evaluation criterion across the 16 sections. Most criteria received scores above 3, indicating that the generated texts were generally of acceptable quality. The exception is Criterion 4, which averaged 2.05, reinforcing the automatic evaluation results reported in Section 4.1 and reflected in Figure 2.

4.3 Baseline Comparison

We compare KLARpsy App against FLEXRAG (Zhuocheng et al., 2025), an off-the-shelf RAG system, using the same set of 99 meta-reviews described in Section 4.1. To ensure a fair comparison, both systems rely on the same underlying model, GPT-4.0. For FLEXRAG, each summary was generated by providing only the meta-analysis and the KLARpsy guideline as prompts. Table 1 reports the BLEU scores and sentence similarity scores (against the 99

Section	FRE	Gunning	SMOG
Title	50.0 (28.5)	12.4 (15.8)	11.5 (12.9)
Key message	41.5 (25.2)	13.8 (16.6)	13.2 (14.7)
Background	37.5 (31.6)	14.9 (15.1)	13.4 (13.9)
Research Question	38.0 (38.6)	16.8 (16.2)	14.8 (14.5)
Selection criteria	44.5 (29.0)	14.3 (17.1)	13.4 (15.1)
Study selection	42.5 (54.7)	14.6 (12.3)	13.5 (11.8)
Study approach	38.1 (25.4)	15.5 (18.7)	14.7 (16.3)
Study variables	17.4 (15.1)	24.7 (28.4)	19.5 (23.3)
Key results	30.4 (31.3)	16.8 (15.0)	15.5 (13.5)
Results reason	29.2 (34.9)	17.1 (15.2)	15.3 (14.3)
Results bias	46.4 (47.5)	11.6 (11.0)	10.9 (10.6)
R. reliability	44.4 (33.1)	13.6 (14.7)	13.2 (13.7)
Everyday relevance	33.1 (31.3)	15.2 (16.2)	14.3 (14.8)
Funding	47.4 (36.0)	13.7 (17.2)	12.8 (15.1)
Conflict of interest	53.7 (60.7)	11.5 (9.8)	11.4 (10.1)
Average	39.6 (35.2)	15.1 (15.5)	13.8 (14.2)

Table 2: Evaluation of KLARpsy App generated text on readability using the Flesch Reading Ease (FRE), Gunning Fog (Gunning) Index, and SMOG Index across the KLARpsy sections. Readability scores for expert-written texts are shown in parentheses.

expert-written summaries) across the 16 sections. Although BLEU scores are low for both systems, KLARpsy App outperforms FLEXRAG across all sections. Sentence similarity scores show a similar trend. KLARpsy App outperforms FlexRAG with an average score of 0.73 compared to 0.20. These results suggest that lay summarization cannot be reliably achieved with an out-of-the-box RAG system.

5 Conclusion and Future Work

We introduced KLARpsy App, a RAG system that supports psychology experts in creating plain language summaries of meta-analyses. Guided and optimized by a 37-point guideline, the system produces layperson-friendly drafts that experts refine for factuality and clarity – in a human-in-the-loop workflow. Automatic evaluation shows that the model produces solid initial drafts, achieving a similarity score of 0.73 compared to expert-written texts. Human evaluations indicated strong overall performance, with scores exceeding 3 out of 5 on most criteria. The only exception was criterion 4 ("uncertainty expression"), which received a score of 2. This finding strengthens the need for experts in the loop, as LLMs tend to produce verbose formulations and overstated claims about findings.

In future work, we will explore automatic prompt-optimization techniques to refine prompts so they better match the domain of each meta-analysis (e.g., education, crime and law, media, mental health). In addition, we plan to investigate reinforcement learning with an expert in the loop and expand the KLARpsy App to additional languages.

Section	Krippendorff's α
Title	0.31
Key message	0.53
Authors	0.59
Background	0.22
Research question	0.85
Study selection	0.77
Selection criteria	0.53
Study approach	0.86
Study variables	0.83
Key results	0.21
Results reason	0.53
Publication bias	0.33
Results reliability	0.77
Everyday relevance	0.53
Funding info	0.81
Conflict of interest	0.93
Average	0.60

Table 3: Inter-annotator agreement between three experts, reported as Krippendorff's α for each section and overall.

Criterion	Avg.
Does the information in this slot correctly reflect the content title?	3.32
Does the text avoid irrelevant information?	3.18
The language is understandable for laypeople.	3.41
Is uncertainty in existing scientific findings adequately reflected in the choice of words (or is the language too assertive)?	2.05
The text is neutral (i.e., without judgemental or advice)	4.31
I would not recognize that the text has been written by an AI.	4.36

Table 4: Average ratings (1–5 scale) for each criterion.

6 Limitations

Summarising scientific texts for a lay audience inevitably involves a trade-off between accessibility and technical accuracy. Making complex findings easier to understand often requires simplifying terminology and concepts, but this can risk omitting important qualifiers or subtly changing the intended meaning. Our design addresses this by positioning KLARpsy App as a tool to assist, rather than replace, domain experts. However, this approach depends on experts being available to review and refine outputs, which may limit scalability in practice.

The system is built around a psychological guideline developed specifically for plain language summaries of meta-analyses in psychology. While this framework could serve as a starting point for other fields, it would require adaptation to the terminology, conventions, and standards of each specific domain. This limits its immediate, "out-of-the-box" applicability beyond psychology.

7 Ethical Considerations

The presented work involves generating plain-language summaries of psychological meta-analyses using large language models. LLMs may introduce hallucinations or overly confident claims that could mislead non-expert readers. Since inaccurate information may affect public understanding of scientific findings, the KLARpsy App outputs are intended only as initial drafts for experts rather than as a fully automatic tool. Moreover, the KLARpsy App is designed specifically for summarizing psychological meta-reviews and has not been tested in other domains. Therefore, the use outside of psychology should be validated by domain experts.

We use GPT-4.0 as the underlying model, and results may vary with other LLMs or future model updates. Summary quality and accuracy may differ across models, so applying the system with alternative LLMs requires additional validation.

References

Center for Drug Evaluation and Research, Center for Biologics Evaluation and Research, and Center for Devices and Radiological Health. 2017. Draft fda guidance on provision of plain language summaries. Accessed: [August 1, 2025].

Lisa Chamberlain James. 2024. Plain language summaries of clinical trial results: What is their role, and should patients and ai be involved? *Medical Writing*, 33(3):34–37.

Anita Chasiotis, Gesa Benz, Martin Kerwer, Pawel Nuwaltzew, Marlene Stoll, and Mark Jonas. 2023. Klarpsy-richtlinie zum verfassen allgemeinverständlicher zusammenfassungen psychologischer metaanalysen.

Wafaa S. El-Kassas, Cherif R. Salama, Ahmed A. Rafea, and Hoda K. Mohamed. 2021. Automatic text summarization: A comprehensive survey. *Expert Systems with Applications*, 165:113679.

European Commission. 2023. Clinical trials– regulation eu no 536/2014. Accessed: [August 1, 2025].

European Medicines Agency. 2022. Clinical trials information system. Accessed: [August 1, 2025].

Biaoyan Fang, Xiang Dai, and Sarvnaz Karimi. 2024. Understanding faithfulness and reasoning of large language models on plain biomedical summaries. In *Findings of the Association for Computational Linguistics: EMNLP 2024*, pages 9890–9911, Miami, Florida, USA. Association for Computational Linguistics.

Rudolph Flesch. 1948. A new readability yardstick. *Journal of applied psychology*, 32(3):221.

Aaron Grattafiori, Abhimanyu Dubey, and Llama Team. 2024. The llama 3 herd of models. *arXiv preprint arXiv:2407.21783*.

Robert Gunning. 1952. *The Technique of Clear Writing*. McGraw–Hill.

Albert Q Jiang, Alexandre Sablayrolles, Antoine Roux, Arthur Mensch, Blanche Savary, Chris Bamford, Devendra Singh Chaplot, Diego de las Casas, Emma Bou Hanna, Florian Bressand, and 1 others. 2024. Mixtral of experts. *arXiv preprint arXiv:2401.04088*.

Nicholas Kloehn, Gondy Leroy, David Kauchak, Yang Gu, Sonia Colina, Nicole P Yuan, and Debra Revere. 2018. Improving consumer understanding of medical text: development and validation of a new subsimplify algorithm to automatically generate term explanations in english and spanish. *Journal of medical Internet research*, 20(8):e10779.

G Harry Mc Laughlin. 1969. Smog grading-a new readability formula. *Journal of reading*, 12(8):639–646.

OpenAI. 2022. Gpt-3.5 model. Accessed: [30.03.2024].

OpenAI. 2023. Gpt-4 technical report.

OpenAI. 2024. Structured outputs. `https://platform.openai.com/docs/guides/structured-outputs`. Accessed: 2025-08-06.

Katharina Otten, Lara Keller, Andrei A. Puiu, Beate Herpertz-Dahlmann, Jochen Seitz, Nils Kohn, J. Christopher Edgar, Lisa Wagels, and Kerstin Konrad. 2022. Pre- and postnatal antibiotic exposure and risk of developing attention deficit hyperactivity disorder–a systematic review and meta-analysis combining evidence from human and animal studies. *Neuroscience and Biobehavioral Reviews*, 140:104776.

Colleen Ovelman, Shannon Kugley, Gerald Gartlehner, and Meera Viswanathan. 2024. The use of a large language model to create plain language summaries of evidence reviews in healthcare: A feasibility study. *Cochrane Evidence Synthesis and Methods*, 2(2):e12041.

Ehud Reiter and Robert Dale. 1997. Building applied natural language generation systems. *Natural Language Engineering*, 3(1):57–87.

Carolina Salazar-Lara, Andrés Felipe Arias Russi, and Rubén Manrique. 2024. Bridging the gap in health literacy: Harnessing the power of large language models to generate plain language summaries from biomedical texts. *medRxiv*.

Chantal Shaib, Millicent Li, Sebastian Joseph, Iain Marshall, Junyi Jessy Li, and Byron Wallace. 2023. Summarizing, simplifying, and synthesizing medical evidence using GPT-3 (with varying success). In *Proceedings of the 61st Annual Meeting of the Association for Computational Linguistics (Volume 2: Short Papers)*, pages 1387–1407, Toronto, Canada. Association for Computational Linguistics.

Cathy Shyr, Randall W Grout, Nan Kennedy, Yasemin Akdas, Maeve Tischbein, Joshua Milford, Jason Tan, Kaysi Quarles, Terri L Edwards, Laurie L Novak, Jules White, Consuelo H Wilkins, and Paul A Harris. 2024. Leveraging artificial intelligence to summarize abstracts in lay language for increasing research accessibility and transparency. *Journal of the American Medical Informatics Association*, 31(10):2294–2303.

Aseem Srivastava, Smriti Joshi, Tanmoy Chakraborty, and Md Shad Akhtar. 2024. Knowledge planning in large language models for domain-aligned counseling summarization. In *Proceedings of the 2024 Conference on Empirical Methods in Natural Language Processing*, pages 17775–17789, Miami, Florida, USA. Association for Computational Linguistics.

Prashant D. Tailor, Haley S. D'Souza, Clara M. Castillejo Becerra, Heidi M. Dahl, Neil R. Patel, Tyler M. Kaplan, Darrell Kohli, Erick D. Bothun, Brian G. Mohney, Andrea A. Tooley, Keith H. Baratz, Raymond Iezzi, Andrew J. Barkmeier, Sophie J. Bakri, Gavin W. Roddy, David Hodge, Arthur J. Sit, Matthew R. Starr, and John J. Chen. 2024. Utilizing ai-generated plain language summaries to enhance interdisciplinary understanding of ophthalmology notes: A randomized trial. *medRxiv*.

Oguzhan Tas and Farzad Kiyani. 2017. A survey automatic text summarization. *PressAcademia Procedia*, 5(1):205–213.

Holly R. Tomlin and 1 others. 2024. Challenges and opportunities for professional medical publications writers to contribute to plain language summaries (pls) in an ai/ml environment – a consumer health informatics systematic review. In *AMIA Annual Symposium Proceedings*, volume 2023, pages 709–717. Symposium held 11 Jan 2024.

Hugo Touvron, Louis Martin, Kevin Stone, Peter Albert, Amjad Almahairi, Yasmine Babaei, Nikolay Bashlykov, Soumya Batra, Prajjwal Bhargava, Shruti Bhosale, and 1 others. 2023. Llama 2: Open foundation and fine-tuned chat models. *arXiv preprint arXiv:2307.09288*.

Oisín Turbitt, Robert Bevan, and Mouhamad Aboshokor. 2023. MDC at BioLaySumm task 1: Evaluating GPT models for biomedical lay summarization. In *Proceedings of the 22nd Workshop on Biomedical Natural Language Processing and BioNLP Shared Tasks*, pages 611–619, Toronto, Canada. Association for Computational Linguistics.

Brandon T Willard and Rémi Louf. 2023. Efficient guided generation for large language models. *arXiv preprint arXiv:2307.09702*.

Zhang Zhuocheng, Yang Feng, and Min Zhang. 2025. FlexRAG: A flexible and comprehensive framework for retrieval-augmented generation. In *Proceedings of the 63rd Annual Meeting of the Association for Computational Linguistics (Volume 3: System Demonstrations)*, pages 621–631, Vienna, Austria. Association for Computational Linguistics.

A Lay Summary Example from the KLARpsy App

In the next sections, we present the same lay summary produced by psychology experts (Section A.1) and by KLARpsy App (Section A.2).[5] All summaries are generated from the meta-analysis reported in Otten et al. (2022).

A.1 Human Generated Summary

```
---
title: "Is the risk of ADHD higher in babies who had early exposure to antibiotics?"

key_message: "Babies do not have an increased risk of ADHD if they receive antibiotics shortly after
    birth. However, babies do have an increased risk of ADHD if their mothers take antibiotics
    during pregnancy."
---
### Background:
"ADHD (Attention-Deficit/Hyperactivity Disorder) is one of the most common developmental disorders of
    the nervous system. The gut microbiota also plays an important role in the development of such
    disorders. It can be disrupted when antibiotics are taken. Therefore, researchers are examining
    whether early exposure to antibiotics can lead to a child developing ADHD."

### Research question:
"With their review, the researchers wanted to find out: Do babies who come into contact with
    antibiotics very early have a higher risk of developing ADHD later on?"

### Which studies did the researchers look for in the review?
"The researchers looked for studies that examined a connection between early exposure to antibiotics
    as a baby and the development of ADHD. The exposure to antibiotics had to occur during the
    mother's pregnancy or up to two years after birth."

### Which studies did the researchers find for the review?
"The researchers found a total of 8 studies from the years 2016 to 2021. Of these, 4 studies from the
    years 2019 to 2021 involved babies who received antibiotics after birth, which they could
    combine into a meta-analysis. These results pertain to 1,863,867 babies. Another 4 studies from
    the years 2019 to 2021 involved babies whose mothers took antibiotics during pregnancy, which
    they could combine into another meta-analysis. These results pertain to 2,398,475 babies."

### What did the researchers do in the review?
"In the 8 studies, the researchers examined whether early exposure to antibiotics increased the risk
    of infants developing ADHD later on."

### What did the researchers investigate in the review?
"The following characteristics of the babies were examined:

- Type and timing of contact with antibiotics
  - Before birth
    - The mother took antibiotics during pregnancy.
    - The mother did not take antibiotics during pregnancy.
  - After birth
    - The baby received antibiotics in the first two years of life.
    - The baby did not receive antibiotics in the first two years of life.
- Development of ADHD in childhood
  - The baby later developed ADHD in childhood.
  - The baby did not develop ADHD later in childhood."

## What are the most important results?
"- When the mothers of the babies took antibiotics during pregnancy, the risk of the babies
    developing ADHD later was significantly higher. The summary risk measure, Hazard Ratio, was 1.23.
    This means that the risk of these babies developing ADHD later was 1.23 times higher compared
    to babies whose mothers did not take antibiotics during pregnancy.
- When the babies received antibiotics after birth, the risk of them developing ADHD later was not
    significantly higher compared to babies who did not receive antibiotics after birth."

### What is the reason for the results?
"The review article observed a correlation between the intake of antibiotics during the mother's
    pregnancy and a subsequent ADHD diagnosis in the child. Due to the types of studies that were
```

[5] For space reasons, we omit all comments and interface-related code that is constant across summaries. The expert version was originally written in German, machine-translated into English, and then double-checked by the experts.

considered, it is only known that this correlation exists. However, it cannot be definitively stated that the antibiotics caused the ADHD."

Are the results biased by limited publication of studies?
- What is the issue? Clear research results are easier to publish than ambiguous results. This is problematic for reviews. They cannot take unpublished results into account.

"- **What is it about?** Clear research findings are easier to publish than ambiguous results. This poses a problem for review articles because they cannot take unpublished results into account.

- **What does this mean for the present review article?** The researchers do not specify whether there are indications of such biases. It remains unclear whether the connection between antibiotics and ADHD is actually smaller than calculated in this review article."

How reliable are the results?
"All the studies examined were observational studies. From these results, it cannot be determined whether antibiotics actually cause ADHD. ADHD could also have been caused by something else, such as the mother's illness, which required her to take antibiotics."

What relevance to everyday life do the researchers see in the review?
"The researchers say that the results are important for the study of ADHD. However, improved studies are needed in order to make clear statements. Experiments with test animals would also help in drawing reliable conclusions."

Who funded the review?
"The creation of the review article was funded by the German Research Foundation. This is an organization that promotes science and research in Germany. It is financed by the federal and state governments."

Do the researchers report their own conflicts of interest in the review?
"The researchers report that there are no conflicts of interest present."

A.2 KLARpsy App Lay Summary

---
title: "**Can Taking Antibiotics During and After Pregnancy Increase a Child's Risk of Developing ADHD?**"

key_message: "The study investigates whether using antibiotics around the time of birth could increase the risk of ADHD in children by affecting gut health and brain development. Animal studies have previously shown that early antibiotic use can change gut health and behavior, implying a connection between the gut and brain development."

Background:
"The study investigates if taking antibiotics around the time of birth could increase a child's risk of developing ADHD. It suggests that antibiotics might alter gut bacteria, potentially impacting brain development and behavior. The research also considers other factors like genetics and the environment that could affect ADHD."

Research question:
With their review, the researchers wanted to find out:"Does exposure to antibiotics before and shortly after birth increase the risk of a child developing ADHD, possibly by affecting gut health and brain development?"

Which studies did the researchers look for in the review?
"Researchers looked at studies to see if taking antibiotics during pregnancy or early childhood is connected to being diagnosed with ADHD later on. They focused on studies involving humans in the first two years of life and some experiments with animals. Only studies written in English before January 2021 were considered, and two experts carefully checked each study to make sure it was relevant and met their criteria."

Which studies did the researchers find for the review?
"The researchers found a total of 21 studies published between 1995 and 2017, involving 2,398,475 subjects who participated in the analysis of prenatal antibiotic exposure and 1,863,867 subjects in the study on postnatal exposure within the first two years of life."

What did the researchers do in the review?
"In the 21 studies, The researchers looked at how giving antibiotics to mothers before and shortly after birth could affect a child's chances of developing ADHD. They gathered information from

different human and animal studies. In human studies, they explored any possible link between antibiotic use and ADHD. The animal studies helped them understand how antibiotics might impact gut health and behavior. By using statistical techniques, they made sure their results were dependable, considering both the direct and indirect effects of antibiotics on the risk of ADHD ."

What did the researchers investigate in the review?
"- Investigating the impact of early antibiotic exposure on the risk of developing ADHD.
- Main variables investigated:
  - Prenatal Antibiotic Exposure
  - Postnatal Antibiotic Exposure
  - ADHD Diagnosis"

What are the most important results?
"The research found that taking antibiotics before birth is linked to a higher risk of a child developing ADHD, likely due to changes in gut health. However, giving antibiotics to young children after they're born doesn't generally increase ADHD risk, except in premature babies, where it might play a role. Scientists suggest that how antibiotics affect gut health could influence brain development, but more studies are needed to fully understand these connections."

What is the reason for the results?
"In the review, relationships between prenatal antibiotic exposure and ADHD risk were observed. Because of the type of studies that were considered, it can be said with a high degree of certainty,
- that prenatal antibiotic exposure is also the cause of an increased risk of developing ADHD in the general population.
- that postnatal antibiotic exposure does not cause increased susceptibility to ADHD, except possibly in preterm infants."

Are the results biased by limited publication of studies?
- What is the issue? Clear research results are easier to publish than ambiguous results. This is problematic for reviews. They cannot take unpublished results into account.

"What does this mean for this review? The researchers provide no information on whether there are indications of such biases. Whether the results indicating an increased risk for ADHD after prenatal antibiotic exposure are actually smaller than calculated in this review thus remains unclear."

How reliable are the results?
"The results of the study aren't very strong because there were only a few studies included, and they weren't all the same. Also, the way the study was designed might have added some confusion. The connections found might actually be due to the infections themselves rather than the antibiotics used."

What relevance to everyday life do the researchers see in the review?
"Taking antibiotics during pregnancy might increase the chances of the child developing ADHD by affecting gut health. After birth, antibiotics generally don't raise ADHD risk, except possibly in premature babies. Changes in gut health may impact brain development, but more research is needed to understand these links."

Who funded the review?
"The preparation of the review was funded by Deutsche Forschungsgemeinschaft (DFG, German Research Foundation)."

Do the researchers report their own conflicts of interest in the review?
"The researchers report that they have no conflicts of interest."

Standardizing the Measurement of Text Diversity: A Tool and Comparative Analysis

Chantal Shaib[1†] **Venkata S Govindarajan**[4] **Joe Barrow**[3†] **Jiuding Sun**[1]
Alexa F. Siu[2] **Byron C. Wallace**[1] **Ani Nenkova**[2]
[1]Northeastern University, [2]Adobe Research, [3]Pattern Data, [4]Ithaca College
shaib.c@northeastern.edu

Abstract

The diversity across outputs generated by LLMs shapes perception of their quality and utility. High lexical diversity is often desirable, but there is no standard method to measure this property. Templated answer structures and "canned" responses across different documents are readily noticeable, but difficult to visualize across large corpora. This work aims to standardize measurement of text diversity. Specifically, we empirically investigate the convergent validity of existing scores across English texts, and release `diversity`, an open-source Python package[1] for measuring and extracting repetition in text. We also build a platform[2] based on `diversity` for users to interactively explore repetition in text. We find that fast compression algorithms capture information similar to what is measured by slow-to-compute n-gram overlap homogeneity scores. Further, a combination of measures—compression ratios, self-repetition of long n-grams, and Self-BLEU—are sufficient to report, as they have low mutual correlation with each other.

1 Introduction

LLM-generated texts are typically evaluated with respect to accuracy or factuality, e.g., as measured via entailment (Tang et al., 2023), or text quality aspects such as coherence and fluency (e.g., estimated using LLMs as evaluators Liu et al. 2023). When reference summaries are available, the similarity of generated outputs to these is also often measured (e.g., via ROUGE; Lin and Och, 2004). A complementary dimension of model performance is *diversity*, or how much "boilerplate" content is repeated *across* LLM outputs.

There is a distinct lack of standardization in reporting diversity in ML datasets (Zhao et al., 2024). We address this by introducing `diversity`, an open-source Python package for evaluating text diversity,[1] along with a web-based UI that allows users to visualize repetition in their corpus,[2] providing an intuitive, efficient tool for text analysis that permits: (i) Viewing repetitive text and Part-of-Speech n-grams; (ii) Quickly computing diversity metrics, and; (iii) Interactively highlighting and matching repetition in documents. Both the package[3] and UI code[4] are open-sourced under the Apache 2.0 license.

We run existing diversity metrics over English language outputs from several LLMs to identify a few (mostly) independent scores that characterize repetition. We also examine diversity in downstream datasets such as instruction tuning. Finally, we show that *compression ratio*—compressed over original texts size—is a fast, easy to compute score sufficient to capture the information in all token/-type ratio related alternatives. But we emphasize text length as an important confounder when assessing diversity: No reliable conclusions can be drawn without taking this into consideration.

Our contributions are as follows. (1) We introduce `diversity`, a Python package implementing diversity metrics. (2) We host and release source code to a user interface to explore repetition and diversity. (3) We evaluate the convergent validity of existing lexical diversity metrics and highlight compression ratios as efficient measures of diversity.

2 Related Work

Lack of diversity in text may result from repetition of lengthy strings or owe to subtle distributional patterns (Holtzman et al., 2019; Meister et al., 2022, 2023a). We focus on scores that aim to capture overt repetition across outputs, and leave for future work similar analysis of semantic and structural diversity scores (Bär et al., 2012; Shaib et al.,

†Partial work completed while at Adobe Research.
[1]https://pypi.org/project/diversity/
[2]`https://ai-templates.app`
[3]`https://github.com/cshaib/diversity`
[4]`https://github.com/cshaib/diversity_demo`

Proceedings of The 14th International Joint Conference on Natural Language Processing and The 4th Conference of the Asia-Pacific Chapter of the Association for Computational Linguistics: System Demonstrations, pages 36–46

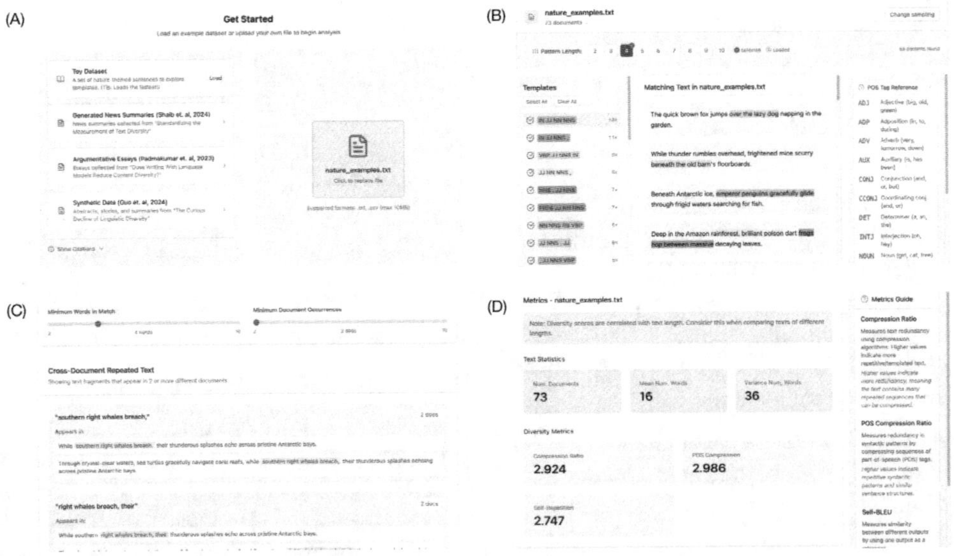

Figure 1: **(A)** Users start by uploading their own dataset on the right or by selecting one of the existing demo datasets on the left. Once uploaded, users can **(B)** interactively visualize part-of-speech patterns in the data, **(C)** interactively search for exact repeated text matches, and **(D)** calculate lexical diversity metrics.

2024). Conditional generation tasks such as image captioning have offered observations regarding the diversity of produced texts. Prior work has shown that models tend to repeat the same text for different contexts in these tasks (Li et al., 2016; Devlin et al., 2015). Self-repetition (Salkar et al., 2022)—exact repetition of the same n-gram ($n \geq 4$) across outputs—is a practical way of measuring repetition in lengthy outputs. In such cases repetition is common, especially relative to training data (Wang et al., 2023a).

We discuss several metrics but it is unclear which of these to use when, and how to efficiently visualize lower diversity in text-only tasks. Further, prior work has shown that human judgments of diversity are difficult to reliably collect. Humans tend to implicitly conflate quality of text with its diversity, and it can be difficult to separate content and lexical diversity in such assessments (Tevet and Berant, 2021). We design an interactive tool to allow users to browse highlighted instances of "lower diversity" text (Figure 1 (B)).

2.1 A Smorgasbord of Text Diversity Scores

Scores used to measure diversity across a corpus of texts derive from two core ideas: Computing average similarity between pairs of outputs produced by the same model for different inputs, and computing variants of token/type ratio. The former are adapted from common approaches to reference-based text generation using standard measures of pairwise similarity; the latter track the diversity of vocabulary measured as the ratio of unique words to total words produced, with outputs from a model concatenated into a single text. We first describe each score, and then present insights regarding their mutual redundancy. All scores are defined for a set of generated texts D, each conditioned on its respective input.

Self-BLEU The quality of text in machine translation, summarization, and image captioning is often reported in terms of overlap with a reference text. This idea can be adapted to measure diversity across different outputs by using one generated text as a "reference" and measuring the similarity of other outputs against this. Self-BLEU measures similarity between all text pairs in D using BLEU (Zhu et al., 2018). BLEU could be replaced with other similarity scores, e.g., ROUGE-L or BERTScore. These variants are called **homogenization scores** and have recently been used to compare the diversity of texts produced under several conditions (Padmakumar and He, 2023).

Homogenization Score (ROUGE-L) All homogenization scores calculate an aggregate similarity across pairs of examples (Equation 1). Here the similarity score of choice is ROUGE-L (Lin and Och, 2004), which quantifies overlap in terms of longest common sub-sequences between all pairs of text in a corpus instead of the fixed n-gram size used in other ROUGE variants:

$$\text{hom}(D) = \frac{1}{|D| - 1} \sum_{d,d' \in D;\, d \neq d'} \text{sim}(d, d') \quad (1)$$

Homogenization Score (BERTScore) This homogenization score uses BERTScore to measure similarity between documents in Equation 1. Unlike the other scores, it does not count the repetition of specific tokens, but instead uses BERT embeddings to (ideally) capture "semantic" similarity beyond verbatim n-gram matches.

Self-repetition Score Self-repetition measures the tendency of LMs to repeat long n-grams across different outputs (Salkar et al., 2022).

$$\text{SRS}(d) = \log\left(\sum_{i=1}^{k} N_i + 1\right) \quad (2)$$

Where k is the total number of 4-grams in a single document d and N_i the number of other summaries in which 4-gram i appears. The final score is the sum of SRS(d) divided by $|D|$.

Moving Average Token-Type Ratio The token-type ratio for a text is the unique token count divided by the total token count. This metric captures the repetition of a given word in segments of text and does not explicitly account for longer repeated sequences (Covington and McFall, 2010).

N-Gram Diversity Score NGD extends the idea of token-type ratio to longer n-grams (Padmakumar and He, 2023; Meister et al., 2023b; Li et al., 2023), taking a ratio of unique to all n-gram counts:

$$\text{NGD}(D) = \sum_{n=1}^{4} \frac{\#\text{ unique } n\text{-grams in } D\oplus}{\#\ n\text{-grams in } D\oplus} \quad (3)$$

Where $D\oplus$ denotes the dataset D concatenated into a single string. We use four as the maximum n-gram length. This method captures repeated *sequences* in addition to single token diversity.

2.2 Compression Ratios for Diversity

Compression Ratios (CRs) The diversity scores introduced so far are all a function of the number of repeated substrings across outputs. We use gZip to compress the concatenated text of all outputs generated by a model. CR is then the ratio between the size of the compressed file to that of the original. High CRs imply more redundancy:

$$\text{CR}(D) = \frac{\text{size of } D\oplus}{\text{compressed size of } D\oplus} \quad (4)$$

Part-of-Speech Compression Ratio To capture repeated syntactic patterns, we also compute compression ratios for part-of-speech (POS) tag sequences. We use the NLTK POS tagger [5] and the Penn Treebank set of 36 tags.

3 Evaluating Repetition with `diversity`

3.1 Design of the Diversity Package

The `diversity` package incorporates measures of diversity including lexical, syntactic, and semantic diversity. For lexical/syntactic diversity, we use NLTK (Bird and Loper, 2004) and SpaCY (Honnibal et al., 2020) to tag text with parts of speech and extract n-grams. We also include implementations of **embedding-based** measures (Cox et al., 2021), and **QUDSim** (Namuduri et al., 2025). Users can install the package via pip (assuming Python 3.10+) and can calculate various diversity metrics over a list of texts as follows:

```
from diversity import *

text = ["I enjoy walking with my cute
    dog...", "I enjoy walking outside
    with...", "I enjoy jogging on a
    sunny..."]
# compression ratios
cr = compression_ratio(text, 'gzip')
cr_pos = compression_ratio(get_pos(
    text)[1], 'gzip')
# homogenization scores
hs_rougel = homogenization_score(text,
    'rougel')
hs_bert = homogenization_score(text,
    'bertscore')
self_bleu = homogenization_score(text,
    'bleu')
# other
self_rep = self_repetition_score(text)
nds = ngram_diversity_score(text, n=4)

# Embedding-based
rc = remote_clique(text, model="Qwen/
    Qwen3-Embedding-0.6B", verbose=
    False)

cd = chamfer_dist(text, model="Qwen/
    Qwen3-Embedding-0.6B", verbose=
    False)

# QUDSim
key = os.environ.get("OPENAI_API_KEY")
    # requires an OpenAI key
qud_alignment = qudsim(text, key=key)
    # list of QUD-based alignments/
    scores
```

[5] `https://www.nltk.org/api/nltk.tag.html`

Users can extract PoS patterns using the `extract_patterns` function by specifying the n-gram length to search for, and the top_n most repeated n-grams to return:

```
extract_patterns(text, n=5, top_n=100)
```

This returns a Python dictionary where the keys are the part-of-speech n-grams and the values are the raw text n-grams matching those patterns. The pattern matches are based on the frequency seen across the entire dataset, i.e., a part-of-speech pattern is only a pattern if it appears in more than 2 texts in the original input. Default values consider the top 100 part-of-speech patterns (sorted by frequency).

Then, using `match_patterns`, a user can identify all patterns in a single text from the input:

```
idx = 2
match_patterns(text[idx], patterns)
```

which returns a list of tuples containing the pattern and matched substring, respectively. Many diversity metrics require pairwise comparisons. With larger datasets, this can become infeasible to compute (see Appendix A). We implement a few methods to increase efficiency: memoization of already computed pairs, and batch pattern searching in the UI.

We also include a function for users to run all metrics and display them in a table to easily compare values:

```
compute_all_metrics(corpus=text)
```

3.2 Metric Visualization and the Web UI

The `diversity` Web UI offers the same functionality as the package via a no-code UI. Figure 1 shows the main pages of the site: users can begin by (A) either uploading their own text file for analysis or selecting one of the demo datasets provided on the site. Then, the user is prompted to select one of three types of analyses: either (B) to explore part-of-speech patterns, (C) to explore verbatim repeated text, or (D) to measure various diversity metrics of the dataset. Datasets are processed upon upload, and nothing is stored on the backend server aside from the existing demo datasets.

(B) Templates The templates tab allows users to explore extracted part-of-speech n-grams in their selected dataset. The left-most column displays pattern length of $n = [2, 10]$. The user can then scroll through all of the templates, select some or all, and see the highlighted text in the middle panel corresponding to the template. The templates are assigned a colour when selected to indicate the corresponding matched text. The right-most column provides a reference for all the part-of-speech tags from SpaCY. [6] The default pattern length is set to $n = 4$. Other lengths will load when selected.

(C) Exact Match The exact matches tab allows a user to explore exact text matches in their dataset. The top provides two sliders: the left slider allows the user to set a string length to search for ($n = [2, 10]$), and the right the minimum number of documents in which the string must appear ($n = [2, 10]$). The minimum document occurrence slider defaults to 2. Once selected, the user can scroll through to see the repeated text in bold, and the full document text in which the string appears, as well as the number of documents.

(D) Diversity Metrics The diversity metrics tabs reports the recommended metrics from our evaluation: Compression Ratio, POS Compression, Self-BLEU, Self-Repetition, and Homogenization with BERTScore. We display these values alongside a guide to the metrics on the right-hand side.

3.3 Use-Cases

Our implementation of compression ratios over PoS tags and tokens (along with BERTScore, Self-BLEU, and self-repetition) have already been used in prior works (by other groups) to evaluate diversity in model evaluation and alignment (Lake et al., 2024; Moon et al., 2024; Fernandez et al., 2024), and for reporting diversity over synthetic datasets (Chang et al., 2024; Hastings et al., 2024). Due to its computational efficiency, compression ratios have also been used as optimization parameters in decoding strategies (Lanchantin et al., 2025).

Shaib et al. (2024) use the pattern analysis in `diversity` to measure and evaluate the prevalence of syntactic patterns in LLMs. Wadhwa et al. (2025) extract PoS patterns in distillation tasks for model attribution. Further, insights from our evaluation of diversity metrics have informed how to report diversity with respect to text length and data sizes (Guo et al., 2023; Hastings et al., 2024).

[6] https://spacy.io/usage/linguistic-features

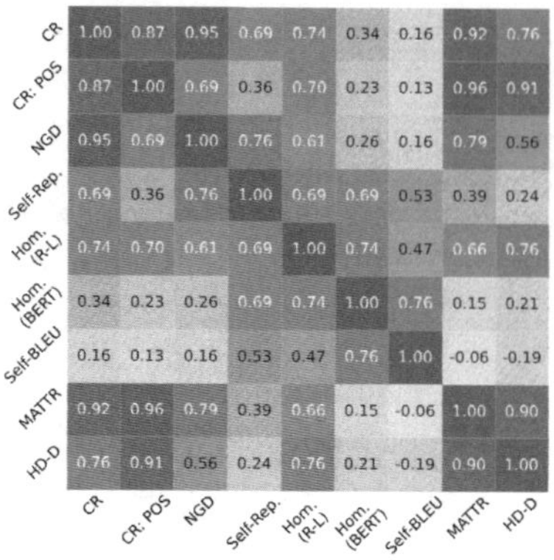

Figure 2: Correlations between diversity scores on CN-N/DM. CR correlates strongly with most other metrics.

4 Platform Evaluation: Comparative Analysis of Diversity Metrics

4.1 Data and Models

We compute diversity scores for the outputs of six instruction tuned models on the CNN/Daily-Mail (Hermann et al., 2015) and XSUM (Narayan et al., 2018) English news summarization datasets: Llama-2 (Touvron et al., 2023a), GPT-4 (OpenAI, 2023), FlanT5-XXL (Longpre et al., 2023), StableLM (Taori et al., 2023; Chiang et al., 2023; Anand et al., 2023), Mistral (Jiang et al., 2023), and StableBeluga (Touvron et al., 2023b; Mukherjee et al., 2023).[7] We selected these models to cover a range of availability (open and closed), and architectures (encoder-decoder, decoder-only). The lengths of texts vary considerably by source, for reference and model-produced text alike, so we also note average lengths when reporting diversity.

5 Text Length as a Confounder

To keep compute time and costs manageable, we randomly sample 500 inputs from CNN/DailyMail and XSUM for analysis. Table 1 reports diversity scores for outputs generated by the six LLMs for these inputs. Table 1 (top) reports scores for human-written texts: The article given as input for summarization, the baseline summary comprising the first three sentences of the news article, and the reference summary. These scores serve as a reference point for the diversity scores of the models.

One would expect that human-authored texts would be more diverse than those produced by LLMs (with the caveat that the texts were scraped from the web, and so may contain HTML and page layout artifacts which might be repetitive (Salkar et al., 2022)). The human texts differ by length and the sources of longer texts appear to be less diverse.

Text length as a confounder for diversity has been reported in prior work (Salkar et al., 2022), along with methods to account for this, e.g., sampling blocks of fixed size (Covington and McFall, 2010).

All scores of the token/type ratio family are highly correlated with length, while the pairwise similarity ones are only moderately correlated. Self-BLEU has low correlation with length.

6 Diversity of Model Summaries

The confound of length complicates reporting. On CNN/DM (cf. Table 1) StableLM produces the longest summaries. All scores indicate that these are the least diverse, probably due to length. Three types of differences are marked in the tables. Model summaries that are shorter but less diverse than human summaries are marked in bold. Human texts here are written by journalists, so the expectation is that they would be more diverse. More bold entries in a column indicate that the score captures differences between human and machine diversity, a desirable trait. Underlined entries denote models that are less diverse than other models that produce longer summaries. The more underlined entries there are for a model, the more indicators there are that its output is less diverse. Asterisks mark models that appear more diverse than a human text of shorter length.

The most interesting diversity scores are those that capture differences between human and automatically produced text. On the CNN/DM dataset, Hom. (BERT) and MATTR are the two scores that detect no differences between human and model texts. Compression ratio for part of speech sequences is the score that identifies the most differences between human and model-generated text. Self-repetition stands out as the only score that identifies model generated text as more diverse on the CNN/DM dataset. From this analysis, CR:POS and self-repetition emerge as prime candidates of reportable scores, while Hom. BERT is less useful.

7 Correlation Analysis

We present three sets of correlation analyses between *(i)* different diversity scores, *(ii)* the same diversity score across datasets, and *(iii)* diversity

[7]All models—except GPT-4—downloaded from HUGGINGFACE (`https://huggingface.co/models`).

Model	Avg. Length	CR (↓)	CR: POS (↓)	NGD (↑)	Self-Rep. (↓)	Hom. (R-L) (↓)	Hom. (BERT) (↓)	Self-BLEU (↓)	MATTR (↑)	HD-D (↑)
Article	452.25	2.615	5.544	2.637	6.216	0.118	0.696	0.003	0.837	0.896
Article (Lead 3)	75.87	2.369	5.497	3.041	4.276	0.105	0.686	0	0.856	0.892
Reference	51.78	2.277	5.330	3.164	3.842	0.074	0.683	0	0.875	0.919
StableLM	132.71	**2.724**	**5.940**	2.673	4.940	**0.126**	0.689	0.002	0.792	0.867
Mistral	114.88	2.499	**5.621**	2.926	4.688	**0.123**	*0.697*	*0.036*	0.831	0.880
Llama-2	106.52	*2.543*	**5.684**	2.874	4.159*	**0.125**	*0.694*	0.001	0.820	*0.873*
StableBeluga	91.17	2.452	**5.644**	3.028	4.467	**0.121**	*0.702*	*0.047*	0.846	0.889
FlanT5	63.84	**2.453**	**5.608**	*2.939*	3.608*	0.084	0.667	0	*0.833*	**0.887**
GPT-4	55.4	2.361	**5.463**	**3.124**	*3.909*	*0.098*	*0.684*	***0.001***	0.853	**0.891**

Table 1: Diversity scores for the CNN/Daily Mail dataset. Arrows indicate direction of *more diversity*. Values indicating less diversity compared to at least one text source that produces longer human texts are bolded; models with scores that are less diverse than those from a model that produces longer summaries are underlined. An asterisk indicates a model more diverse than a shorter human text.

scores and standard reference-based evaluations. Despite the large number of diversity scores in our list, they all revolve around n-gram repetition. Do these capture different (complementary) information? To assess this we compute the correlations between all pairs of scores, reported in Figure 2.

Compression ratio is highly to moderately correlated with other n-gram scores. The only weak correlations are with Self-BLEU and Hom. (BERT). Given the degenerate behavior of Hom. (BERT) on the analysis of summaries, reporting Self-BLEU only is advisable. Finally, self-repetition is only moderately correlated with other scores, and is therefore informative to report. Correlations are similar on XSUM summaries (Appendix 5).

8 Truncating to Control for Length

We truncate all summaries to the length of the shortest one produced by any source as a crude means to control scores for length. The resulting scores are directly comparable (see Table 5 in the Appendix). CRs and Self-BLEU scores indicate that model-generated text is less diverse than human text. Hom. (BERT) scores barely vary across sources. On the CNN/DM dataset, Self-BLEU indicates that Llama-2 and StableLM are the most repetitive models. CR also ranks these two models as the least diverse. The results are consistent on XSUM, but for that dataset Flan-T5 is also highly ranked and the most repetitive.

Truncation to control for length is impractical for published research or leaderboards. Introducing a new source of texts would require recomputing scores for other sources for comparison, which is sometimes impossible (when outputs from other sources are not available). Future research might search for more practical alternatives.

9 Discussion and Recommendations

The `diversity` package and platform provides a useful way to analyze and visualize diversity in datasets. Our analyses of metrics reveal that compression ratio (CR) is an excellent score to report, easy to compute and strongly correlated with other scores used in past work. CR of PoS sequences captures differences between human and model-generated text. Self-repetition focusses on repetition of longer n-grams across generations, and is only moderately correlated with CRs. Finally Self-BLEU is only weakly correlated with the previous three, so is a good complement score to report. We found BERTScore limited: It does not show differences between human and model-generated text and barely varies when adjusted for length.

Length of the analyzed text has to be reported alongside all these scores. When length differs, scores are not meaningfully comparable. Truncating text is one way to control for this. Different random draws of the sample chosen to represent a dataset may differ in diversity, in turn leading to unwarranted conclusions. Truncating texts prevents quantifying repetition towards the end of longer texts. Finally, `diversity` offers a platform and package in which researchers from a variety of domains can use to facilitate evaluation and gather insights about diversity between human- and model-produced texts.

10 Limitations

In this work, we do not attempt to measure human judgments of diversity, which are straightforward for short texts (e.g., questions) but far more difficult for longer summaries or large instruction datasets (Tevet and Berant, 2021); we leave this for future work. All evaluations are conducted in English.

Acknowledgements

We gratefully acknowledge the National Science Foundation (RI 2211954) for supporting this work. We thank Ramya Namuduri for contributing the QUDSim framework to the repository, and extend our appreciation to all other contributors.

References

Yuvanesh Anand, Zach Nussbaum, Brandon Duderstadt, Benjamin Schmidt, and Andriy Mulyar. 2023. Gpt4all: Training an assistant-style chatbot with large scale data distillation from gpt-3.5-turbo. `https://github.com/nomic-ai/gpt4all`.

Daniel Bär, Torsten Zesch, and Iryna Gurevych. 2012. Text reuse detection using a composition of text similarity measures. In *Proceedings of COLING 2012*, pages 167–184, Mumbai, India. The COLING 2012 Organizing Committee.

Steven Bird and Edward Loper. 2004. NLTK: The natural language toolkit. In *Proceedings of the ACL Interactive Poster and Demonstration Sessions*, pages 214–217, Barcelona, Spain. Association for Computational Linguistics.

Ernie Chang, Matteo Paltenghi, Yang Li, Pin-Jie Lin, Changsheng Zhao, Patrick Huber, Zechun Liu, Rastislav Rabatin, Yangyang Shi, and Vikas Chandra. 2024. Scaling parameter-constrained language models with quality data. *ArXiv*, abs/2410.03083.

Wei-Lin Chiang, Zhuohan Li, Zi Lin, Ying Sheng, Zhanghao Wu, Hao Zhang, Lianmin Zheng, Siyuan Zhuang, Yonghao Zhuang, Joseph E. Gonzalez, Ion Stoica, and Eric P. Xing. 2023. Vicuna: An open-source chatbot impressing gpt-4 with 90%* chatgpt quality.

Mike Conover, Matt Hayes, Ankit Mathur, Jianwei Xie, Jun Wan, Sam Shah, Ali Ghodsi, Patrick Wendell, Matei Zaharia, and Reynold Xin. 2023. Free dolly: Introducing the world's first truly open instruction-tuned llm.

Michael A. Covington and Joe D. McFall. 2010. Cutting the gordian knot: The moving-average type–token ratio (mattr). *Journal of Quantitative Linguistics*, 17:100 – 94.

Samuel Rhys Cox, Yunlong Wang, Ashraf Abdul, Christian von der Weth, and Brian Y. Lim. 2021. Directed diversity: Leveraging language embedding distances for collective creativity in crowd ideation. In *Proceedings of the 2021 CHI Conference on Human Factors in Computing Systems*, CHI '21, page 1–35. ACM.

Jacob Devlin, Hao Cheng, Hao Fang, Saurabh Gupta, Li Deng, Xiaodong He, Geoffrey Zweig, and Margaret Mitchell. 2015. Language models for image captioning: The quirks and what works. In *Proceedings of the 53rd Annual Meeting of the Association for Computational Linguistics and the 7th International Joint Conference on Natural Language Processing (Volume 2: Short Papers)*, pages 100–105, Beijing, China. Association for Computational Linguistics.

Nigel Fernandez, Alexander Scarlatos, Wanyong Feng, Simon Woodhead, and Andrew Lan. 2024. Divert: Distractor generation with variational errors represented as text for math multiple-choice questions. *arXiv preprint arXiv:2406.19356*.

Yanzhu Guo, Guokan Shang, Michalis Vazirgiannis, and Chloé Clavel. 2023. The curious decline of linguistic diversity: Training language models on synthetic text. *CoRR*, abs/2311.09807.

John D. Hastings, Sherri Weitl-Harms, Joseph Doty, Zachary L. Myers, and Warren Thompson. 2024. Utilizing large language models to synthesize product desirability datasets. *2024 IEEE International Conference on Big Data (BigData)*, pages 5352–5360.

Karl Moritz Hermann, Tomás Kociský, Edward Grefenstette, Lasse Espeholt, Will Kay, Mustafa Suleyman, and Phil Blunsom. 2015. Teaching machines to read and comprehend. *ArXiv*, abs/1506.03340.

Ari Holtzman, Jan Buys, Li Du, Maxwell Forbes, and Yejin Choi. 2019. The curious case of neural text degeneration. *arXiv preprint arXiv:1904.09751*.

Matthew Honnibal, Ines Montani, Sofie Van Landeghem, and Adriane Boyd. 2020. spaCy: Industrial-strength Natural Language Processing in Python.

Or Honovich, Thomas Scialom, Omer Levy, and Timo Schick. 2023. Unnatural instructions: Tuning language models with (almost) no human labor. In *Proceedings of the 61st Annual Meeting of the Association for Computational Linguistics (Volume 1: Long Papers)*, pages 14409–14428, Toronto, Canada. Association for Computational Linguistics.

Albert Qiaochu Jiang, Alexandre Sablayrolles, Arthur Mensch, Chris Bamford, Devendra Singh Chaplot, Diego de Las Casas, Florian Bressand, Gianna Lengyel, Guillaume Lample, Lucile Saulnier, L'elio Renard Lavaud, Marie-Anne Lachaux, Pierre Stock, Teven Le Scao, Thibaut Lavril, Thomas Wang, Timothée Lacroix, and William El Sayed. 2023. Mistral 7b. *ArXiv*, abs/2310.06825.

Andreas Köpf, Yannic Kilcher, Dimitri von Rütte, Sotiris Anagnostidis, Zhi Rui Tam, Keith Stevens, Abdullah Barhoum, Duc Nguyen, Oliver Stanley, Richárd Nagyfi, et al. 2024. Openassistant conversations-democratizing large language model alignment. *Advances in Neural Information Processing Systems*, 36.

Thom Lake, Eunsol Choi, and Greg Durrett. 2024. From distributional to overton pluralism: Investigating large language model alignment. *ArXiv*, abs/2406.17692.

Jack Lanchantin, Angelica Chen, Shehzaad Dhuliawala, Ping Yu, Jason Weston, Sainbayar Sukhbaatar, and Ilia Kulikov. 2025. Diverse preference optimization. *ArXiv*.

Jiwei Li, Michel Galley, Chris Brockett, Jianfeng Gao, and Bill Dolan. 2016. A diversity-promoting objective function for neural conversation models. In *Proceedings of the 2016 Conference of the North American Chapter of the Association for Computational Linguistics: Human Language Technologies*, pages 110–119, San Diego, California. Association for Computational Linguistics.

Xiang Lisa Li, Ari Holtzman, Daniel Fried, Percy Liang, Jason Eisner, Tatsunori Hashimoto, Luke Zettlemoyer, and Mike Lewis. 2023. Contrastive decoding: Open-ended text generation as optimization. In *Proceedings of the 61st Annual Meeting of the Association for Computational Linguistics (Volume 1: Long Papers)*, pages 12286–12312, Toronto, Canada. Association for Computational Linguistics.

Chin-Yew Lin and Franz Josef Och. 2004. Automatic evaluation of machine translation quality using longest common subsequence and skip-bigram statistics. In *Proceedings of the 42nd Annual Meeting of the Association for Computational Linguistics (ACL-04)*, pages 605–612, Barcelona, Spain.

Yang Liu, Dan Iter, Yichong Xu, Shuo Wang, Ruochen Xu, and Chenguang Zhu. 2023. G-eval: Nlg evaluation using gpt-4 with better human alignment. In *Conference on Empirical Methods in Natural Language Processing*.

S. Longpre, Le Hou, Tu Vu, Albert Webson, Hyung Won Chung, Yi Tay, Denny Zhou, Quoc V. Le, Barret Zoph, Jason Wei, and Adam Roberts. 2023. The flan collection: Designing data and methods for effective instruction tuning. In *International Conference on Machine Learning*.

Clara Meister, Tiago Pimentel, Gian Wiher, and Ryan Cotterell. 2023a. Locally typical sampling. *Trans. Assoc. Comput. Linguistics*, 11:102–121.

Clara Meister, Tiago Pimentel, Gian Wiher, and Ryan Cotterell. 2023b. Locally typical sampling. *Transactions of the Association for Computational Linguistics*, 11:102–121.

Clara Meister, Gian Wiher, and Ryan Cotterell. 2022. On decoding strategies for neural text generators. *Trans. Assoc. Comput. Linguistics*, 10:997–1012.

Swaroop Mishra, Daniel Khashabi, Chitta Baral, and Hannaneh Hajishirzi. 2022. Cross-task generalization via natural language crowdsourcing instructions. In *Proceedings of the 60th Annual Meeting of the Association for Computational Linguistics (Volume 1: Long Papers)*, pages 3470–3487, Dublin, Ireland. Association for Computational Linguistics.

JiHwan Moon, Jihoon Park, Jungeun Kim, Jongseong Bae, Hyeongwoo Jeon, and Ha Young Kim. 2024. Diffslt: Enhancing diversity in sign language translation via diffusion model. *ArXiv*, abs/2411.17248.

Subhabrata Mukherjee, Arindam Mitra, Ganesh Jawahar, Sahaj Agarwal, Hamid Palangi, and Ahmed Awadallah. 2023. Orca: Progressive learning from complex explanation traces of gpt-4. *Preprint*, arXiv:2306.02707.

Ramya Namuduri, Yating Wu, Anshun Asher Zheng, Manya Wadhwa, Greg Durrett, and Junyi Jessy Li. 2025. QUDsim: Quantifying discourse similarities in LLM-generated text. In *Second Conference on Language Modeling*.

Shashi Narayan, Shay B. Cohen, and Mirella Lapata. 2018. Don't give me the details, just the summary! topic-aware convolutional neural networks for extreme summarization. *ArXiv*, abs/1808.08745.

OpenAI. 2023. Gpt-4 technical report. *ArXiv*, abs/2303.08774.

Vishakh Padmakumar and He He. 2023. Does writing with language models reduce content diversity? *ArXiv*, abs/2309.05196.

Vishakh Padmakumar, Behnam Hedayatnia, Di Jin, Patrick Lange, Seokhwan Kim, Nanyun Peng, Yang Liu, and Dilek Hakkani-Tur. 2023. Investigating the representation of open domain dialogue context for transformer models. In *Proceedings of the 24th Annual Meeting of the Special Interest Group on Discourse and Dialogue*, pages 538–547, Prague, Czechia. Association for Computational Linguistics.

Nikita Salkar, Thomas Trikalinos, Byron C Wallace, and Ani Nenkova. 2022. Self-repetition in abstractive neural summarizers. In *Proceedings of the Conference of the Asia-Pacific Chapter of the Association for Computational Linguistics and the International Joint Conference on Natural Language Processing (AACL)*, volume 2022, pages 341–350.

Victor Sanh, Albert Webson, Colin Raffel, Stephen H. Bach, Lintang Sutawika, Zaid Alyafeai, Antoine Chaffin, Arnaud Stiegler, Arun Raja, Manan Dey, M Saiful Bari, Canwen Xu, Urmish Thakker, Shanya Sharma Sharma, Eliza Szczechla, Taewoon Kim, Gunjan Chhablani, Nihal V. Nayak, Debajyoti Datta, Jonathan Chang, Mike Tian-Jian Jiang, Han Wang, Matteo Manica, Sheng Shen, Zheng Xin Yong, Harshit Pandey, Rachel Bawden, Thomas Wang, Trishala Neeraj, Jos Rozen, Abheesht Sharma, Andrea Santilli, Thibault Févry, Jason Alan Fries, Ryan Teehan, Teven Le Scao, Stella Biderman, Leo Gao, Thomas Wolf, and Alexander M. Rush. 2022. Multitask prompted training enables zero-shot task generalization. In *The Tenth International Conference on Learning Representations, ICLR 2022, Virtual Event, April 25-29, 2022*. OpenReview.net.

Chantal Shaib, Yanai Elazar, Junyi Jessy Li, and Byron C Wallace. 2024. Detection and measurement of syntactic templates in generated text. In *Proceedings of the 2024 Conference on Empirical Methods in Natural Language Processing*, pages 6416–6431, Miami, Florida, USA. Association for Computational Linguistics.

Liyan Tang, Tanya Goyal, Alex Fabbri, Philippe Laban, Jiacheng Xu, Semih Yavuz, Wojciech Kryscinski, Justin Rousseau, and Greg Durrett. 2023. Understanding factual errors in summarization: Errors, summarizers, datasets, error detectors. In *Proceedings of the 61st Annual Meeting of the Association for Computational Linguistics (Volume 1: Long Papers)*, pages 11626–11644, Toronto, Canada. Association for Computational Linguistics.

Rohan Taori, Ishaan Gulrajani, Tianyi Zhang, Yann Dubois, Xuechen Li, Carlos Guestrin, Percy Liang, and Tatsunori B. Hashimoto. 2023. Stanford alpaca: An instruction-following llama model. `https://github.com/tatsu-lab/stanford_alpaca`.

Guy Tevet and Jonathan Berant. 2021. Evaluating the evaluation of diversity in natural language generation. In *Proceedings of the 16th Conference of the European Chapter of the Association for Computational Linguistics: Main Volume*, pages 326–346, Online. Association for Computational Linguistics.

Hugo Touvron, Thibaut Lavril, Gautier Izacard, Xavier Martinet, Marie-Anne Lachaux, Timothée Lacroix, Baptiste Rozière, Naman Goyal, Eric Hambro, Faisal Azhar, Aurelien Rodriguez, Armand Joulin, Edouard Grave, and Guillaume Lample. 2023a. Llama: Open and efficient foundation language models. *ArXiv*, abs/2302.13971.

Hugo Touvron, Louis Martin, Kevin Stone, Peter Albert, Amjad Almahairi, Yasmine Babaei, Nikolay Bashlykov, Soumya Batra, Prajjwal Bhargava, Shruti Bhosale, Dan Bikel, Lukas Blecher, Cristian Canton Ferrer, Moya Chen, Guillem Cucurull, David Esiobu, Jude Fernandes, Jeremy Fu, Wenyin Fu, Brian Fuller, Cynthia Gao, Vedanuj Goswami, Naman Goyal, Anthony Hartshorn, Saghar Hosseini, Rui Hou, Hakan Inan, Marcin Kardas, Viktor Kerkez, Madian Khabsa, Isabel Kloumann, Artem Korenev, Punit Singh Koura, Marie-Anne Lachaux, Thibaut Lavril, Jenya Lee, Diana Liskovich, Yinghai Lu, Yuning Mao, Xavier Martinet, Todor Mihaylov, Pushkar Mishra, Igor Molybog, Yixin Nie, Andrew Poulton, Jeremy Reizenstein, Rashi Rungta, Kalyan Saladi, Alan Schelten, Ruan Silva, Eric Michael Smith, Ranjan Subramanian, Xiaoqing Ellen Tan, Binh Tang, Ross Taylor, Adina Williams, Jian Xiang Kuan, Puxin Xu, Zheng Yan, Iliyan Zarov, Yuchen Zhang, Angela Fan, Melanie Kambadur, Sharan Narang, Aurelien Rodriguez, Robert Stojnic, Sergey Edunov, and Thomas Scialom. 2023b. Llama 2: Open foundation and fine-tuned chat models. *Preprint*, arXiv:2307.09288.

Somin Wadhwa, Chantal Shaib, Silvio Amir, and Byron C Wallace. 2025. Who taught you that? tracing teachers in model distillation. In *Findings of the Association for Computational Linguistics: ACL 2025*, pages 3307–3315, Vienna, Austria. Association for Computational Linguistics.

Lucy Lu Wang, Yulia Otmakhova, Jay DeYoung, Thinh Hung Truong, Bailey Kuehl, Erin Bransom, and Byron Wallace. 2023a. Automated metrics for medical multi-document summarization disagree with human evaluations. In *Proceedings of the 61st Annual Meeting of the Association for Computational Linguistics (Volume 1: Long Papers)*, pages 9871–9889, Toronto, Canada. Association for Computational Linguistics.

Yizhong Wang, Yeganeh Kordi, Swaroop Mishra, Alisa Liu, Noah A. Smith, Daniel Khashabi, and Hannaneh Hajishirzi. 2023b. Self-instruct: Aligning language models with self-generated instructions. In *Proceedings of the 61st Annual Meeting of the Association for Computational Linguistics (Volume 1: Long Papers)*, pages 13484–13508, Toronto, Canada. Association for Computational Linguistics.

Yizhong Wang, Swaroop Mishra, Pegah Alipoormolabashi, Yeganeh Kordi, Amirreza Mirzaei, Atharva Naik, Arjun Ashok, Arut Selvan Dhanasekaran, Anjana Arunkumar, David Stap, Eshaan Pathak, Giannis Karamanolakis, Haizhi Lai, Ishan Purohit, Ishani Mondal, Jacob Anderson, Kirby Kuznia, Krima Doshi, Kuntal Kumar Pal, Maitreya Patel, Mehrad Moradshahi, Mihir Parmar, Mirali Purohit, Neeraj Varshney, Phani Rohitha Kaza, Pulkit Verma, Ravsehaj Singh Puri, Rushang Karia, Savan Doshi, Shailaja Keyur Sampat, Siddhartha Mishra, Sujan Reddy A, Sumanta Patro, Tanay Dixit, and Xudong Shen. 2022. Super-NaturalInstructions: Generalization via declarative instructions on 1600+ NLP tasks. In *Proceedings of the 2022 Conference on Empirical Methods in Natural Language Processing*, pages 5085–5109, Abu Dhabi, United Arab Emirates. Association for Computational Linguistics.

Dora Zhao, Jerone Andrews, Orestis Papakyriakopoulos, and Alice Xiang. 2024. Position: Measure dataset diversity, don't just claim it. In *Proceedings of the 41st International Conference on Machine Learning*, volume 235 of *Proceedings of Machine Learning Research*, pages 60644–60673. PMLR.

Yaoming Zhu, Sidi Lu, Lei Zheng, Jiaxian Guo, Weinan Zhang, Jun Wang, and Yong Yu. 2018. Texygen: A benchmarking platform for text generation models. *The 41st International ACM SIGIR Conference on Research & Development in Information Retrieval*.

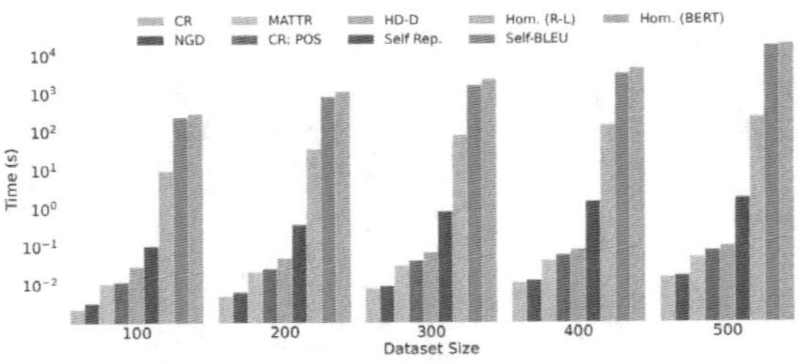

Figure 3: Mean run time **(log-scale)** on CNN/DM summaries. Run times increase with the number of text for the analysis. Even for small datasets, Self-BLEU and BERTScore homogenization are slow.

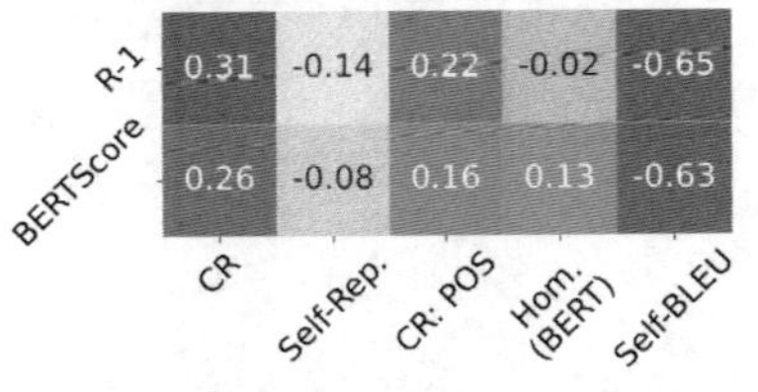

Figure 4: Correlations between diversity metrics, BERTScore, and ROUGE-1. Both reference-based metrics are weakly correlated with CR and Hom. (BERT), and moderately anti-correlated with Self-BLEU.

Appendix

A Run-Time Considerations

Figure 3 provides insights about the feasibility of obtaining scores for large samples.[8] The compression ratio scores are fast compared to other diversity measures.

B Correlations with Evaluation Metrics

Output diversity and self-repetition are aspects of model behavior that are not captured by existing evaluation approaches. We compute the system level correlation between the diversity scores and the traditional BERTScore and ROUGE evaluations, shown in Figure 4.

C Controlling for Length

Scores on CNN/DM summaries truncated to the shortest summary reveal a different model order with respect to diversity (Table 2).

D Additional Evaluations

Story Writing Padmakumar et al. (2023) presented an analysis of human-written stories, where people wrote either by themselves or with the help of GPT-3 or GPT-3.5 Turbo. We also find that all diversity scores agree that people writing independently produce the more diverse texts (cf. Table 5). Length is not an issue because the average length of stories in each setting are comparable: 375 words for writing without help, 372 words when writing with GPT-3 and 370 when writing with GPT-3.5.

[8]Run on a single NVIDIA Quadro RTX 8000 GPU.

Model	CR (↓)	CR: POS (↓)	Self-Rep. (↓)	Hom. (BERT) (↓)	Self-BLEU (↓)
Article	2.268	5.25	2.763	0.676	0
Article (Lead 3)	2.274	5.25	2.762	0.658	0
Reference	2.189	5.179	2.763	0.674	0
Llama-2	2.96	5.627	2.847	0.674	0.001
GPT-4	**2.287**	5.376	2.761	0.672	**0**
FlanT5	2.288	5.389	2.779	0.673	**0**
StableLM	2.393	5.537	2.884	0.672	0.001
Mistral	2.32	5.415	2.812	**0.67**	**0**
StableBeluga	2.288	5.46	2.766	0.671	**0**

Table 2: Scores on CNN/DM summaries truncated to the shortest summary length for a given input.

Dataset	CR (↓)	CR: POS (↓)	Self-Rep. (↓)
Open Assistant	2.886	6.731	3.969
Unnatural Instructions	4.191	7.278	9.868
Alpaca	3.119	6.61	3.105
Super-NaturalInstructions	2.675	5.749	3.456
Dolly	2.578	6.214	2.935

Table 3: Diversity scores for instruction datasets. We do not include Self-BLEU nor Hom. (BERT) due to long run times.

Instruction-tuning Datasets The quality and diversity of instructions are likely to result in more robust and capable systems (Sanh et al., 2022; Mishra et al., 2022). We analyze the diversity of five instruction-tuning datasets: Open Assistant (Köpf et al., 2024), Super-NaturalInstructions (Wang et al., 2022), Unnatural Instructions (Honovich et al., 2023), Alpaca (Wang et al., 2023b),

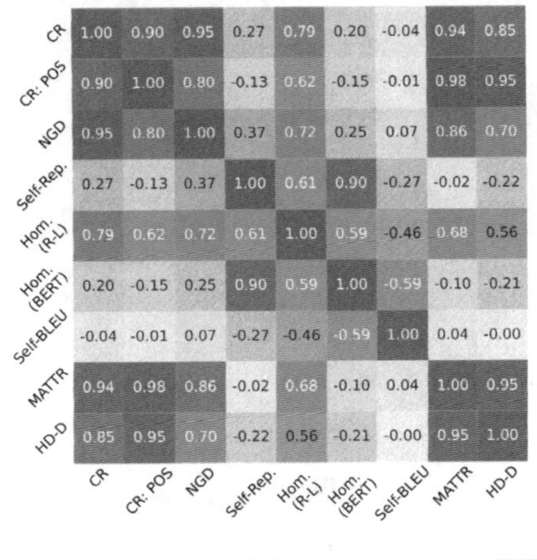

Figure 5: Correlation table between scores on XSUM.

Model	Avg. Length	CR (↓)	CR: POS (↓)	NGD (↑)	Self-Rep. (↓)	Hom. (R-L) (↓)	Hom. (BERT) (↓)	Self-BLEU (↓)	MATTR (↑)	HD-D (↑)
Article	310.20	2.511	5.555	2.756	5.643	0.110	0.695	0.002	0.838	0.892
Article (Lead-3)	55.94	2.316	5.454	3.107	3.999	0.103	0.683	0	0.860	0.891
Reference	21.04	2.276	5.409	3.211	2.914	0.081	0.673	0	0.877	0.888
StableLM	109.20	2.745	6.008	2.636	4.687	0.130	0.695	0.002	0.78	0.854
Llama-2	102.48	2.634	5.802	2.795	4.618	0.128	0.687	0.002	0.795	0.858
Mistral	95.18	2.531	5.708	2.911	4.495	*0.132*	*0.698*	*0.044*	0.819	0.867
StableBeluga	88.46	2.461	5.673	2.992	4.418	0.124	*0.698*	*0.046*	0.837	0.88
GPT-4	62.15	2.394	5.531*	3.079	4.041	0.104	0.682	0	0.848	0.886
FlanT5	20.93	***2.666***	***6.222***	***2.743***	***2.868***	***0.114***	0.665	0.001	***0.756***	**0.842**

Table 4: Diversity scores for XSUM summaries. Arrow indicate the direction of more diverse texts for each score.

Dataset	CR (↓)	CR: POS (↓)	Self-Rep. (↓)	Hom. (BERT) (↓)	Self-BLEU (↓)
Solo	2.901	5.314	5.873	0.604	0.018
GPT-3	2.940	5.371	5.911	0.613	0.020
InstructGPT	3.064	5.462	5.966	0.631	0.022

Table 5: Diversity scores over essays. Working with an LLM correlates with lower diversity.

Model	CR (↓)	CR: POS (↓)	Self-Rep. (↓)	Hom. (BERT) (↓)	Self-BLEU (↓)
Article	2.162	5.095	2.719	0.666	0
Article (Lead 3)	2.179	5.093	2.719	0.663	0
Reference	2.230	5.314	2.663	0.667	0
Llama-2	2.345	5.636	2.919	0.663	0.002
GPT-4	2.213	5.425	2.666	0.663	0
FlanT5	2.490	5.737	2.707	0.665	0.001
StableLM	2.342	5.521	2.823	0.664	0.001
Mistral	2.308	5.689	2.736	0.659	0
StableBeluga	2.210	5.436	2.663	0.659	0

Table 6: Diversity metrics for XSUM summaries, with outputs from each model truncated to the length of the shortest. All scores are directly comparable.

and Dolly (Conover et al., 2023) (Table 3).

Open Assistant instructions are remarkably diverse compared to the other datasets across all diversity scores. Unnatural instructions are remarkable in the opposite direction. We provide an analysis of the diversity scores with the length controlled in Appendix D.2.

Given the large dataset sizes, ranging from 15-80k data points, we do not compute the homogenization scores nor Self-BLEU, as the computation time is infeasible. For approximately 50k instructions, the estimated computation times ranged from 48 to 800 hours for these scores. This case study highlights the relevancy of the run-time analysis for computing score that we presented in the previous section.

D.1 Correlation Between Metrics

Self-BLEU scores are almost perfectly correlated between the two datasets; they appear to not be affected by text source. The other scores are still moderately to highly correlated but as already observed, models are ranked differently. When reporting diversity, source of analyzed data also has to be taken into account, in addition to length.

Dataset	CR (↓)	CR: POS (↓)	Self-Rep. (↓)
Open Assistant	2.370	5.402	1.741
Unnatural Instructions	6.036	8.421	5.595
Alpaca	3.301	6.044	2.020
Super-NaturalInstructions	2.458	1.844	4.859
Dolly	2.832	5.504	2.235

Table 7: Truncated diversity scores for instruction datasets.

D.2 Instruction Datasets, Length Controlled

Table 7 shows scores for instructions downsampled to the size of the smallest dataset, and truncated to the length of the shortest instructions in the remaining data. Again, the Open Assistant dataset stand out as most diverse, while the Unnatural Instructions dataset is markedly less diverse than the others. Self-repetition in the related Super-Natural and Unnatural instructions is notably high. The human instructions in Dolly compare favorably with automatic instructions, especially when bearing in mind that only eight tasks are covered in it. CR:POS points to Super-natural instructions as the most diverse. We do not have a convincing explanation of why it compares so favorably against others on this score.

D.3 XSUM Metrics

Tables 4, 6 show the full diversity metrics over XSUM with and without controlling for length.

Figure 5 shows the correlations between all pairs of metrics for the XSUM dataset. The correlations show that compression ratio is highly to moderately correlated with other n-gram scores, similar to the findings for the CNN/DM dataset.

LITMUS++ : An Agentic System for Predictive Analysis of Low-Resource Languages Across Tasks and Models

Avni Mittal[1] **Shanu Kumar**[2] **Sandipan Dandapat**[3] **Monojit Choudhury**[2]
[1]Microsoft Corporation, India
[2]Mohamed bin Zayed University of Artificial Intelligence (MBZUAI)
[3]Indian Institute of Technology Hyderabad
avnimittal@microsoft.com {shanu.kumar, monojit.choudhury}@mbzuai.ac.ae sdandapat@cse.iith.ac.in

Abstract

We present LITMUS++, an agentic system for *predicting* language-model performance for queries of the form "How will a *Model* perform on a *Task* in a *Language*?", a persistent challenge in multilingual and low-resource settings, settings where benchmarks are incomplete or unavailable. Unlike static evaluation suites or opaque LLM-as-judge pipelines, LITMUS++ implements an agentic, auditable workflow: a Directed Acyclic Graph of specialized *Thought Agents* that generate hypotheses, retrieve multilingual evidence, select predictive features, and train lightweight regressors with calibrated uncertainty. The system supports interactive querying through a chat-style interface, enabling users to inspect reasoning traces and cited evidence. Experiments across six tasks and five multilingual scenarios show that LITMUS++ delivers accurate and interpretable performance predictions, including in low-resource and unseen conditions. Code is available at https://github.com/AvniMittal13/litmus_plus_plus.

1 Introduction

Large Language Models (LLMs) now support diverse tasks such as reasoning, summarization, code synthesis, and multilingual communication across more than a hundred languages (OpenAI, 2023; Huang et al., 2024). Yet, evaluating their performance remains a critical bottleneck. Benchmark-driven resources such as XTREME-R and XGLUE (Ruder et al., 2021; Liang et al., 2020), along with broader stress tests like BIG-Bench and HELM (Srivastava et al., 2023; Liang et al., 2023), provide systematic measurement but cannot scale to the vast *Task–Model–Language* space, especially in low-resource settings. LLM-as-judge approaches (Zhou et al., 2024; Tan et al., 2024) offer scalability but raise concerns about bias, opacity, and reproducibility.

Predictive multilingual analysis has gained traction as an alternative to direct evaluation. Early methods like LangRank leveraged typological and corpus features for transfer prediction (Lin et al., 2019), while lightweight proxies such as LEEP and LogME offered fast transferability estimates (Nguyen et al., 2020; You et al., 2021). The foundational **LITMUS** predictor (Srinivasan et al., 2022) combined diverse linguistic and task features but required expert feature design and manual setup. More recent approaches, including Bayesian factorization and information-parity models (Schram et al., 2023; Tsvetkov and Kipnis, 2024), and multi-task zero-shot prediction frameworks (Ahuja et al., 2022b), improved scalability but still rely on predefined features and static configurations. Overall, existing predictors struggle to generalize under data scarcity and lack automation.

We introduce **LITMUS++**, an agentic system that transforms predictive evaluation into a fully autonomous workflow. A Directed Acyclic Graph (DAG) of specialized Thought Agents (Zhang et al., 2024) hypothesizes, gather multilingual evidence, select predictive features, and train lightweight regressors with calibrated uncertainty. This design enables interpretable and auditable predictions for unseen *Task–Model–Language* combinations, including challenging low- and zero-resource cases. The system is accessible through a browser-based interface (Figure 1), which combines three complementary views: a chat entry point for user queries, a live reasoning trace of DAG orchestration, and an evidence panel showing citations and exportable reports. Users can pose questions such as "How will a *Model* perform on a *Task* in a *Language*?", observe autonomous reasoning unfold in real time, and inspect the provenance of predictions.

We evaluate LITMUS++ across six representative tasks in five multilingual settings, measuring predictive accuracy, Q&A correctness, and reasoning quality dimensions such as plausibility, co-

Proceedings of The 14th International Joint Conference on Natural Language Processing and The 4th Conference of the Asia-Pacific Chapter of the Association for Computational Linguistics: System Demonstrations, pages 47–54

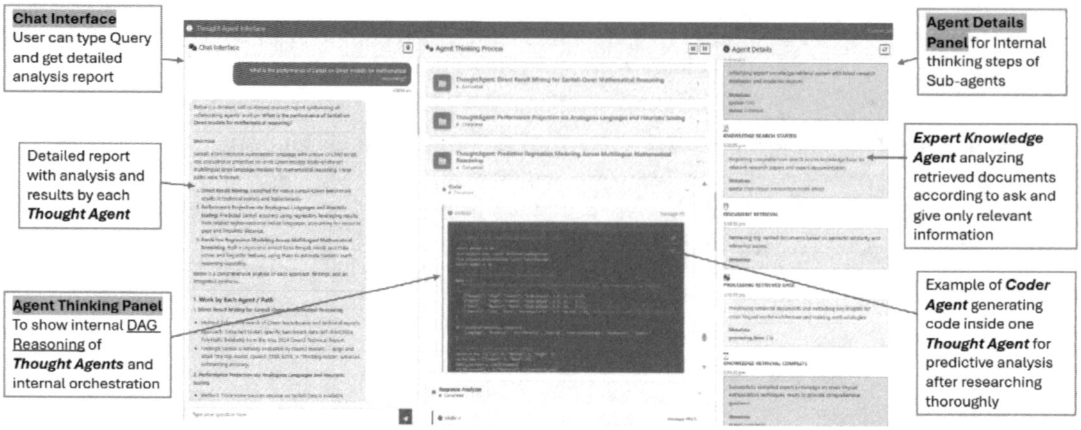

Figure 1: The interactive interface of LITMUS++. The system is organized into three coordinated panels: (left) the chat interface where users submit queries and receive structured analysis reports, (center) the DAG reasoning view showing the orchestration of *Thought Agents* and their outputs, and (right) the agent details panel exposing internal reasoning steps and expert knowledge retrieval. This design emphasizes transparency, allowing users to follow how predictions are generated and to inspect the provenance of evidence used in multilingual evaluation.

herence, and hallucination control. Our results show that DAG-based orchestration consistently reduces errors and enhances reasoning quality compared to single-agent and generalist multi-agent baselines. We have hosted a live demo at `https://litmusplusplus.azurewebsites.net/`.

2 System Overview

LITMUS++ is a multi-agent orchestration framework for automated, interpretable, and extensible evaluation of language models in multilingual and low-resource settings. The system transforms what is traditionally a manual research process into a fully autonomous workflow. At its core, a DAG architecture of collaborative *ThoughtAgents* enables structured decomposition of queries, parallel investigation of hypotheses, and traceable reasoning paths. By allowing multiple branches to expand or be pruned dynamically, the DAG ensures both efficiency and transparency. This design provides scalability across languages and tasks while preserving auditability.

2.1 End-to-End Workflow

Query Ingestion and Initialization: A natural language query (e.g., *"How will model X perform on task Y in language Z?"*) is first received by the *MainAgent*, which distinguishes between new and follow-up queries. For new queries, the *ThoughtCreatorAgent* generates hypotheses and spawns corresponding *ThoughtAgents* as nodes in the DAG. For the follow-up queries, the *ThoughtAnalyzerAgent* routes new information, spawns additional nodes, or prunes irrelevant ones to refine the DAG.

DAG-Based Reasoning: Each node in the DAG corresponds to a *ThoughtAgent*, which validates a single hypothesis. Dependencies across nodes allow for both parallel and conditional reasoning. The DAG evolves dynamically, expanding when new evidence emerges and pruning branches that are unproductive. Figure 3 illustrates the internal pipeline of a single *ThoughtAgent*, which itself orchestrates multiple specialized sub-agents.

Agent Internal Structure: A ThoughtAgent is in itself a groupchat of multiple collaborative sub-agents. The *Research Planner* coordinates investigations and decides what should be done next based on the current evidence provided by other agents such as *Web Search and Crawl*, *Expert Knowledge* and *Coder* agents. Creating these as separate agents, rather than just providing tools for web search, coding, and querying the curated multilingual knowledge base, leads to improved context management and allows individual iterative reasoning of sub agents with only relevant context for the groupchat. The *Send User Message* observes the conversation and produces a detailed report of the conversation at the end when either the hypothesis testing is complete successfully or some clarification is needed from the User. Together, they maintain a shared history of tool calls, reasoning steps, and outputs, ensuring reproducibil-

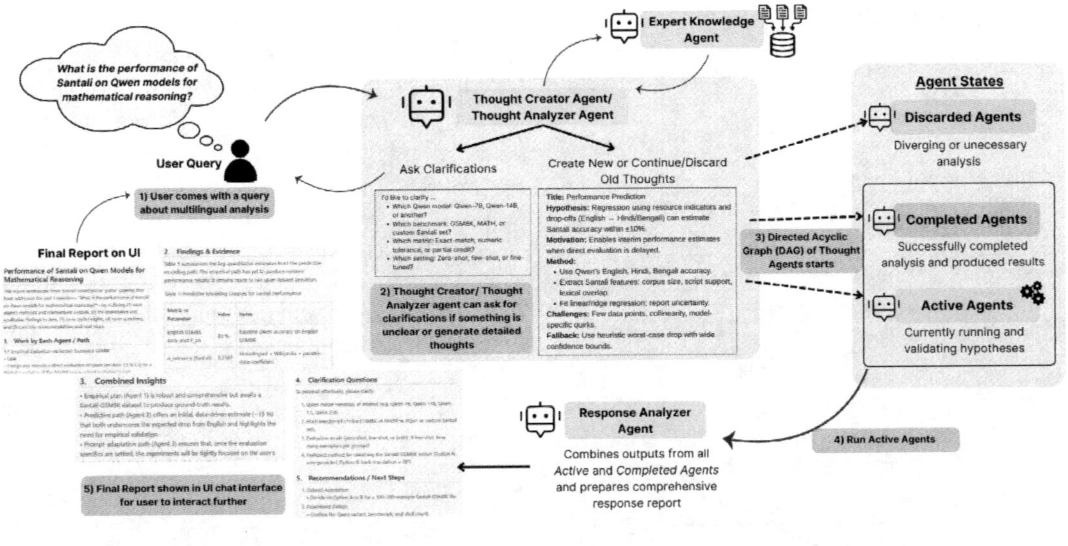

Figure 2: LITMUS++ pipeline: a user query triggers orchestration that initializes and refines a DAG of *ThoughtAgents*. Each agent retrieves evidence from the curated knowledge base, web search, and benchmarks, and may perform predictive modelling with lightweight regressors. The *Response Analyzer* aggregates results with uncertainty estimates and delivers both predictions and full reasoning traces to the user interface.

ity and transparency. More details on the design and curation of the knowledge base are provided in Appendix C.

Iterative Management: The *ThoughtAnalyzerAgent* monitors active hypotheses and manages progression. It routes clarifications, creates new agents, marks completed ones, and discards irrelevant branches. This iterative refinement keeps the system aligned with evolving queries while maintaining focus on the evaluation goal. The full lifecycle of *ThoughtAgents* is detailed in Appendix A.

Execution and Aggregation: Active *ThoughtAgents* run in parallel, producing validated hypotheses, predictive outputs, and evidence traces. Results are aggregated by the *ResponseAnalyzerAgent*, which synthesizes a final response that includes predictions, supporting evidence, confidence measures, and tradeoffs.

2.2 User Interface

The browser-based interface is organized into three coordinated panels as shown in Figure 1. The *Chat Window* (left) displays user queries and final system responses. The *Agent Reasoning View* (middle) logs the main orchestration flow, with expandable views of ThoughtAgents. The *Sub-agent Panel* (right) exposes detailed conversations of *Web Search and Crawl* and *Expert Knowledge* Agents. This design promotes transparency, allowing researchers to inspect intermediate reasoning and intervene when needed. The interface outputs comprehensive reports that combine retrieved evidence, predictions, and uncertainty estimates. These reports can be exported for reproducibility and integration into research workflows.

Implementation: LITMUS++ runs locally or in-browser with minimal setup, requiring only an API key for external search. The agentic backend uses *Autogen*[1] for orchestration, *ChromaDB*[2] as the curated knowledge base, and *Firecrawl*[3] for web search and scraping. Further details are provided in Appendix B.

3 Evaluation Framework

We design an evaluation framework to probe both the predictive accuracy and the reasoning quality of LITMUS++ in realistic multilingual conditions. The framework combines representative tasks, controlled scenarios, constrained knowledge access, and multi-dimensional evaluation metrics, balancing correctness with interpretability.

3.1 Evaluation Tasks and Scenarios

The benchmark spans six tasks: code generation, mathematical reasoning, question answering, text classification, text summarization, and machine

[1] https://microsoft.github.io/autogen/stable/index.html
[2] https://github.com/chroma-core/chroma
[3] https://www.firecrawl.dev/

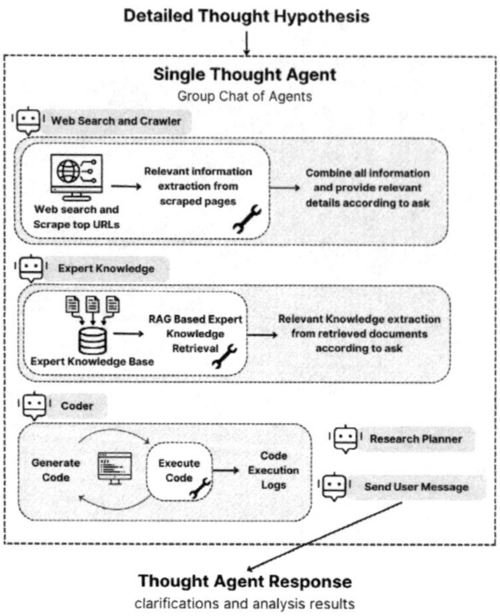

Figure 3: Single *ThoughtAgent* pipeline. Each agent operates as a group chat of specialized sub-agents (e.g., Web Search, Expert Knowledge, Coder) that validate a hypothesis and return structured results. These agents form the nodes of the DAG.

translation. To reflect practical multilingual challenges, each task is evaluated under five controlled scenarios: *Scenario 1 (Same Lang + Same Model)*: the same language and model are available. *Scenario 2 (Same Lang + Diff Model)*: the language is available but only with a different model. *Scenario 3 (Similar Lang + Same Model)*: transfer from a typologically related language using the same model. *Scenario 4 (Distant Lang + Same Model)*: transfer from a distant language with the same model. *Scenario 5 (No Lang + No Model)*: neither the language nor the model is represented.

Each scenario contains 60 questions (10 per task), covering high- to zero-resource conditions and testing how well the system adapts as prior evidence decreases. Scenario labels are used consistently in the Results.

3.2 Evaluation Sets and Knowledge Access Constraints

We evaluate the system using two complementary query sets, each consisting of 150 questions. The *PredSet* contains predictive analysis questions of the form "How will a model perform on a task in a language?", probing the system's ability to generate quantitative performance estimates. The *QnASet* contains comparative and factoid-style questions about models, languages, and benchmarks. Figure 4 shows representative examples.

While the system supports unrestricted web access, we constrain evidence sources during evaluation. The web-search tool is redirected to a fixed corpus of research papers, retrieving the top candidate via a retrieval-augmented setup that ranks paper abstracts by embedding similarity to the generated query. This ensures consistent, controlled conditions across scenarios while providing a realistic retrieval signal for multilingual evaluation.

Q1: *How does cross-lingual summarization work for low-resource Ukrainian?*
Answer: 13.5

Q2: *What is the performance of GPT-4o on MT for Amharic?*
Answer: 14

Q3: *Which models have been benchmarked on code generation in Sanskrit?*
Answer: Gemini 1.5, Gemini 2.0, LLaMA 7B

Q4: *Which model performs best for Math Reasoning in Italian?*
Answer: LLaMA 3.1 70B

Q5: *Compare Aquila-VL2 and Aria-MoE for QA/VQA in German.*
Answer: Aria-MoE

Figure 4: Illustrative queries from *PredSet* (predictive analysis) and *QnASet* (Q&A).

3.3 Evaluation Metrics

Outputs are judged using the LLM-as-Judge paradigm (Şahinuç et al., 2025; Li et al., 2024), complemented with task-specific correctness. For the *PredSet*, we measure *mean absolute error (MAE)* between predicted and ground truth performance values. For the *QnASet*, we report *accuracy* based on exact or task-appropriate matching.

Ground-truth values come from the fixed corpus of research papers. Scenario conditions are simulated by removing papers containing the target language–task–model results, the values in these removed papers serve as ground truth. In *Scenario 1*, the relevant paper remains in the corpus, making the task a retrieval case. In all other scenarios, ground-truth papers are excluded, creating controlled evidence scarcity for prediction. We plan to release additional dataset details in future work.

Beyond correctness, we evaluate multiple aspects of reasoning quality, including predictive plausibility under low-resource settings, citation verification (whether cited works exist and are relevant), citation emphasis (how strongly reasoning is grounded in citations), the depth of feature selection and modeling choices, and overall coherence in logical flow and linguistic fluency. We further conduct human validation of the LLM judge's outputs, with details provided in Appendix D.

4 Results

We present quantitative results of LITMUS++, evaluating its predictive accuracy and Q&A performance under the five controlled scenarios introduced in Section 3. All experiments use GPT-4.1[4] as the underlying LLM. Detailed task-level numbers are provided in the supplementary material due to space constraints.

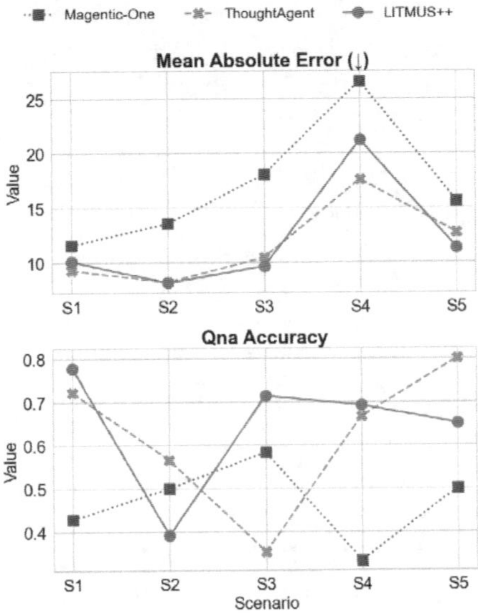

Figure 5: Quantitative results for *PredSet* (Mean Absolute Error, top) and *QnASet* (Accuracy, bottom) across the five scenarios (S1–S5). Lower is better for *PredSet*, higher is better for *QnASet*.

We compare against two baselines. The first, *ThoughtAgent*, is a simplified variant that processes the full query with a single agent, isolating the benefits of DAG-based coordination. The second, *Magentic-One*, is a generalist multi-agent framework from Microsoft,[5] included as a strong open-ended, general-purpose baseline.

4.1 Predictive and Q&A Performance

Figure 5 shows results on the two evaluation sets. On the *PredSet* (left), we report mean absolute error (↓). We observe that error generally increases from Scenario 1 to Scenario 4 as the prediction task becomes harder: in S1 and S2, the target language and model are available, so predictions are relatively straightforward; in S3 and especially S4, the system must rely on increasingly distant evidence and construct more complex transfer paths, which increases error. Interestingly, S5 shows a drop compared to S4: since neither language nor model is available, most systems fall back to predicting consistently low performance, which reduces variance and makes the case less challenging than S4 where nuanced feature-based modeling is required.

Across systems, *Magentic-One* shows the highest errors, especially in mid- and low-resource conditions, reflecting its lack of task-specific orchestration. Both LITMUS++ and *ThoughtAgent* maintain mean absolute error below or close to 12 in all scenarios except S4, highlighting the effectiveness of specialized reasoning even in harder conditions. Between the two, LITMUS++ achieves lower errors on average, showing the benefit of orchestrated DAG reasoning over a single-agent baseline.

On the *QnASet* (bottom in Figure 5), there is no uniform trend across scenarios: accuracy fluctuates depending on the combination of task and resource availability. Overall, LITMUS++ achieves the best performance in most scenarios, while *Magentic-One* consistently underperforms. *ThoughtAgent* remains competitive, often close to LITMUS++, but falls behind in scenarios requiring more complex reasoning (e.g., S3 and S4). These results confirm that orchestration in LITMUS++ provides a measurable advantage, though the single *ThoughtAgent* performs strongly, likely because the queries are relatively simple, reducing the need for multi-step reasoning and causing LITMUS++ to occasionally overdo the reasoning.

4.2 Reasoning Quality

We evaluate reasoning quality across five dimensions: predictive plausibility, feature selection, coherence, citation emphasis, and hallucination rate (Figure 6). Starting with *Predictive Plausibility*, LITMUS++ achieves the strongest and most stable scores (∼4.0–4.5), consistently producing reasonable and interpretable predictions even in challenging scenarios. *ThoughtAgent* remains competitive but slightly weaker (∼3.4–3.6), while *Magentic-One* trails at ∼3.0 across all scenarios, highlighting the value of structured orchestration.

On *Feature Selection*, the advantages of or-

[4]https://openai.com/index/gpt-4-1/

[5]https://microsoft.github.io/autogen/stable//user-guide/agentchat-user-guide/magentic-one.html

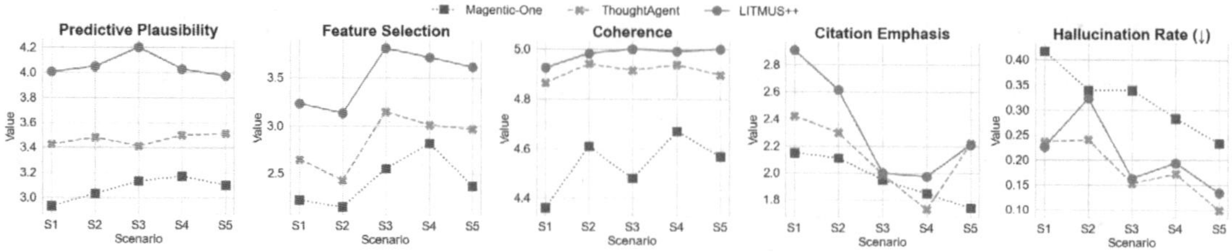

Figure 6: Qualitative results across non-accuracy metrics. Each subplot reports performance averaged across all tasks and scenarios, enabling comparison of model behavior under multiple evaluation dimensions.

chestration become even clearer. LITMUS++ reaches as high as ∼3.8 in S3–S4, precisely the settings where feature-driven reasoning is essential. *ThoughtAgent* improves under the same conditions but stays ∼0.5 points behind, while *Magentic-One* struggles at ∼2.2–2.8. For *Coherence*, both LITMUS++ and *ThoughtAgent* maintain excellent fluency and logical consistency (∼4.9–5.0), with LITMUS++ slightly ahead. *Magentic-One*, however, lags behind with lower scores of ∼4.3–4.6, underscoring its weaker reasoning discipline.

For *Citation Emphasis*, LITMUS++ grounds its outputs more consistently in cited evidence, scoring ∼2.5–3.0 in S1–S2. Although this decreases in S3–S4, it remains above both baselines. *ThoughtAgent* follows the same trend at lower levels, while *Magentic-One* is lowest throughout. *Hallucination Rate* shows an unexpected pattern: instead of rising as evidence grows scarcer, hallucinations actually decrease from S1 to S5. In high-resource cases like S1, models sometimes hallucinate nonexistent papers due to strong priors, whereas in low-resource cases they adhere strictly to constrained citations. *Magentic-One* hallucinates the most (42%→24%), while LITMUS++ and *ThoughtAgent* remain substantially lower (23%→10%). Overall, while *ThoughtAgent* stays close to LITMUS++ in surface-level coherence, it lags behind on citation grounding, feature-driven reasoning, and hallucination control, whereas *Magentic-One* underperforms across all dimensions.

4.3 Ablation Study

To examine the impact of the underlying LLM in LITMUS++, we ran an ablation study in the Web Search configuration, testing o3-mini,[6] a model reported to have stronger reasoning than GPT-4.1 on 30 questions. Table 1 reports results across plausibility, feature selection, citation emphasis, and coherence. Despite o3-mini's reasoning-oriented design, results were highly competitive: GPT-4.1 achieved stronger citation grounding, while o3-mini offered slight gains in feature selection. Overall, LITMUS++ remains robust across backbones, indicating that orchestration matters more than the choice of a single LLM. Extending this to open-source LLMs is left for future work.

Model	Predictive Plausibility	Feature Selection	Citation Emphasis	Coherence
o3-mini	3.97	3.68	1.19	5.00
GPT-4.1	3.90	3.10	2.10	4.97

Table 1: Ablation study of LITMUS++ with different underlying LLMs in the Web Search configuration, evaluated on reasoning quality metrics.

5 Conclusion

We introduced LITMUS++, a demo system for multilingual performance prediction that combines DAG-based orchestration of thought agents with transparent reasoning and uncertainty-aware outputs. The system enables users to query tasks, inspect evidence traces, and obtain plausible predictions even under distant and zero-resource conditions. Compared to strong baselines such as *ThoughtAgent* and *Magentic-One*, LITMUS++ achieves lower prediction error, higher Q&A accuracy, and stronger reasoning quality, making it both effective and trustworthy. The demo illustrates how complex evaluation workflows can be transformed into interactive, auditable experiences, lowering the barrier for researchers and practitioners to explore multilingual model behavior. We have hosted a live demo for review while a broader public release is under active development. Future work will focus on optimizing latency, expanding task coverage, and extending the curated knowledge base to further strengthen the system's utility.

[6]https://openai.com/index/openai-o3-mini/

References

Kabir Ahuja, Sandipan Dandapat, Sunayana Sitaram, and Monojit Choudhury. 2022a. Beyond static models and test sets: Benchmarking the potential of pre-trained models across tasks and languages. *arXiv preprint arXiv:2205.06356*.

Kabir Ahuja, Shanu Kumar, Sandipan Dandapat, and Monojit Choudhury. 2022b. Multi task learning for zero shot performance prediction of multilingual models. In *Proceedings of the 60th Annual Meeting of the Association for Computational Linguistics (Volume 1: Long Papers)*, pages 5454–5467, Dublin, Ireland. Association for Computational Linguistics.

Błażej Dolicki and Gerasimos Spanakis. 2021. Analysing the impact of linguistic features on cross-lingual transfer. *arXiv preprint arXiv:2105.05975*.

Kaiyu Huang, Fengran Mo, Xinyu Zhang, Hongliang Li, You Li, Yuanchi Zhang, Weijian Yi, Yulong Mao, Jinchen Liu, Yuzhuang Xu, and 1 others. 2024. A survey on large language models with multilingualism: Recent advances and new frontiers. *arXiv preprint arXiv:2405.10936*.

Shanu Kumar, Soujanya Abbaraju, Sandipan Dandapat, Sunayana Sitaram, and Monojit Choudhury. 2023. Ditto: A feature representation imitation approach for improving cross-lingual transfer. In *Proceedings of the 17th Conference of the European Chapter of the Association for Computational Linguistics*, pages 385–406.

Anne Lauscher, Vinit Ravishankar, Ivan Vulić, and Goran Glavaš. 2020. From zero to hero: On the limitations of zero-shot language transfer with multilingual Transformers. In *Proceedings of the 2020 Conference on Empirical Methods in Natural Language Processing (EMNLP)*, pages 4483–4499, Online. Association for Computational Linguistics.

Haitao Li, Qian Dong, Junjie Chen, Huixue Su, Yujia Zhou, Qingyao Ai, Ziyi Ye, and Yiqun Liu. 2024. Llms-as-judges: a comprehensive survey on llm-based evaluation methods. *arXiv preprint arXiv:2412.05579*.

Percy Liang, Rishi Bommasani, Tony Lee, Dimitris Tsipras, Dilara Soylu, Michihiro Yasunaga, Yian Zhang, Deepak Narayanan, Yuhuai Wu, Ananya Kumar, Benjamin Newman, Binhang Yuan, Bobby Yan, Ce Zhang, Christian Cosgrove, Christopher D Manning, Christopher Re, Diana Acosta-Navas, Drew A. Hudson, and 31 others. 2023. Holistic evaluation of language models. *Transactions on Machine Learning Research*. Featured Certification, Expert Certification, Outstanding Certification.

Yaobo Liang, Nan Duan, Yeyun Gong, Ning Wu, Fenfei Guo, Weizhen Qi, Ming Gong, Linjun Shou, Daxin Jiang, Guihong Cao, Xiaodong Fan, Ruofei Zhang, Rahul Agrawal, Edward Cui, Sining Wei, Taroon Bharti, Ying Qiao, Jiun-Hung Chen, Winnie Wu, and 5 others. 2020. XGLUE: A new benchmark dataset for cross-lingual pre-training, understanding and generation. In *Proceedings of the 2020 Conference on Empirical Methods in Natural Language Processing (EMNLP)*, pages 6008–6018, Online. Association for Computational Linguistics.

Yu-Hsiang Lin, Chian-Yu Chen, Jean Lee, Zirui Li, Yuyan Zhang, Mengzhou Xia, Shruti Rijhwani, Junxian He, Zhisong Zhang, Xuezhe Ma, Antonios Anastasopoulos, Patrick Littell, and Graham Neubig. 2019. Choosing transfer languages for cross-lingual learning. In *Proceedings of the 57th Annual Meeting of the Association for Computational Linguistics*, pages 3125–3135, Florence, Italy. Association for Computational Linguistics.

Cuong Nguyen, Tal Hassner, Matthias Seeger, and Cedric Archambeau. 2020. Leep: A new measure to evaluate transferability of learned representations. In *International Conference on Machine Learning*, pages 7294–7305. PMLR.

OpenAI. 2023. Gpt-4 technical report. `https://cdn.openai.com/papers/gpt-4.pdf`.

Sebastian Ruder, Noah Constant, Jan Botha, Aditya Siddhant, Orhan Firat, Jinlan Fu, Pengfei Liu, Junjie Hu, Dan Garrette, Graham Neubig, and Melvin Johnson. 2021. XTREME-R: Towards more challenging and nuanced multilingual evaluation. In *Proceedings of the 2021 Conference on Empirical Methods in Natural Language Processing*, pages 10215–10245, Online and Punta Cana, Dominican Republic. Association for Computational Linguistics.

Furkan Şahinuç, Subhabrata Dutta, and Iryna Gurevych. 2025. Expert preference-based evaluation of automated related work generation. *arXiv preprint arXiv:2508.07955*.

Viktoria Schram, Daniel Beck, and Trevor Cohn. 2023. Performance prediction via bayesian matrix factorisation for multilingual natural language processing tasks. In *Proceedings of the 17th Conference of the European Chapter of the Association for Computational Linguistics*, pages 1790–1801.

Anirudh Srinivasan, Gauri Kholkar, Rahul Kejriwal, Tanuja Ganu, Sandipan Dandapat, Sunayana Sitaram, Balakrishnan Santhanam, Somak Aditya, Kalika Bali, and Monojit Choudhury. 2022. Litmus predictor: An ai assistant for building reliable, high-performing and fair multilingual nlp systems. In *Proceedings of the AAAI Conference on Artificial Intelligence*, volume 36, pages 13227–13229.

Aarohi Srivastava, Abhinav Rastogi, Abhishek Rao, Abu Awal Md Shoeb, Abubakar Abid, Adam Fisch, Adam R. Brown, Adam Santoro, Aditya Gupta, Adrià Garriga-Alonso, Agnieszka Kluska, Aitor Lewkowycz, Akshat Agarwal, Alethea Power, Alex Ray, Alex Warstadt, Alexander W. Kocurek, Ali Safaya, Ali Tazarv, and 431 others. 2023. Beyond the imitation game: Quantifying and extrapolating the capabilities of language models. *Transactions on Machine Learning Research*. Featured Certification.

S. Tan and 1 others. 2024. Judgebench: A benchmark for evaluating llm-based judges. https://openreview.net/forum?id=G0dksFayVq.

Alexander Tsvetkov and Alon Kipnis. 2024. Information parity: Measuring and predicting the multilingual capabilities of language models. In *Findings of the Association for Computational Linguistics: EMNLP 2024*, pages 7971–7989.

Kaichao You, Yong Liu, Jianmin Wang, and Mingsheng Long. 2021. Logme: Practical assessment of pre-trained models for transfer learning. In *International Conference on Machine Learning*, pages 12133–12143. PMLR.

Yifan Zhang, Yang Yuan, and Andrew Chi-Chih Yao. 2024. On the diagram of thought. *arXiv preprint arXiv:2409.10038*.

R. Zhou and 1 others. 2024. Is llm a reliable reviewer? a comprehensive evaluation of llm on automatic paper reviewing tasks. In *LREC-COLING 2024 (Proceedings)*.

Ethical Considerations

LITMUS++ operates in sensitive settings such as multilingual fairness. Although evaluated under controlled evidence access, it provides predictive estimates and is not a replacement for ground-truth benchmarks. We mitigate risks through curated knowledge bases and transparent reasoning traces and will extend coverage responsibly in future.

A Agent Lifecycle Details

Each *ThoughtAgent* transitions between three core states: **Active**: investigating a hypothesis with assigned tools; **Completed**: finished investigation and returned validated evidence; **Discarded**: pruned when deemed irrelevant, redundant, or divergent. State transitions are managed by the *ThoughtAnalyzerAgent*, which monitors progress and determines whether to continue, complete, or discard a *ThoughtAgent*. This lifecycle ensures only relevant outputs contribute to the final analysis, while providing auditable reasoning paths.

B Implementation Details

Tooling. Agents access a modular suite of reusable tools, including web search and scraping utilities, knowledge-base retrieval functions, and code executor. Tools are independently registered and can be added, replaced, or modified without altering agent logic, enabling easy integration of new APIs or analysis modules. **Deployment.** The system supports both local and hosted execution, running via a command-line interface or local server, with a hosted variant for reproducible experiments. External search and LLM calls require user-provided API keys; all other components run offline. **Performance.** Predictions include evidence traces and calibrated uncertainty estimates, offering transparent and confidence-aware reasoning. **Extensibility.** The DAG orchestration is model- and task-agnostic. New agents or tools are added by registering them within the *MainAgent* or *ThoughtAgent* logic, without modifying control flow, supporting ongoing extensibility as evaluation needs evolve.

C Knowledge Base Curation

A curated multilingual knowledge base grounds LITMUS++ in linguistic and computational evidence. It integrates (i) **literature-derived resources** from peer-reviewed papers, benchmarks, and typological databases (Lauscher et al., 2020; Dolicki and Spanakis, 2021; Srinivasan et al., 2022; Ahuja et al., 2022a; Kumar et al., 2023), and (ii) **expert annotations** for under-documented or low-resource languages. It is organized as detailed reports over language–task–model combinations, combining few-shot examples, known failure modes, and best-practice guidelines. We employ a retrieval-augmented generation setup, where top-K chunks from this knowledge base are passed as tool outputs to the Expert Knowledge Agent, which synthesizes answers for the current query. The knowledge base can be expanded as new research, experimental findings, and expert inputs become available, supporting hypothesis generation, feature selection, and provenance tracking.

D Human Validation of LLM-as-Judge Evaluation

To assess the reliability of LLM-as-Judge, we ran a human validation study on a subset of reports. Annotators received the report, LLM reasoning, rating criteria and scores (1–5) on four metrics: predictive plausibility, coherence, feature selection, and emphasis on citations. Their task was to mark agreement or disagreement (binary 1/0) with each score. The results showed that an annotator agreed with the LLM evaluations in 81.25% of the cases, while the second annotator agreed in 78.1% of the cases. The high agreement indicates that the LLM-as-Judge framework provides evaluations that are generally consistent with human judgment, though some divergences remain.

SIMAGENTS: Bridging Literature and the Universe Via A Multi-Agent Large Language Model System

Xiaowen Zhang[♠*], Zhenyu Bi[♡*], Patrick Lachance[♠],
Xuan Wang[♡], Tiziana Di Matteo[♠], Rupert A. C. Croft[♠†]
[♠]Department of Physics, Carnegie Mellon University, Pittsburgh, PA, USA
[♡]Department of Computer Science, Virginia Tech, Blacksburg, VA, USA
[♠](xiaowen4,plachanc,tizianad)@andrew.cmu.edu, rcroft@cmu.edu,
[♡](zhenyub,xuanw)@vt.edu

Abstract

As cosmological simulations and their associated software become increasingly complex, physicists face the challenge of searching through vast amounts of literature and user manuals to extract simulation parameters from dense academic papers, each using different models and formats. Translating these parameters into executable scripts remains a time-consuming and error-prone process. To improve efficiency in physics research and accelerate the cosmological simulation process, we introduce SIMAGENTS, a multi-agent system designed to automate both parameter configuration from the literature and preliminary analysis for cosmology research. SIMAGENTS is powered by specialized LLM agents capable of physics reasoning, simulation software validation, and tool execution. These agents collaborate through structured communication, ensuring that extracted parameters are physically meaningful, internally consistent, and software-compliant. We also construct a cosmological parameter extraction evaluation dataset by collecting over 40 simulations in published papers from Arxiv and leading journals that cover diverse simulation types. Experiments on the dataset demonstrate a strong performance of SIMAGENTS, highlighting its effectiveness and potential to accelerate scientific research for physicists. Our demonstration video is available at: https://youtu.be/w1zLpm_CaWA. The complete system and dataset are publicly available at https://github.com/xwzhang98/SimAgents.

1 Introduction

Modern cosmological simulations are essential tools for advancing our understanding of the universe, enabling researchers to study the formation of galaxies and the evolution of structures. Setting up such simulations is a highly manual, time-consuming, and error-prone process. Researchers must extract parameters from dense scientific papers, convert values between units, interpret context-specific model assumptions, and then format them into executable scripts compatible with domain-specific software such as MP-GADGET (Feng et al., 2018), GADGET-4 (Springel et al., 2022), Arepo (Springel et al., 2019), GIZMO code (Hopkins, 2015) and ENZO (Bryan et al., 2014). In addition to the diversity of the simulations themselves, the complexity of using the software adds another layer of difficulty. Software user manuals are often dozens of pages long and filled with intricate rules about parameter dependencies, default settings, and strict formatting requirements.

As a result, even experienced physics researchers face a steep learning curve when trying to adopt a new simulation tool. For example, when given a cosmology paper covering several simulations, the average time cost for a human researcher to formulate the correct parameter files is in the range of hours to days, depending on the familiarity with the software. Ideally, we want this labor-intensive process to be done in minutes. The above challenges raise a crucial question: **How can we design a highly professional automated toolkit to assist cosmologists with the lengthy and complex task of setting up simulations?**

Large Language Model (LLM) agents have demonstrated significant potential on many scientific tasks (Zhao et al., 2023). Recently, researchers have proposed multi-agent reasoning frameworks that enable collaborative debates among multiple LLM agents to enhance their problem-solving abilities (Wu et al., 2023; Liang et al., 2024; Zhuge et al., 2024; Bi et al., 2025). Following this path, researchers have explored LLM-agent-based workflows on several highly professional scientific and technical applications, such as biomedical tasks and clinical tasks (Bi et al., 2024; Lu et al., 2024).

In the field of cosmology, researchers have ex-

[*]Equal contribution
[†]Corresponding author.

Proceedings of The 14th International Joint Conference on Natural Language Processing and The 4th Conference of the Asia-Pacific Chapter of the Association for Computational Linguistics: System Demonstrations, pages 55–66
December 20-24, 2025 ©2025 Association for Computational Linguistics

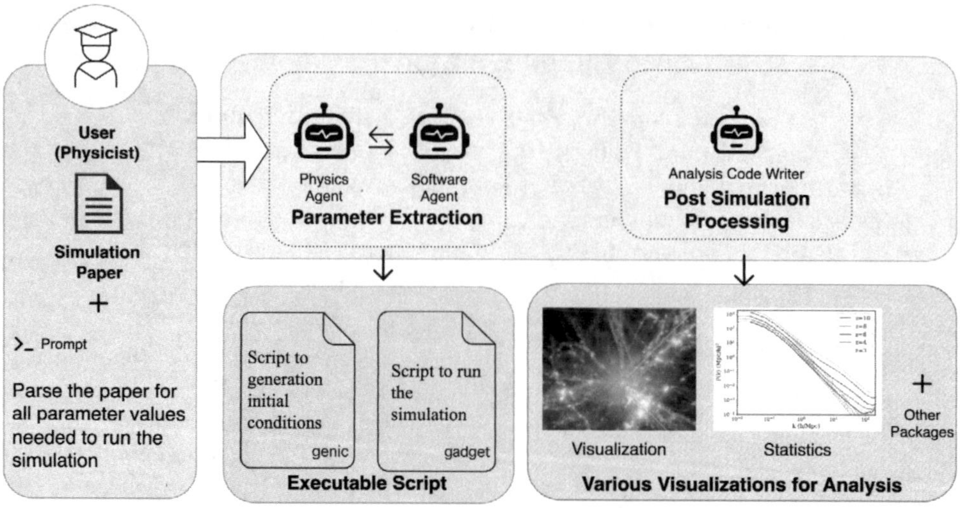

Figure 1: The workflow of our proposed multi-agent system, SIMAGENTS.

plored various LLM agent tools to provide assistance to researchers, targeting several tasks, such as a programming assistant specialized in different cosmology tasks. For example, CLAPP[1] is a single LLM agent that specializes in the CLASS cosmology code. CAMEL agents [2] provide a suite of AI-powered agents designed specifically to navigate and analyze the extensive CAMELS cosmological simulation dataset, automating tasks such as data exploration and code generation. In addition, CMBAgent (Laverick et al., 2024) and Mephisto (Sun et al., 2024) utilize a multi-agent LLM system to aid physicists in cosmological parameter analysis. Each of these systems focuses on a different scope of research, ranging from coding support to data analysis research directions. **However, to our knowledge, no prior LLM agent system automates the whole workflow from parameter configuration from the literature to initial simulation output analysis on cosmology simulation software.**

Toward this end, we introduce SIMAGENTS, a multi-agent system that automates parameter extraction, validation and configuration for cosmological simulations. The system is composed of specialized LLM agents with different distinct roles:

- **Physics Agent** that reads and interprets simulation papers using domain knowledge
- **Software Agent** that parses and enforces the constraints specified in the software user manual
- **Analysis Code Writer** that provides codes for result visualization and produces preliminary analysis (e.g. power spectra and density fields plot)

These agents collaborate through structured communication, ensuring that extracted parameters are physically meaningful, internally consistent, and software-complaint. To assess the effectiveness of SIMAGENTS, we construct a benchmark dataset of 41 simulations and evaluate the system's performance using metrics such as precision and recall, and error-specific breakdowns (e.g. Value Error, Type Error and Hallucinations). Our results show that SIMAGENTS achieves high accuracy while significantly reducing the manual workload typically required for simulation setup.

2 SIMAGENTS

In this section, we present the structure and implementations of SIMAGENTS. As illustrated in Figure 1, SIMAGENTS is composed of the following key components:

- **Parameter extraction:** This module automates the process of generating simulation scripts by extracting relevant parameters from user-uploaded papers and formatting them according to the internal requirements of the target simulation software. The extraction is performed through iterative communication between a dual-agent setup, ensuring accuracy and consistency.

[1] https://github.com/santiagocasas/clapp/

[2] https://github.com/franciscovillaescusa/CAMELS_Agents/

- **Post Simulation Processing:** This module handles code generation and execution for preliminary simulation analysis, including power spectra and density field plotting.

Together, the simulation preparation and preliminary analysis step allows users to move quickly from a published paper to actionable simulation output, closing the loop from literature reading to research insight.

2.1 Parameter Extraction

The parameter extraction module is responsible for transforming scientific papers into structured simulation-ready configurations. Given a user-uploaded paper, the system initiates a dual-agent collaboration between **Physics Agent** and **Software Agent**. The **Physics Agent** reads the input paper using domain knowledge in cosmology to identify relevant parameters such as cosmological constants, simulation box size, redshift and simulation types (dark matter, gas, stars and neutrinos). The **Software Agent** utilizes the simulation software's official user manual to query all required and optional parameters, including their default values, units, and inter-parameter dependencies.

These two agents collaborate through participation in multiple rounds of discussions based on the provided material, including a research paper and the software manual, to refine the parameter extraction process. Specifically, after Physics Agent reads the paper and extracts the parameters, the results will be sent to the Software Agent, which will then use the software user manual to check the coverage and validity of the extracted parameters. Then Software Agent will generate the parameter file following the required format and constraints. The generated file will then be sent to Physics Agent for another round of refinement. This iterative process, together with specialized task assignment on each agent, ensures:

- **High accuracy**, including scientific parameter accuracy and software requirement compliance, through task-specific expertise;
- **Modular adaptability**, as the formatting agent can be extended to support different simulation software by referencing alternative user manuals without altering the extraction logic.

2.2 Post-Simulation Processing

Once parameter extraction is completed, the generated script is passed to the simulation software for execution. After obtaining the output, the system transitions to the post-simulation processing stage, where an **Analysis Code Writer** automatically generates Python scripts to assist users with early-stage analysis of the simulation output. These generated scripts support:

- **Visualization:** Generating 2D/3D density plots from slices of the simulation box.
- **Statistical Analysis:** Generating code to plot summary statistics like matter power spectrum.
- **Custom Post-Processing:** Capability to use user-provided custom packages

The scripts are designed to be executable with minimal modification and make use of standard Python libraries such as NumPy, Matplotlib. For specialized cosmology packages, the system generates code based on example usage provided to the agent. This stage helps researchers validate simulations, identify issues early and prepare for deeper scientific investigation.

3 Experimental Setup

Our experiments are conducted in two parts: the first focuses on parameter extraction, where we evaluate quantitative accuracy; the second addresses simulation post-processing, which is more subjective and demonstrated through a representative pipeline. In our paper, we use MP-GADGET as our simulation software. In the following, we describe the experimental setup for parameter extractions.

Dataset We construct a dataset for the evaluation of cosmological parameter extraction by collecting more than 40 different simulations from published articles from ArXiv and leading journals (e.g. *ApJ*, *MNRAS*). To run MP-GADGET, two input files are required: a .genic file and a .gadget file. The .genic file generates the initial positions and velocities of particles, along with essential simulation metadata. The .gadget file evolves the initial particle distribution over time and contains numerous configuration options for selecting and enabling various physical models. Each paper is manually annotated with all MP-GADGET relevant parameter value pairs, covering cosmological parameters (Ω_m, Ω_b, Ω_Λ, h, σ_8, n_s), initial-condition settings (`BoxSize`, `Ngrid`, `Redshift`), and key model switches (e.g. `StarformationOn`, `WindOn`). To our knowledge, this is the first publicly released dataset of cosmological simulations with parameters derived directly from published text.

Implementation We use OpenAI GPT-4 (OpenAI et al., 2023) for our zero-shot extraction experiments. Our `SimAgents` framework utilizes the publicly available Autogen framework[3]. We also conduct an ablation study of our SIMAGENTS using the Qwen3-4B model (Yang et al., 2025). We set the temperature to 0.01 and *top_p* to 0.1. For the simulation software, we use MP-GADGET as an example in this paper. All outputs are formatted directly in MP-GADGET configuration syntax. We conduct all the experiments with user manual since the LLM does not have sufficient knowledge of current simulation software.

Baselines We compare our methods against two baseline methods.

- **Chain-of-thought (CoT)** (Kojima et al., 2022) We implement zero-shot CoT prompting with a single LLM agent. The agent is provided with both the literature and the manual.
- **Exchange-of-thought (EoT)** (Yin et al., 2023) We implement EoT using two agents with the same initialization, and provide them both with the literature and the manual. The agents engage in a discussion with one another.
- **SIMAGENTS** Our approach employs two task-specific agents: Physics Agent and Software Agent, each with role-specialized profiling. We provide Physics Agent with only the literature and Software Agent with only the manual. The agents engage in a discussion with one another.

We recognize that there are other LLM-based retrieval augmented generation frameworks (Gao et al., 2023). However, these RAG methods are unnecessary for our current work, as the information we provide is straightforward and does not need special design on the RAG techniques. Other LLM-based multi-agent tools in the field of cosmology (Laverick et al., 2024; Sun et al., 2024) do not fit into the scope of the current work. Thus, we do not compare with these methods in our baselines.

Evaluation We evaluate our framework using F1-score and different error metrics and provide the details of these metrics in Appendix B. Due to time constraints, we only annotated one version of the executable files. For each simulation, there exist multiple variants that contain parameters not covered in the original paper, but which could still yield the same output. To facilitate a fair comparison with the baselines, we conduct a human evaluation covering as many variants as possible and report the results in Table 1 and Table 2. The automated evaluation against the annotated dataset is reported in Section C.

[3]`https://microsoft.github.io/autogen/`

Method	Micro-F1	Precision	Recall
CoT (1-Agent)	93.64	92.46	94.84
EoT (2-Agent)	<u>94.95</u>	<u>93.87</u>	<u>96.05</u>
Ours (2-Agent)	**98.67**	**97.80**	**99.55**

Table 1: Performance comparison of SIMAGENTS with baseline methods on the cosmological simulation dataset. We report Micro-F1 score, Precision, and Recall as percentages. **Higher values indicate better performance.** The best-performing methods are bolded, and the second-best are underlined.

Method	Value Error	Type Error	Hallucination
CoT (1-Agent)	<u>0.97</u>	0.51	**0.21**
EoT (2-Agent)	1.21	<u>0.21</u>	0.34
Ours (2-Agent)	**0.46**	**0.02**	<u>0.30</u>

Table 2: Performance comparison of SIMAGENTS with baseline methods on the cosmological simulation dataset, in terms of average number of errors made per simulation. Each error type is reported as the average number of errors per case. **Lower values indicate better performance.** The best-performing methods are bolded, and the second-best are underlined.

4 Results

In this section, we first present the quantitative results, which contains baseline comparisons, detailed error analysis, ablation studies, and cost analysis. We then present a brief overview of the post-simulation processing capabilities of our system.

4.1 Main Results

The performance of our system compared to the baseline methods is shown in Table 1. Our proposed method, SIMAGENTS, outperforms CoT and EoT, achieving improvements of 5.03% and 3.72% in Micro-F1 score, respectively. Reduces the overall error rate by 80% compared to CoT and 70% compared to EoT, demonstrating significantly improved reliability in parameter extraction.

Comparison with Baseline Methods We examine the reasoning process of the CoT method and find that it struggles to handle excessive task instructions and information at input time, consistently making errors, and is unable to complete any tasks effectively. Simply involving multiple agents is not sufficient for optimal performance: EoT benefits from multi-agent interaction, but its lack of specialized task decomposition and clear communication structures results in imprecise outcomes. In contrast, SIMAGENTS incorporates task-specialized agents with specialized inputs, significantly reducing critical error types and leading to more accurate and robust parameter extraction.

Error Analysis In detailed error analysis, we observe that both CoT-based extraction and EoT-based extraction exhibits a higher frequency of both value error and type errors as shown in Table 2. Although our system exhibits slightly higher hallucination per case than the other baselines, these hallucinated parameters are easier to detect and filter (we provide an example in Appendix A). In contrast, value errors involve plausible-looking parameters whose values or units are subtly incorrect, often bypassing sanity checks and undetected during the simulation stage. Figure 2 shows that a single value error leads to drastically different structures, due to the different unit convention between the literature and simulation software.

4.2 Ablation study

Rounds of Discussion We conduct an ablation study to investigate the optimal number of discussion rounds between Physics Agent and Software Agent. In our parameter extraction module, each agent contributes domain-specific expertise to achieve high extraction accuracy while maintaining computational efficiency. By varying the number of discussions between these agents, we observe that two iterations yield the highest Micro-F1 score, as shown in Figure 3.

Smaller Backbone Model We also conduct experiments using Qwen3-4B as the backbone model to examine the generalizability of SIMAGENTS on Small Language Models. We provide the detailed results in Table 5 and Table 6 in Appendix C. Compared with GPT-4 which is significantly larger in model size, Qwen3-4B has inferior reasoning ability, leading to a decreased performance of an 81.23 F1 score, and an average of 3.05 value errors and 2.59 type errors per simulation.

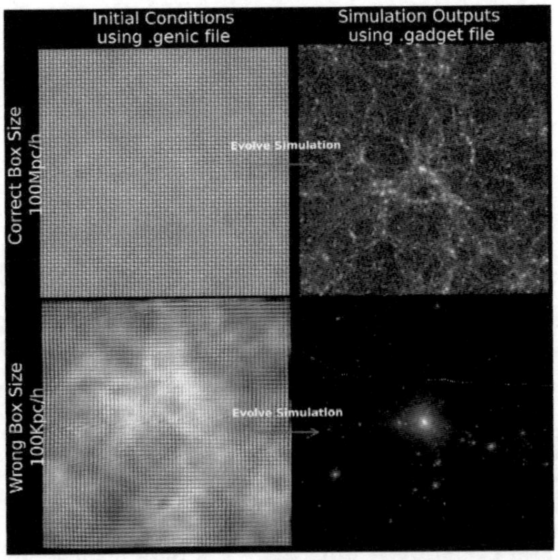

Figure 2: Impact of incorrect parameters (Value Error) on cosmological simulation outputs. Varying a single parameter, such as box size (correct top row: 100 Mpc/h; incorrect bottom row: 100 Kpc/h), while keeping all others fixed, can result in drastically different structures.

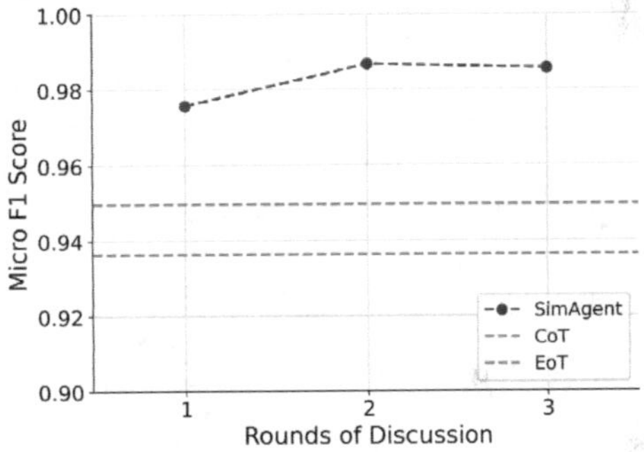

Figure 3: Results for the ablation study on the number of rounds of discussion.

4.3 Time and Cost Analysis

We conducted a survey of researchers to estimate the time cost of using simulation software. Results show that first-time users require an average of 166 minutes to replicate experiments, while experienced users average 44.4 minutes. In contrast, SIMAGENTS completes the same step in about 2 min per simulation, giving an $83\times$ speedup (-98.8%) for first-time users and $22.2\times$ (-95.5%) speed up for familiar users. At current GPT-4 API rates, a full extraction consumes around \$0.25 per paper. Additionally, SIMAGENTS can run on smaller, locally executable language models with no monetary cost and an increased time cost. We report detailed numbers in Table 7 and 8 in Appendix D.

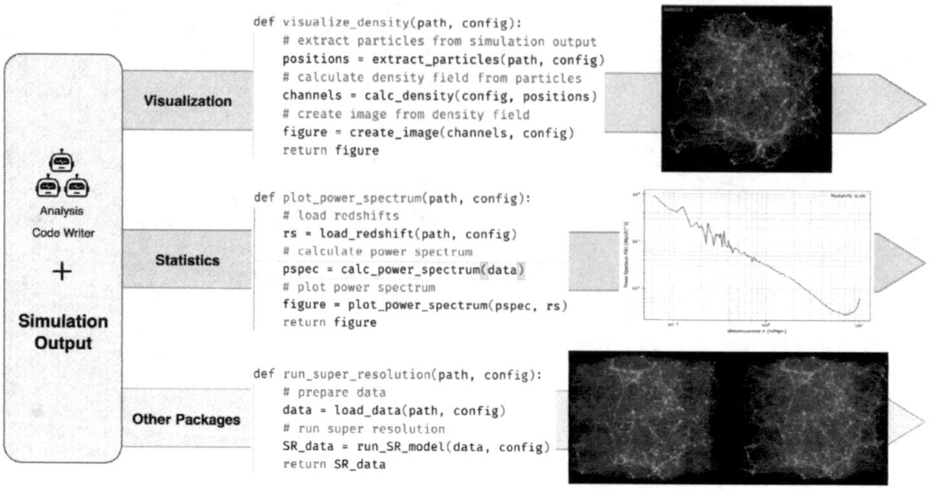

Figure 4: Illustration of post-simulation processing pipeline

4.4 Post-Simulation Processing

The output of simulation software typically consists of particle data, including positions, velocities, masses and optional quantities such as internal energy and star formation rate depending on the physical models enabled. These particles represent matter components in the universe, and the evolution over cosmic time encodes the formation of large-scale structures such as filaments, voids and halos. Some preliminary analysis are crucial for validating and interpreting simulation results:

- **Matter Power Spectrum:** Quantifies the statistical distribution of matter at different scales, sensitive to cosmological parameters such as Ω_m, σ_8, and n_s. Comparing the measured power spectrum with theoretical expectations helps to assess whether the simulation correctly reproduces the output we want.
- **Density Visualization:** Provides intuitive insight into particle distribution, particularly useful for identifying issues like incorrect box sizes or physical model settings.
- **Specialized Packages:** Generates code for specialized cosmology tools using sample code or minimal user input.

The Analysis Code Writer agent automatically provides the user with Python scripts designed to facilitate preliminary analysis of the complex and non-straightforward simulation output. As shown in Figure 4, the generated code processes the simulation output using various packages to produce the figures described above. Due to the lengthy running time of the simulation software, we were only able to perform visualization analysis and evaluation on a subset of our annotate dataset. The code provided by the Analysis Code Writer agent is highly reliable, with an execution rate of 100% in the evaluation subset.

5 Conclusions

In this paper, we propose SIMAGENTS, a multi-agent system that could accelerate physicist research for cosmological research by automatically performing parameter extraction from user-uploaded paper and simulation setup with preliminary analysis. We demonstrate the system's ability to accurately extract parameters from various simulations and translate them into valid software configuration files. Through benchmark evaluations, SIMAGENTS achieves F1 score of 98%, showing its utility in improving reproducibility, reducing human workload and accelerating the research pipeline. We envision extending SIMAGENTS to support additional simulation engines, incorporating more advanced reasoning techniques to interactively assist the researcher during post-simulation analysis. Our system and dataset are released to support further development.

Limitations

Due to time constraints, we annotated only one executable variant per paper. SIMAGENTS currently supports a small set of pretrained models and simulation codes, we will expand both datasets and coverage in the future.

Acknowledgments

This work was supported by The Block Center for Technology and Society at Carnegie Mellon University, the NSF NAIRR Pilot with PSC Neocortex and NCSA Delta, Commonwealth Cyber Initiative, Children's National Hospital, Fralin Biomedical Research Institute (Virginia Tech), Sanghani Center for AI and Data Analytics (Virginia Tech), Virginia Tech Innovation Campus, and generous gifts from Nivida, Cisco, and the Amazon + Virginia Tech Center for Efficient and Robust Machine Learning.

Ethics Statement

All models used in our system are commercially available and operated via the OpenAI API under their usage policies. No private, sensitive data were used in this paper. To ensure reproducibility and transparency, we use only publicly available papers, software and user manuals.

References

Zhenyu Bi, Sajib Acharjee Dip, Daniel Hajialigol, Sindhura Kommu, Hanwen Liu, Meng Lu, and Xuan Wang. 2024. Ai for biomedicine in the era of large language models.

Zhenyu Bi, Daniel Hajialigol, Zhongkai Sun, Jie Hao, and Xuan Wang. 2025. StoC-TOT: Stochastic tree-of-thought with constrained decoding for complex reasoning in multi-hop question answering. In *Proceedings of the 4th International Workshop on Knowledge-Augmented Methods for Natural Language Processing*, pages 141–151, Albuquerque, New Mexico, USA. Association for Computational Linguistics.

G. L. Bryan, M. L. Norman, B. W. O'Shea, T. Abel, J. H. Wise, M. J. Turk, D. R. Reynolds, D. C. Collins, P. Wang, S. W. Skillman, B. Smith, R. P. Harkness, J. Bordner, J.-h. Kim, M. Kuhlen, H. Xu, N. Goldbaum, C. Hummels, A. G. Kritsuk, E. Tasker, S. Skory, C. M. Simpson, O. Hahn, J. S. Oishi, G. C. So, F. Zhao, R. Cen, Y. Li, and The Enzo Collaboration. 2014. ENZO: An Adaptive Mesh Refinement Code for Astrophysics. *apjs*, 211:19.

Yu Feng, Simeon Bird, Lauren Anderson, Andreu Font-Ribera, and Chris Pedersen. 2018. Mp-gadget/mp-gadget: A tag for getting a doi.

Yunfan Gao, Yun Xiong, Xinyu Gao, Kangxiang Jia, Jinliu Pan, Yuxi Bi, Yi Dai, Jiawei Sun, Qianyu Guo, Meng Wang, and Haofen Wang. 2023. Retrieval-augmented generation for large language models: A survey. *ArXiv*, abs/2312.10997.

Philip F. Hopkins. 2015. A new class of accurate, mesh-free hydrodynamic simulation methods. *mnras*, 450(1):53–110.

Takeshi Kojima, Shixiang Shane Gu, Machel Reid, Yutaka Matsuo, and Yusuke Iwasawa. 2022. Large Language Models are Zero-Shot Reasoners. *arXiv e-prints*, page arXiv:2205.11916.

Andrew Laverick, Kristen Surrao, Inigo Zubeldia, Boris Bolliet, Miles Cranmer, Antony Lewis, Blake Sherwin, and Julien Lesgourgues. 2024. Multi-Agent System for Cosmological Parameter Analysis. *arXiv e-prints*, page arXiv:2412.00431.

Tian Liang, Zhiwei He, Wenxiang Jiao, Xing Wang, Yan Wang, Rui Wang, Yujiu Yang, Shuming Shi, and Zhaopeng Tu. 2024. Encouraging divergent thinking in large language models through multi-agent debate. In *Proceedings of the 2024 Conference on Empirical Methods in Natural Language Processing*, pages 17889–17904, Miami, Florida, USA. Association for Computational Linguistics.

Meng Lu, Brandon Ho, Dennis Ren, and Xuan Wang. 2024. TriageAgent: Towards better multi-agents collaborations for large language model-based clinical triage. In *Findings of the Association for Computational Linguistics: EMNLP 2024*, pages 5747–5764, Miami, Florida, USA. Association for Computational Linguistics.

OpenAI, Josh Achiam, Steven Adler, Sandhini Agarwal, Lama Ahmad, Ilge Akkaya, Florencia Leoni Aleman, Diogo Almeida, Janko Altenschmidt, Sam Altman, Shyamal Anadkat, Red Avila, Igor Babuschkin, Suchir Balaji, Valerie Balcom, Paul Baltescu, Haiming Bao, Mohammad Bavarian, Jeff Belgum, Irwan Bello, Jake Berdine, Gabriel Bernadett-Shapiro, Christopher Berner, Lenny Bogdonoff, Oleg Boiko, Madelaine Boyd, Anna-Luisa Brakman, Greg Brockman, Tim Brooks, Miles Brundage, Kevin Button, Trevor Cai, Rosie Campbell, Andrew Cann, Brittany Carey, Chelsea Carlson, Rory Carmichael, Brooke Chan, Che Chang, Fotis Chantzis, Derek Chen, Sully Chen, Ruby Chen, Jason Chen, Mark Chen, Ben Chess, Chester Cho, Casey Chu, Hyung Won Chung, Dave Cummings, Jeremiah Currier, Yunxing Dai, Cory Decareaux, Thomas Degry, Noah Deutsch, Damien Deville, Arka Dhar, David Dohan, Steve Dowling, Sheila Dunning, Adrien Ecoffet, Atty Eleti, Tyna Eloundou, David Farhi, Liam Fedus, Niko Felix, Simón Posada Fishman, Juston Forte, Isabella Fulford, Leo Gao, Elie Georges, Christian Gibson, Vik Goel, Tarun Gogineni, Gabriel Goh, Rapha Gontijo-Lopes, Jonathan Gordon, Morgan Grafstein, Scott Gray, Ryan Greene, Joshua Gross, Shixiang Shane Gu, Yufei Guo, Chris Hallacy, Jesse Han, Jeff Harris, Yuchen He, Mike Heaton, Johannes Heidecke, Chris Hesse, Alan Hickey, Wade Hickey, Peter Hoeschele, Brandon Houghton, Kenny Hsu, Shengli Hu, Xin Hu, Joost Huizinga, Shantanu Jain, Shawn Jain, Joanne Jang, Angela Jiang, Roger Jiang, Haozhun Jin, Denny Jin, Shino Jomoto, Billie Jonn, Heewoo Jun, Tomer Kaftan, Łukasz Kaiser, Ali Kamali, Ingmar Kanitscheider, Nitish Shirish Keskar, Tabarak Khan, Logan Kilpatrick, Jong Wook Kim, Christina Kim, Yongjik Kim, Jan Hendrik Kirchner, Jamie Kiros, Matt Knight, Daniel Kokotajlo,

Łukasz Kondraciuk, Andrew Kondrich, Aris Konstantinidis, Kyle Kosic, Gretchen Krueger, Vishal Kuo, Michael Lampe, Ikai Lan, Teddy Lee, Jan Leike, Jade Leung, Daniel Levy, Chak Ming Li, Rachel Lim, Molly Lin, Stephanie Lin, Mateusz Litwin, Theresa Lopez, Ryan Lowe, Patricia Lue, Anna Makanju, Kim Malfacini, Sam Manning, Todor Markov, Yaniv Markovski, Bianca Martin, Katie Mayer, Andrew Mayne, Bob McGrew, Scott Mayer McKinney, Christine McLeavey, Paul McMillan, Jake McNeil, David Medina, Aalok Mehta, Jacob Menick, Luke Metz, Andrey Mishchenko, Pamela Mishkin, Vinnie Monaco, Evan Morikawa, Daniel Mossing, Tong Mu, Mira Murati, Oleg Murk, David Mély, Ashvin Nair, Reiichiro Nakano, Rajeev Nayak, Arvind Neelakantan, Richard Ngo, Hyeonwoo Noh, Long Ouyang, Cullen O'Keefe, Jakub Pachocki, Alex Paino, Joe Palermo, Ashley Pantuliano, Giambattista Parascandolo, Joel Parish, Emy Parparita, Alex Passos, Mikhail Pavlov, Andrew Peng, Adam Perelman, Filipe de Avila Belbute Peres, Michael Petrov, Henrique Ponde de Oliveira Pinto, Michael, Pokorny, Michelle Pokrass, Vitchyr H. Pong, Tolly Powell, Alethea Power, Boris Power, Elizabeth Proehl, Raul Puri, and Alec Radford. 2023. GPT-4 Technical Report. *arXiv e-prints*, page arXiv:2303.08774.

Volker Springel, Rüdiger Pakmor, and Rainer Weinberger. 2019. AREPO: Cosmological magnetohydrodynamical moving-mesh simulation code. Astrophysics Source Code Library, record ascl:1909.010.

Volker Springel, Rüdiger Pakmor, Oliver Zier, and Martin Reinecke. 2022. GADGET-4: Parallel cosmological N-body and SPH code. Astrophysics Source Code Library, record ascl:2204.014.

Zechang Sun, Yuan-Sen Ting, Yaobo Liang, Nan Duan, Song Huang, and Zheng Cai. 2024. Interpreting Multi-band Galaxy Observations with Large Language Model-Based Agents. *arXiv e-prints*, page arXiv:2409.14807.

Qingyun Wu, Gagan Bansal, Jieyu Zhang, Yiran Wu, Beibin Li, Erkang Zhu, Li Jiang, Xiaoyun Zhang, Shaokun Zhang, Jiale Liu, Ahmed Hassan Awadallah, Ryen W. White, Doug Burger, and Chi Wang. 2023. Autogen: Enabling next-gen llm applications via multi-agent conversation.

An Yang, Anfeng Li, Baosong Yang, Beichen Zhang, Binyuan Hui, Bo Zheng, Bowen Yu, Chang Gao, Chengen Huang, Chenxu Lv, Chujie Zheng, Dayiheng Liu, Fan Zhou, Fei Huang, Feng Hu, Hao Ge, Haoran Wei, Huan Lin, Jialong Tang, Jian Yang, Jianhong Tu, Jianwei Zhang, Jianxin Yang, Jiaxi Yang, Jing Zhou, Jingren Zhou, Junyang Lin, Kai Dang, Keqin Bao, Kexin Yang, Le Yu, Lianghao Deng, Mei Li, Mingfeng Xue, Mingze Li, Pei Zhang, Peng Wang, Qin Zhu, Rui Men, Ruize Gao, Shixuan Liu, Shuang Luo, Tianhao Li, Tianyi Tang, Wenbiao Yin, Xingzhang Ren, Xinyu Wang, Xinyu Zhang, Xuancheng Ren, Yang Fan, Yang Su, Yichang Zhang, Yinger Zhang, Yu Wan, Yuqiong Liu, Zekun Wang, Zeyu Cui, Zhenru Zhang, Zhipeng Zhou, and Zihan Qiu. 2025. Qwen3 technical report.

Zhangyue Yin, Qiushi Sun, Cheng Chang, Qipeng Guo, Junqi Dai, Xuanjing Huang, and Xipeng Qiu. 2023. Exchange-of-Thought: Enhancing Large Language Model Capabilities through Cross-Model Communication. *arXiv e-prints*, page arXiv:2312.01823.

Xiaowen Zhang, Patrick Lachance, Yueying Ni, Yin Li, Rupert A. C. Croft, Tiziana Di Matteo, Simeon Bird, and Yu Feng. 2024. AI-assisted super-resolution cosmological simulations III: time evolution. *mnras*, 528(1):281–293.

Wayne Xin Zhao, Kun Zhou, Junyi Li, Tianyi Tang, Xiaolei Wang, Yupeng Hou, Yingqian Min, Beichen Zhang, Junjie Zhang, Zican Dong, Yifan Du, Chen Yang, Yushuo Chen, Zhipeng Chen, Jinhao Jiang, Ruiyang Ren, Yifan Li, Xinyu Tang, Zikang Liu, Peiyu Liu, Jian-Yun Nie, and Ji-Rong Wen. 2023. A Survey of Large Language Models. *arXiv e-prints*, page arXiv:2303.18223.

Mingchen Zhuge, Wenyi Wang, Louis Kirsch, Francesco Faccio, Dmitrii Khizbullin, and Jürgen Schmidhuber. 2024. Language agents as optimizable graphs. *ArXiv*, abs/2402.16823.

A Example script and type of errors

A correct version of the MP-GADGET simulation script to match the low-resolution simulation in Zhang et al., 2024.

```
"genic": {
    "OutputDir": "./ICs/",
    "FileBase": "LR_100Mpc_64",
    "BoxSize": 100000.0,
    "Ngrid": 64,
    "WhichSpectrum": 2,
    "FileWithInputSpectrum": "./
  WMAP9_CAMB_matterpower.dat",
    "Omega0": 0.2814,
    "OmegaBaryon": 0.0464,
    "OmegaLambda": 0.7186,
    "HubbleParam": 0.697,
    "ProduceGas": 0,
    "Redshift": 99,
    "Seed": 12345
  }
"gadget": {
    "InitCondFile": "./ICs/
  LR_100Mpc_64",
    "OutputDir": "./output/",
    "OutputList": "0.333,1.0",
    "TimeLimitCPU": 86400,
    "MetalReturnOn": 0,
    "CoolingOn": 0,
    "SnapshotWithFOF": 0,
    "BlackHoleOn": 0,
    "StarformationOn": 0,
    "WindOn": 0,
    "MassiveNuLinRespOn": 0,
    "DensityIndependentSphOn": 0,
    "Omega0": 0.2814
  }
```

An example script with an incorrect simulation box size (Value Error), caused by a mismatch between the units used in the paper and those expected by the simulation software.

```
"genic": {
    "OutputDir": "./ICs/",
    "FileBase": "LR_100Mpc_64",
    "BoxSize": 100.0,
    "Ngrid": 64,
    "WhichSpectrum": 2,
    "FileWithInputSpectrum": "./
  WMAP9_CAMB_matterpower.dat",
    "Omega0": 0.2814,
    "OmegaBaryon": 0.0464,
    "OmegaLambda": 0.7186,
    "HubbleParam": 0.697,
    "ProduceGas": 0,
    "Redshift": 99,
    "Seed": 12345
  }
......
```

An example script containing an incorrect option that enables gas production in a dark matter only simulation (Type Error), caused by a mismatch between the paper specifications and the generated script.

```
"genic": {
    "OutputDir": "./ICs/",
    "FileBase": "LR_100Mpc_64",
    "BoxSize": 100.0,
    "Ngrid": 64,
    "WhichSpectrum": 2,
    "FileWithInputSpectrum": "./
  WMAP9_CAMB_matterpower.dat",
    "Omega0": 0.2814,
    "OmegaBaryon": 0.0464,
    "OmegaLambda": 0.7186,
    "HubbleParam": 0.697,
    "ProduceGas": 1,
    "Redshift": 99,
    "Seed": 12345
  }
  ......
```

An example of script containing an incorrect variable name that mismatch with the one in software user manual. (Hallucination)

```
"genic": {
    "OutputDir": "./ICs/",
    "FileBase": "LR_100Mpc_64",
    "BoxSize": 100.0,
    "Ngrid": 64,
    "WhichSpectrum": 2,
    "FileWithInputSpectrum": "./
  WMAP9_CAMB_matterpower.dat",
    "Omega0": 0.2814,
    "OmegaBaryon": 0.0464,
    "OmegaLambda": 0.7186,
    "HubbleParam": 0.697,
    "ProduceGas": 1,
    "Redshift": 99,
    "Seed": 12345,
    "FinalRedshift": 0
  }
......
```

B Evaluation Protocol

We define our parameter-level metrics as follows:

- **True Positives (TP):** Number of extracted parameters whose names and values are exactly correct.
- **False Positives (FP):** Number of extracted parameters with incorrect values/settings .
- **False Negatives (FN):** Number of required parameters that are missing from the extraction out-

put.

Our primary evaluation metric is the **F_1 Score**, which captures the overall balance between precision and recall in all extracted parameter instances.

$$F_1 = 2 \times \frac{\text{Precision} \times \text{Recall}}{\text{Precision} + \text{Recall}}.$$

Precision and recall are defined as:

$$\text{Precision} = \frac{\text{TP}}{\text{TP} + \text{FP}}$$

$$\text{Recall} = \frac{\text{TP}}{\text{TP} + \text{FN}}.$$

A higher F_1 indicates more accurate extractions with fewer missing or incorrect parameters.

We categorize error cases into the following types:

- **Value Error:** The extracted parameter exists but its numerical value is incorrect. This includes errors due to unit mismatch, incorrect scaling, or misinterpretation of scientific notation.
- **Type Error:** A parameter is extracted from an incompatible simulation context. (e.g. hydrodynamic settings mistakenly used in a dark matter only simulation)
- **Hallucination:** The system outputs parameters that do not appear in the user manual, inventing values or name unsupported by the source.

Each of these types of error is reported as the average number of errors per simulation.

C Additional Experiments and Results

We provide the automatic evaluation results on SIMAGENTS and the baselines in Table 3 and Table 4. The evaluation results are slightly worse for the baselines compared to the human evaluation, as the automatic evaluation does not consider all possible executable variations of the input file. We provide the automatic evaluation results on SIMAGENTS using different backbone models in Table 5 and Table 6.

D Time and Cost Analysis

We provide the average time and cost of SIMAGENTS using GPT-4 and Qwen3-4B as the backbone model, respectively. For GPT-4, we do direct API calling; for Qwen3-4B, we run experiments on a single NVIDIA A40 GPU and report the time cost.

Method	Micro-F1	Precision	Recall
CoT (1-Agent)	91.27	85.84	97.44
EoT (2-Agent)	90.69	84.94	97.27
Ours (2-Agent)	**98.13**	**97.77**	**98.50**

Table 3: Performance comparison of SIMAGENTS with baseline methods on the cosmological simulation dataset. We report Micro-F1 score, Precision, and Recall as percentages. Higher values indicate better performance. The best-performing methods are bolded, and the second-best are underlined.

Method	Value Error	Type Error
CoT (1-Agent)	1.76	1.00
EoT (2-Agent)	1.97	0.95
Ours (2-Agent)	**0.40**	**0.05**

Table 4: Performance comparison of SIMAGENTS with baseline methods on the cosmological simulation dataset, in terms of average number of errors made per simulation. Each error type is reported as the average number of errors per simulation. Lower values indicate better performance. The best-performing methods are bolded, and the second-best are underlined.

E Additional Discussion and Clarifications

In this appendix, we provide additional details and clarifications in response to reviewer questions.

E.1 Manual Inspection and Physical Equivalence

For simulations that can be completed within a few days on our available compute resources, we manually inspected the outputs, focusing primarily on the matter power spectrum and density fields. For huge simulations that would require months of computation, we did not rerun the full simulations from published results. Instead, we verified that the automatically generated configurations (e.g., cosmological parameters, resolution, and activated physical modules) match those described in the corresponding publications.

As a future validation goal, we plan to move toward more systematic checks of *physical equivalence* between SIMAGENTS-generated simulations and published benchmarks. This includes extending our current limited manual inspection on smaller runs to broader, human-verified comparisons on standardized benchmark setups, once additional compute resources are available.

Method	Micro-F1	Precision	Recall
SIMAGENTS (GPT-4)	98.13	97.77	98.50
SIMAGENTS (Qwen3-4B)	81.23	70.16	96.10

Table 5: Performance comparison of SIMAGENTS using Qwen3-4B as the backbone model and GPT-4 as the backbone model. Experiments are conducted on the cosmological simulation dataset. We report Micro-F1 score, Precision, and Recall as percentages.

Method	Value Error	Type Error
SIMAGENTS (GPT-4)	0.40	0.05
SIMAGENTS (Qwen3-4B)	3.05	2.59

Table 6: Error analysis of SIMAGENTS using Qwen3-4B as the backbone model and GPT-4 as the backbone model. Experiments are conducted on the cosmological simulation dataset. Each error type is reported as the average number of errors per simulation.

E.2 Definition of Simulation Success

In our evaluation, success requires both executability and basic physical consistency. First, the simulation script must run to completion without errors raised by the simulation software. Second, we perform lightweight checks of physical consistency, such as verifying units and ensuring that critical physical parameters and models are set in a way that is compatible with the problem specification. These considerations are reflected in the examples and analyses presented in the main paper.

E.3 Agent Decomposition and Coordination

We did consider alternative agent decompositions when designing SIMAGENTS. The current two-agent setup is chosen to balance information distribution and domain expertise: both agents are prompted to use physics knowledge, while the Software Agent focuses on interacting with the code and its manual. In a two-agent interaction, there is limited room for different coordination strategies and patterns in a two-agent interaction. We will explore this in future work as we implement more varieties of agent groups.

E.4 Generalizability to Other Simulation Codes

Our framework is designed to be largely adaptable to different simulation codes. Many widely used codes (e.g., Arepo, ENZO, GIZMO, GADGET-4)

	Manual	Paper/rel.	Draft+dbg	Iter	Total
First-time	64	42	60	5.2	166
Familiar	12	19	13.4	2	44.4
SIMAGENTS		*2 (total only)*			2

Table 7: Average setup effort. Times are averages in minutes. **Manual** = reading the software manual; **Paper/rel.** = reading the paper or related materials and extracting needed parameters; **Draft+dbg** = drafting and debugging the configuration; **Iter** = iterations/debug cycles to first successful run. For SIMAGENTS, only the total time applies (no per-step times).

Backbone Model	Average Time (seconds)	Average Cost ($)
GPT-4	124	**0.25**
Qwen3-4B	406	-

Table 8: Average time and cost per paper of SIMAGENTS using GPT4 and Qwen3-4B, respectively

share similar high-level physical models and workflows (configuration $\rightarrow$ initial conditions $\rightarrow$ run $\rightarrow$ analysis), but differ in file structures, parameter names, units, and other conventions.

In principle, the overall multi-agent structure of SIMAGENTS can be reused across codes. Adapting to a new code primarily requires:

- Providing the Software Agent with the corresponding manuals and documentation.
- Adding code-specific guidance about file formats, execution commands, and key parameters.
- Performing modest prompt engineering to account for different naming conventions, error messages, and pipeline structures.

Thus, extending SIMAGENTS to other simulation environments is not a matter of re-engineering the entire framework, but of combining new documentation with few adaptations.

E.5 Model Dependency and Smaller Open-Source Models

We observe a substantial performance gap between GPT-4 and the smaller open-source model Qwen3-4B (F1 score dropping from 98.13% to 81.23%). A key limitation of Qwen3-4B in our setting is its weaker long-context reasoning ability: given very long inputs such as a ~100-page software manual, it struggles to fully interpret and integrate the necessary information. Thus, giving it more examples would not be that helpful, as we are feeding it with more contexts, which are usually dozens of pages of physics papers. Fine-tuning on the dataset could be beneficial, but it would be very time-consuming and dataset-specific. We will explore light fine-tuning in later works.

E.6 Error Analysis and Hallucination Errors

As noted in Section 3 of the main paper, all baselines, including SIMAGENTS, have access to the user manual, since current LLMs do not possess sufficient built-in knowledge of cosmological simulation software. In SIMAGENTS, we prompt the specialized Software Agent to focus particularly on parameter explanations rather than just parameter names, because type and value errors are especially critical from a physicist's perspective. As a result, many of the hallucination errors made are errors that a physicist can understand which physical parameter they correspond to. Still, the naming is different from that of the software. We expect these errors to be reducible by prompting the agents to pay closer attention to exact parameter names during inter-agent communication and by strengthening consistency checks between proposed configurations and the documentation. Such improvements are a natural direction for future iterations of the framework.

StanceMining: An open-source stance detection library supporting time-series and visualization

Benjamin D. Steel
McGill University
benjamin.steel@mail.mcgill.ca

Derek Ruths
McGill University
derek.ruths@mcgill.ca

Abstract

Despite the size of the field, stance detection has remained inaccessible to most researchers due to implementation barriers. Here we present a library that allows easy access to an end-to-end stance modelling solution. This library comes complete with everything needed to go from a corpus of documents, to exploring stance trends in a corpus through an interactive dashboard. To support this, we provide stance target extraction, stance detection, stance time-series trend inference, and an exploratory dashboard, all available in an easy-to-use library. We hope that this library can increase the accessibility of stance detection for the wider community of those who could benefit from this method.

1 Introduction

The field of stance detection —the identification of the attitude of a document author to a target, as represented by a topic, claim, entity, etc. (Mohammad et al., 2016) —has produced a number of methods critical to the understanding of social behaviour. However, it remains a method that requires a committed natural language processing (NLP) expert to apply. While other NLP fields have successfully made their technology available for general practitioners, with topic modelling being a prime example, stance detection remains off limits to general use. Beyond this, stance detection has thus far focused on the situation of having a set of documents with pre-defined stance targets (the idea or issue a stance is expressed on, here in the form of noun-phrases or claims, as used previously (Zhao and Caragea, 2024)). We present a library that uses a combination of new and prior methods to allow a user to go from a raw corpus of documents, to an organised set of stance targets and stance target trends, with little-to-no tuning needed.

Stance detection is frequently used in a temporal context to understand how attitudes are changing over time. In prior work, the outputs have been naively assembled into a time series using a moving average (Introne, 2023; Almadan et al., 2023). We account for the error in the stance classifier and the noisiness of the data by using Gaussian processes (GPs) with a custom likelihood to model the temporal trends of stance. We show an explanation of this problem in Fig. 1.

Our library contains an easy-to-deploy web-app that allows for the exploration of the features output from our library. In addition, it comes with small fine-tuned models and defaults that allow it to run on consumer-grade GPUs [1], making it accessible to researchers with modest compute budgets. We have seen the value that accessible topic modelling has provided to the larger community that can benefit from using topic modelling but does not have the technical capacity to implement their own topic models, and we hope that, similarly, this library can benefit the larger community of social scientists who have much to gain from easily accessible stance detection.

We present two novel contributions: First, to our knowledge, no stance detection method is available in a library/package form, only as research repositories specific to a context and dataset. We go beyond this and release a library that is designed to be generally usable. Second, no prior work has produced a method that can take stance labels with timestamps, and infer a continuous time-varying stance, considering the error of the classifier.

We release this library under an MIT license at `https://github.com/bendavidsteel/stancemining`. Scripts to reproduce our results are available in `https://github.com/bendavidsteel/stancemining/tree/main/experiments`. In addition, we present a video demonstrating the system at this link: `https://youtu.be/4tvqq8GTUHU`.

[1] Here defined as having less than 16GB VRAM

Proceedings of The 14th International Joint Conference on Natural Language Processing and The 4th Conference of the Asia-Pacific Chapter of the Association for Computational Linguistics: System Demonstrations, pages 67–76
December 20-24, 2025 ©2025 Association for Computational Linguistics

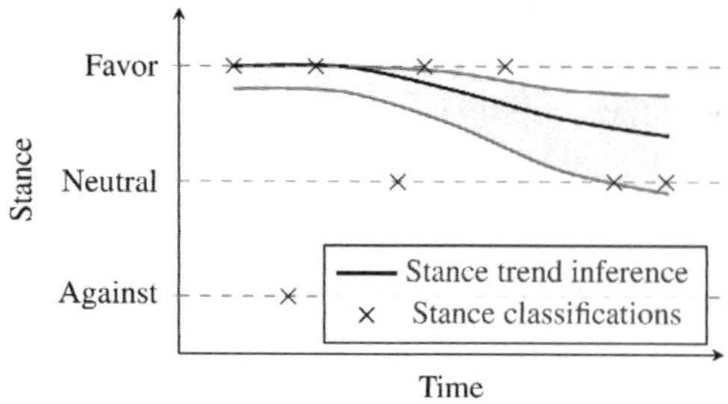

Figure 1: Given the ordinal stance classifications as $\times$, with labels 'Favor', 'Neutral', and 'Against', arrayed in time, how should we infer the latent stance? We propose to use a Gaussian process with a customized ordinal likelihood to infer the latent stance trend. This will allow us to infer the latent stance from the stance classifications as shown in the figure - that is, in a smoothly varying manner that balances fitting signal and avoiding noise. This allows us to factor in the error of the stance detection classifier into our inference, alongside setting a prior on the extent to which the stance trend will vary, allowing us to ignore noise.

2 Background

Services exist to provide stance-detection-like models to a practitioner audience, but they are either proprietary (sum) or domain specific (Stab et al., 2018). Methods for inferring stance trends from stance observations have been limited to rolling averages (Introne, 2023), or aggregation on a time interval basis (Almadan et al., 2023). We produce models that can both interpolate, and consider the error of the classifier.

For stance detection output visualization, previous work has produced solutions (Wu et al., 2014; Martins et al., 2017; Kucher et al., 2020, 2016), but all are either not open-source/publicly available, or are specific to a particular domain, or both.

3 Implementation

We depict the system in Fig. 2, showing the functionality that the library affords. By default, for cases where the specific stance-targets of a corpus are not known a priori, the fine-tuned stance target extraction model will extract stance targets from each document. The fine-tuned stance detection models will then find the stance of each document on each stance target mapped to that document. Additional stance targets can optionally be discovered via clustering, using the method detailed in **?**. Alternately, pre-defined stance targets can be provided, in which case the library will find the stance of each document on each pre-defined stance targets.

For out-of-the-box use, we use our two fine-tuned models by default, hosted on HuggingFace model storage to allow distribution. In practice, stance detection frequently needs custom models for domain specific data, so the library allows using any local transformers compatible fine-tuned model. We train our base stance extraction model on VAST (Allaway and Mckeown, 2020) and EZ-STANCE noun-phrase (Zhao and Caragea, 2024). Stance targets represented by claims are popular in stance detection (Küçük and Can, 2020; Zhao and Caragea, 2024), so we additionally provide fine-tuned claim extraction models. This choice of noun-phrases or claims for extracted stance targets is configurable by the user in the library.

Since cross-dataset generalization in stance detection is poor (Ng and Carley, 2022; Zhao and Caragea, 2024), we fine-tuned a modern small language model on several datasets to produce a model that has more generalizability. While this comes at the risk of each dataset's slightly different definition of stance distorting the learned signal, it should improve the generalizability of the model. Specifically, we use the following datasets: SemEval Task 6 dataset (Mohammad et al., 2016), VAST (Allaway and Mckeown, 2020), EZ-STANCE noun-phrase and claim datasets (Zhao and Caragea, 2024), P-STANCE (Li et al., 2021), and the multi-turn conversational stance detection datasets MT-CSD (Niu et al., 2024) and CTSDT (Li et al., 2023). The use of the multi-turn datasets means that our library supports documents with contextual threads, common in media data. Corresponding to the datasets we select, the specific form of stance detection we focus on is topic/entity stance detection (Zhu et al., 2025).

We use 16-bit models to maintain high throughput on older GPUs [2]. We use vLLM (Kwon et al., 2023) for fast LLM inference. This enables processing of a dataset of $\sim$1300 posts in 4 minutes.

Stance detection using inputs from audio data, whether from social media videos or podcasts, is a common use-case. We therefore provide helper functions to transcribe audio and video files, using WhisperX (Bain et al., 2023) and pyannote (Plaquet and Bredin, 2023). Our library does not currently support image/video inputs.

Stance Trend Inference GP models use a base model that outputs a set of Gaussian distributions corresponding to input points, and a likelihood, that

[2]https://docs.vllm.ai/en/latest/features/quantization/supported_hardware.html

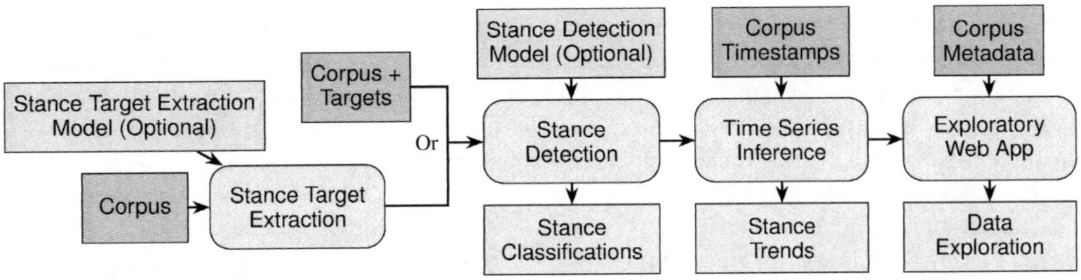

Figure 2: System diagram of *stancemining*. Origin items in blue are inputs to the system, origin items in orange are optional models (*stancemining* provides these models by default), intermediate items in green are components of the *stancemining* library, and endpoint items in red are outputs from the library.

takes as input samples from the base model, and defines how those signals correspond to the actual data seen. In our case, the base model is modelling the function between time and true latent stance, and the likelihood is modelling the relationship between the true latent stance and the observed stance classifications. Stance classifications are ordinal in nature: a 'neutral' post favors a target more than an 'against' post, and an 'favor' post favors a target more than a 'neutral' post. We therefore use an ordinal likelihood (Chu et al., 2005), and model the stance as a continuous time-varying value between -1 ('against') and 1 ('favor').

There are two conditions specific to our use-case. First and most importantly, stance detection is done with classification models that make errors. If a stance detection model is better at classifying 'favor' posts than 'against' posts, we will have a systematic error in our trend inferences if we do not account for this error. We can estimate the error of the classifier from its performance on an evaluation set. The ordinal likelihood function for the 3 true stance labels would generally be defined as:

$$p(Y = \text{Fav.}|F) = \phi\left(\frac{a_0 - F}{\sigma}\right)$$

$$p(Y = \text{Neu.}|F) = \phi\left(\frac{a_1 - F}{\sigma}\right) - \phi\left(\frac{a_0 - F}{\sigma}\right)$$

$$p(Y = \text{Aga.}|F) = 1 - \phi\left(\frac{a_1 - F}{\sigma}\right)$$

where ϕ is the cumulative density function of a Gaussian (the inverse probit function), σ is a parameter to be learned, the data are integer values from 0 to k, and the bin edges where the labels switch are $[a_0, a_1]$, which we set to $[-0.5, 0.5]$

However, we want to model the observed probabilities. So first we normalize the confusion matrix $\mathbf{C}$ such that each row sums to 1: $\sum_{j=1}^{3} c_{ij} = 1$ for all $i \in 1, 2, 3$. We then multiply the true stance probability vector $p_S = [p(Y = \text{Fav.}|F), p(Y = \text{Neu.}|F), p(Y = \text{Aga.}|F)]$ with the normalized confusion matrix to obtain the final observed stance probabilities $\hat{p}_S = Cp_S$, which are used as the probabilities of the likelihood categorical output.

The second condition specific to our use-case is that the stance should be clamped between -1 and 1. Without this, for an array of 'favor' observations, the GP model could reasonably infer a stance of any value over 1, whereas we want to limit the stance at 1 for the sake of trend comparison. We model this by inferring the inverse hyperbolic tangent with the GP base model, and then transform the output of this model for predictions and the likelihood by applying a hyperbolic tangent transform.

We use a GP model with constant mean and the radial basis function for the covariance kernel, with a log-normal prior for the lengthscale parameter. In this case, we are inferring the time-varying trend of a person's stance on an issue (as opposed to an organization etc.), so we choose a lengthscale prior of $\mu = 2, \sigma = 0.1$ based on prior work studying the correlation of user attitudes over time in Krosnick (1988). We use the ordinal likelihood developed by Chu et al. (2005), and optimize the model using stochastic variational inference, using natural gradient descent (Salimbeni et al., 2018).

A critical aspect of getting the model to train fast and effectively is the learning rates of the natural gradient optimizer, and the learning rate and learning rate scheduler of the hyperparameter and likelihood parameter optimizer. We run hyperparameter sweeps of these three variables in Section C. To implement the model, we use GPyTorch (Gardner et al., 2018). To improve training speed, we add a number of optimizations, including compiling the model using PyTorch [3], converting functions to TorchScript, and a batching process which trains models of comparable size in parallel.

When calling the infer trends function on the library, the user can specify filter columns. These are columns in the dataframe where trends should be calculated for each unique value. This is useful for when a user wants to calculate time series trends for different users, sources, accounts etc.

4 Application Use

Once stance features have been extracted from the corpus using *stancemining*, it is useful to be able to quickly explore them using an interactive application. We therefore include a ready-to-use web-app for this purpose. This web-app can be easily deployed via Docker Compose for any user data via the use of environment variables, as long as the data has been saved in the format and structure specified in the documentation. There is an option to enable authentication in the application if necessary for sensitive data. The backend of the application uses FastAPI [4], and the frontend uses React [5].

The user is presented with two main views in the app: a stance target map view, and a timeline view. The map view (Fig. 3a) shows a 2-dimensional map of stance targets, where stance targets are embedded using the 'GIST-small-Embedding-v0' text embedding model (Solatorio, 2024), those embeddings are reduced to 2-dimensions using UMAP (McInnes et al., 2018), and plotted as a scatter plot. Points are coloured with the mean stance of documents on that target, and hovering over the point shows the proportions of each stance on that target. This plot allows the user to explore stance targets in a 2D semantic space, and the discovery of more stance targets than semantic search alone. If a user clicks on a point, they are shown the temporal trends of that target in the timeline view.

The timeline view (Fig. 3b) shows the inferred trend mean for each stance target, alongside its confidence intervals as computed by the GP model. When we load the trend data, the backend automatically finds filter types, and allows the user to display trends broken down by filter value side by side, or one at a time. This is useful when breaking down stance target trends into individual users or sources.

We summarise the full use of the *stancemining* library and web app in the following steps. While each component of the system can be used separately, this sequence represents its full potential:

1. **Extract Targets (Optional)**: Extract stance targets (noun-phrases or claims) from corpus, using default model or custom model if there are specific domain requirements.
2. **Stance Detection**: Detect stance of documents on targets using default models, or custom models if there are specific domain requirements.
3. **Stance Trend Inference**: Do stance trend inference if corpus has timestamps.
4. **Load Web App**: Load web app using saved *stancemining* outputs, specify options via environment variables.
5. **Explore Target Map**: Explore stance targets in the target map view.
6. **View Target Trend**: Zoom in on a specific target timeline, filter by metadata attributes.

5 Evaluation

Where possible, we evaluate components of our system against prior work. Otherwise, we provide multiple competing methods to add context to the range of possible metrics. We did not do any formal evaluation of the web application with end users.

Stance Target Extraction We evaluate the model using BERTScore (Zhang et al., 2019) and BLEU (using the SacreBLEU package) (Post, 2018), and show our results in Table 1. We compare to the smallest open-source model evaluated in Akash et al. (2024). No other direct task and dataset comparisons exist. For the task of noun-phrase stance target extraction, we fine-tune our models on a combined dataset of the document - stance target noun phrases from VAST (Allaway and Mckeown, 2020) and the noun-phrase targets of EZ-STANCE (Zhao and Caragea, 2024). We do not compare against prior work here, as previous work has only evaluated one extracted stance target per document (Akash et al., 2024), as opposed to extracting multiple targets per document. For these tasks we use Qwen 3 models (Yang et al., 2025) and SmolLM2 models (Allal et al., 2025), with specific sizes reported in the tables. For our claim extraction models, we fine-tune them on the document - stance target claims pairs from EZ-STANCE (Zhao and Caragea, 2024). We show metrics from this fine-tuning in Table 2. No comparable results are available for this task on this dataset to our knowledge.

[3]https://pytorch.org/

[4]https://fastapi.tiangolo.com/

[5]https://react.dev/

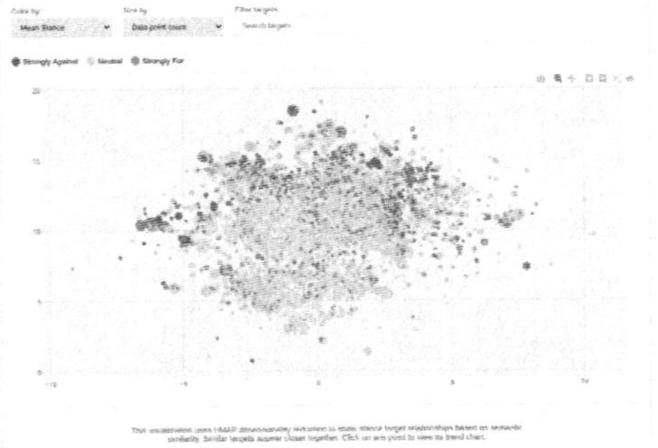

(a) 2-dimensional map view of stance targets.

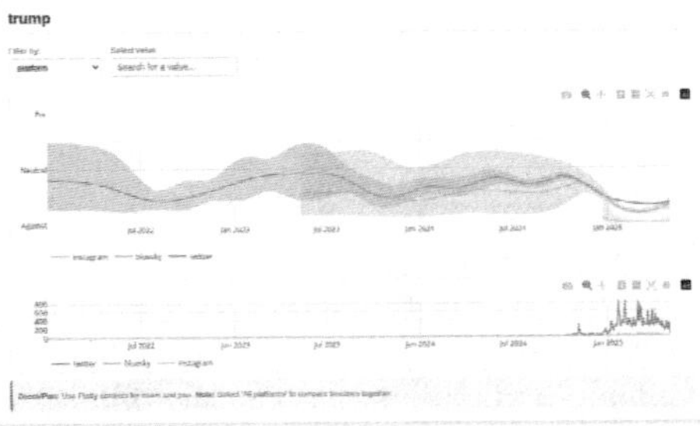

(b) Trend timelines view of a stance target broken down by filter values.

Figure 3: Two screenshots from the *stancemining* dashboard.

Model	Num. params.	EZ-STANCE		VAST	
		BERTScore F1	BLEU F1	BERTScore F1	BLEU F1
Llama-3-8B (Akash et al., 2024)	8B	0.78	-	0.84	-
Qwen3-0.6B (ours)	752M	0.90	0.67	0.91	0.33
SmolLM2-360M-Instruct (ours)	360M	0.90	0.67	0.92	0.20

Table 1: Noun-phrase stance target extraction evaluation results. We compare to the smallest open-source model evaluated in Akash et al. (2024). No other direct task and dataset comparisons exist.

Model	Num. params.	EZ-STANCE	
		BERTScore F1	BLEU F1
Qwen3-1.7B (ours)	2.03B	0.89	0.16
Qwen3-0.6B (ours)	752M	0.88	0.04

Table 2: Claim stance target extraction evaluation. No comparable results are available for this task on this dataset to our knowledge.

Stance Detection We evaluate our fine-tuned stance detection models using the macro F1 score, as is typical in stance detection (Zhao and Caragea, 2024; Allaway and Mckeown, 2020), and show our results in Table 3. We experimented with several hyperparameters and report the best results here, using 4 epochs, $batch\_size \times grad\_accumulation\_size = 32$, a learning rate of 0.0001, and classifying using a classification head (instead of using causal language modelling to generate the label). We report other hyperparameters experimented with in App. A. In the table we also highlight the number of parameters in each model, given that part of the aim of *stancemining* is to make it accessible, thereby necessitating small models that work with limited resources.

Stance Trend Inference To test the GP model, we use synthetic data. This also allows us to model the relationship between a true latent stance and stance classifications across time, lacking a dataset for fine-grained stance over time. We detail our synthetic data generation process in Section B. We use 3 parameters to parameterize our synthetic data, the number of observations n_d, the random walk scale σ_{walk} which determines how much the latent stance trend varies, and σ_{noise} which determines the amount of noise in the stance expressions (i.e. someone who consistently favors a stance target or producing varied views on it).

To improve training time and model performance, we ran hyperparameter sweeps on the learning rates of the natural gradient optimizer for the GP model, and the learning rate and scheduler for the likelihood parameters and model hyperparameters. We averaged across several synthetic data configurations, including n_d, σ_{noise}, and σ_{walk}. We determine scheduler performance by averaging across all learning rate values, and then sorting by minimum loss achieved in 1000 epochs. We detail this experiment in Sec. C. Using no scheduler achieves the best loss, but a cosine scheduler achieves the fastest convergence. We therefore use no learning rate scheduler in our library. When using no learning rate scheduler, the most effective learning rate was 0.2 for both learning rates.

Next, we evaluate our method of inferring stance trends against other regression methods. Other methods have used a rolling average to smooth user stance observations (Introne, 2023) or simply

Model	Num. params.	SemEval	VAST	EZ-STANCE	$F1_{macro}$ EZ-STANCE claim	P-STANCE	MT-CSD	CTSDT
TGA Net	111M	-	0.665	-	-	-	-	-
BART-MNLI-e_p	205M	-	-	0.669	0.885	-	-	-
COLA	Prop.	-	0.73	-	-	-	-	
SmolLM2-135M-Instruct (Ours)	135M	0.57	0.71	0.61	0.81	0.78	0.56	0.67
SmolLM2-360M-Instruct (Ours)	360M	0.59	0.75	0.64	0.85	0.82	0.60	0.64

Table 3: Stance detection F1 scores for each dataset. With models BART-MNLI-e_p (Zhao and Caragea, 2024), TGA Net (Allaway and Mckeown, 2020), and COLA (Lan et al., 2024) (COLA uses GPT 3.5 Turbo, hence the proprietary label in the number of parameters cell.) (While COLA evaluates on P-Stance and SemEval, they report separate macro F1s for each target, making comparison here difficult).

aggregate user stance observations on a time period basis (Almadan et al., 2023), but we consider it very useful to be able to interpolate the values, and as such, we only use methods capable of interpolation here. We evaluate LOWESS (Cleveland, 1979) and a spline model (De Boor and De Boor, 1978). Specifically, we found using a cubic smoothing spline with ridge regression with $\alpha = 0.1$ as a regularization parameter to produce the best data fits. We evaluated each method at 10 values of σ_{noise} between 0.05 and 0.5, 10 values of σ_{walk} between 0.005 and 0.05, and n_d randomly sampled from the range $(5, 30)$ (Detailed in App. D). Our GP method consistently obtains lower mean squared error (MSE) values than the other two methods evaluated. To obtain the overall MSEs, we simply take all MSEs measured for each point in the noise and random walk scales, and obtain their mean. We show these results, plotted against training time, in Fig. 4, showing that our GP method obtains a better mean MSE overall compared to the two methods.

However, this is not without a cost in training time: the process of training and obtaining predictions from GPs is much slower than for LOWESS and splines. This training time is acceptable when we want to have confidence in the stance trends we obtain for further modelling, but we provide LOWESS as a faster alternative in the library for those who want faster stance trend inference. Actual numbers are in Appendix D.

6 Conclusion

We developed a library that allows a user to provide a document corpus expressing stance on unknown issues, optionally with associated timestamps and metadata, and detect the stance of the texts on the discovered targets. We believe that —just as easy-to-use topic modelling tools have enabled widespread use of these tools where they were previously inaccessible —easy-to-access stance detection can unlock new experimental approaches for

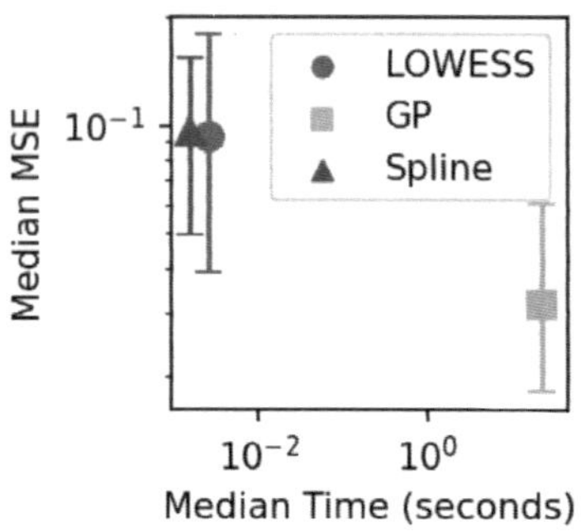

Figure 4: Comparison of median training time and median MSE between our GP, LOWESS, and splines over 100 runs with varying synthetic data parameters. Error bars indicate quartiles. Error bars for runtime are not visible as the runtime variance is small relative to marker size. Our GP method outperforms the other methods, but at the cost of increased training time.

groups where stance detection was previously inaccessible. We hope this tool unlocks improved understanding of opinion and attitude processes for a larger community of social scientists.

7 Ethical Considerations

Stance detection enables inference of attitudes from unconsenting text authors on issues they discuss, which is privacy-violating. It also allows greater insight into social processes, allowing researchers to work towards understanding social processes. However, the current nature of stance detection is that it requires dedicated work from an NLP engineer to implement, in addition to compute resources to train models, meaning that only large incumbents can use it. Our library aims to democratize access to stance detection, such that groups with fewer resources can use it in their studies, while larger groups were always able to use it.

References

SUMMITX. `https://www.summetix.com/`. Accessed: 2025-09-10.

Abu Ubaida Akash, Ahmed Fahmy, and Amine Trabelsi. 2024. Can large language models address open-target stance detection? *arXiv preprint arXiv:2409.00222*.

Loubna Ben Allal, Anton Lozhkov, Elie Bakouch, Gabriel Martín Blázquez, Guilherme Penedo, Lewis Tunstall, Andrés Marafioti, Hynek Kydlíček, Agustín Piqueres Lajarín, Vaibhav Srivastav, and 1 others. 2025. Smollm2: When smol goes big–data-centric training of a small language model. *arXiv preprint arXiv:2502.02737*.

Emily Allaway and Kathleen Mckeown. 2020. Zero-shot stance detection: A dataset and model using generalized topic representations. In *Proceedings of the 2020 Conference on Empirical Methods in Natural Language Processing (EMNLP)*, pages 8913–8931.

Ali Almadan, Mary Lou Maher, and Jason Windett. 2023. Stance detection for gauging public opinion: A statistical analysis of the difference between tweet-based and user-based stance in twitter. In *Future of Information and Communication Conference*, pages 358–374. Springer.

Max Bain, Jaesung Huh, Tengda Han, and Andrew Zisserman. 2023. Whisperx: Time-accurate speech transcription of long-form audio. *INTERSPEECH 2023*.

Wei Chu, Zoubin Ghahramani, and Christopher KI Williams. 2005. Gaussian processes for ordinal regression. *Journal of machine learning research*, 6(7).

William S Cleveland. 1979. Robust locally weighted regression and smoothing scatterplots. *Journal of the American statistical association*, 74(368):829–836.

Carl De Boor and Carl De Boor. 1978. *A practical guide to splines*, volume 27. springer New York.

Jacob Gardner, Geoff Pleiss, Kilian Q Weinberger, David Bindel, and Andrew G Wilson. 2018. Gpytorch: Blackbox matrix-matrix gaussian process inference with gpu acceleration. *Advances in neural information processing systems*, 31.

Joshua Introne. 2023. Measuring belief dynamics on twitter. In *Proceedings of the International AAAI Conference on Web and Social Media*, volume 17, pages 387–398.

Jon A Krosnick. 1988. Attitude importance and attitude change. *Journal of Experimental Social Psychology*, 24(3):240–255.

Kostiantyn Kucher, Rafael M Martins, Carita Paradis, and Andreas Kerren. 2020. Stancevis prime: visual analysis of sentiment and stance in social media texts. *Journal of Visualization*, 23(6):1015–1034.

Kostiantyn Kucher, Teri Schamp-Bjerede, Andreas Kerren, Carita Paradis, and Magnus Sahlgren. 2016. Visual analysis of online social media to open up the investigation of stance phenomena. *Information Visualization*, 15(2):93–116.

Dilek Küçük and Fazli Can. 2020. Stance detection: A survey. *ACM Computing Surveys (CSUR)*, 53(1):1–37.

Woosuk Kwon, Zhuohan Li, Siyuan Zhuang, Ying Sheng, Lianmin Zheng, Cody Hao Yu, Joseph E. Gonzalez, Hao Zhang, and Ion Stoica. 2023. Efficient memory management for large language model serving with pagedattention. In *Proceedings of the ACM SIGOPS 29th Symposium on Operating Systems Principles*.

Xiaochong Lan, Chen Gao, Depeng Jin, and Yong Li. 2024. Stance detection with collaborative role-infused llm-based agents. In *Proceedings of the international AAAI conference on web and social media*, volume 18, pages 891–903.

Yingjie Li, Tiberiu Sosea, Aditya Sawant, Ajith Jayaraman Nair, Diana Inkpen, and Cornelia Caragea. 2021. P-stance: A large dataset for stance detection in political domain. In *Findings of the association for computational linguistics: ACL-IJCNLP 2021*, pages 2355–2365.

Yupeng Li, Dacheng Wen, Haorui He, Jianxiong Guo, Xuan Ning, and Francis CM Lau. 2023. Contextual target-specific stance detection on twitter: Dataset and method. In *2023 IEEE International Conference on Data Mining (ICDM)*, pages 359–367. IEEE.

Rafael Martins, Vasiliki Simaki, Kostiantyn Kucher, Carita Paradis, Andreas Kerren, and 1 others. 2017. Stancexplore: Visualization for the interactive exploration of stance in social media. In *2nd Workshop on Visualization for the Digital Humanities*.

Leland McInnes, John Healy, and James Melville. 2018. Umap: Uniform manifold approximation and projection for dimension reduction. *arXiv preprint arXiv:1802.03426*.

Saif Mohammad, Svetlana Kiritchenko, Parinaz Sobhani, Xiaodan Zhu, and Colin Cherry. 2016. Semeval-2016 task 6: Detecting stance in tweets. In *Proceedings of the 10th international workshop on semantic evaluation (SemEval-2016)*, pages 31–41.

Lynnette Hui Xian Ng and Kathleen M Carley. 2022. Is my stance the same as your stance? a cross validation study of stance detection datasets. *Information Processing & Management*, 59(6):103070.

Fuqiang Niu, Min Yang, Ang Li, Baoquan Zhang, Xiaojiang Peng, and Bowen Zhang. 2024. A challenge dataset and effective models for conversational stance detection. In *Proceedings of the 2024 Joint International Conference on Computational Linguistics, Language Resources and Evaluation (LREC-COLING 2024)*, pages 122–132.

Alexis Plaquet and Hervé Bredin. 2023. Powerset multi-class cross entropy loss for neural speaker diarization. In *Proc. INTERSPEECH 2023*.

Matt Post. 2018. A call for clarity in reporting BLEU scores. In *Proceedings of the Third Conference on Machine Translation: Research Papers*, pages 186–191, Belgium, Brussels. Association for Computational Linguistics.

Hugh Salimbeni, Stefanos Eleftheriadis, and James Hensman. 2018. Natural gradients in practice: Non-conjugate variational inference in gaussian process models. In *International Conference on Artificial Intelligence and Statistics*, pages 689–697. PMLR.

Aivin V. Solatorio. 2024. Gistembed: Guided in-sample selection of training negatives for text embedding fine-tuning. *arXiv preprint arXiv:2402.16829*.

Christian Stab, Johannes Daxenberger, Chris Stahlhut, Tristan Miller, Benjamin Schiller, Christopher Tauchmann, Steffen Eger, and Iryna Gurevych. 2018. ArgumenText: Searching for arguments in heterogeneous sources. In *Proceedings of the 2018 Conference of the North American Chapter of the Association for Computational Linguistics: Demonstrations*, pages 21–25, New Orleans, Louisiana. Association for Computational Linguistics.

Yingcai Wu, Shixia Liu, Kai Yan, Mengchen Liu, and Fangzhao Wu. 2014. Opinionflow: Visual analysis of opinion diffusion on social media. *IEEE transactions on visualization and computer graphics*, 20(12):1763–1772.

An Yang, Anfeng Li, Baosong Yang, Beichen Zhang, Binyuan Hui, Bo Zheng, Bowen Yu, Chang Gao, Chengen Huang, Chenxu Lv, and 1 others. 2025. Qwen3 technical report. *arXiv preprint arXiv:2505.09388*.

Tianyi Zhang, Varsha Kishore, Felix Wu, Kilian Q Weinberger, and Yoav Artzi. 2019. Bertscore: Evaluating text generation with bert. *arXiv preprint arXiv:1904.09675*.

Chenye Zhao and Cornelia Caragea. 2024. Ez-stance: A large dataset for english zero-shot stance detection. In *Proceedings of the 62nd Annual Meeting of the Association for Computational Linguistics (Volume 1: Long Papers)*, pages 15697–15714.

Zhengyuan Zhu, Zeyu Zhang, Haiqi Zhang, and Chengkai Li. 2025. Ratsd: Retrieval augmented truthfulness stance detection from social media posts toward factual claims. In *Findings of the Association for Computational Linguistics: NAACL 2025*, pages 3366–3381.

A Stance Detection Training

We tested several models and hyperparameters to improve our final fine-tuned stance detection model, results shown in Table 4. In some cases where epochs are low we aborted training early due to low evaluation set metrics.

B Synthetic Data Generation

Then sample the observed post stances by sampling them from categoricals indexed by the true quantized post stances, using categorical probabilities obtained by normalizing the confusion matrix of the stance detection classifier on the test set.

We start with our timestamps representing each day in a year of 365 days.

$$t = [0, 1, 2, ..., 365]$$

We then sample the stance on the first day.

$$z_0 \sim \mathcal{U}(-1, 1)$$

Then simulate a random walk for each timestamp.

$$z_i = max(min((\mathcal{N}(z_{i-1}, \sigma^2_{\text{walk}}), -1), 1)$$

$$i = 1, 2, \ldots, n_{\text{time}} - 1$$

We then draw n_{obs} elements from the vectors t and z to serve as our observations t_{obs} and z_obs. We model diversity of stance expression (i.e. someone in favor of something will sometimes say things neutral or even against that thing) by sampling the latent user post stance values from normal distributions centred at the true stance, with scale σ_{noise}:

$$y_i \sim \mathcal{N}(z_i, \sigma_{noise}) \forall i$$

We then clamp these values between -1 and 1, and round them to the nearest integer to simulate the quantizing nature of classification.

$$s_i = round(min(max((y_i, -1), 1)) \forall i$$

where $s_j \in \{-1, 0, 1\}$

Then, using the normalized confusion matrix of the classifier, let $P_{k,\ell}$ be the probability of predicting class ℓ given true class k:

$$P = \begin{pmatrix} P_{-1,-1} & P_{-1,0} & P_{-1,1} \\ P_{0,-1} & P_{0,0} & P_{0,1} \\ P_{1,-1} & P_{1,0} & P_{1,1} \end{pmatrix}$$

where each row sums to 1: $\sum_{\ell \in \{-1,0,1\}} P_{k,\ell} = 1$

We get the classification probabilities as indexed by the true latent classifications to obtain the observed classifications:

$$\hat{s}_j \sim \text{Categorical}(P_{s_j,\cdot}), \quad j = 1, 2, \ldots, n_{\text{obs}}$$

Model Name	Epochs	Grad Accum Steps	Batch Size	LR.	Classification Method	$F1_{macro}$
SmolLM2-360M-Instruct	4	8	4	1.0e-4	head	0.744
SmolLM2-360M-Instruct	2	8	4	1.0e-4	head	0.738
SmolLM2-360M-Instruct	1	8	4	1.0e-4	head	0.724
SmolLM2-135M-Instruct	4	4	8	1.0e-4	head	0.715
SmolLM2-135M-Instruct	8	4	8	1.0e-4	head	0.709
SmolLM-135M-Instruct	4	4	8	1.0e-4	head	0.708
SmolLM2-135M-Instruct	4	4	8	1.0e-4	head	0.708
SmolLM2-135M-Instruct	4	4	8	1.0e-4	head	0.707
SmolLM-135M-Instruct	8	8	8	1.0e-4	head	0.705
SmolLM-135M-Instruct	8	4	8	5.0e-5	head	0.703
SmolLM-135M-Instruct	1	4	8	1.0e-4	head	0.651
SmolLM2-135M	2	8	4	1.0e-4	head	0.621
SmolLM2-135M-Instruct	1	8	4	1.0e-4	generation	0.562
SmolLM2-135M	2	2	4	1.0e-4	head	0.473

Table 4: Hyperparameter sweep with $F1_{macro}$ across all datasets.

Hyperparameter	Tested values
LR.	[0.001, 0.01, 0.1, 0.2, 0.5, 1.0]
NGD LR.	[0.05, 0.1, 0.2, 0.5]
Num. Data Points	[20, 100, 200]
σ_{noise}	[0.2, 0.5]
σ_{walk}	[0.1, 0.5]

Table 5: NGD LR. stands for natural gradient descent optimizer learning rate. It is typical to use a large learning rate for the learning rate of natural gradient descent (Salimbeni et al., 2018).

We then use the observed classifications $\hat{s}$ and observed timestamps t_{obs} as the observations, and the full timestamp vector t as the timestamps to infer the latent stance on.

C Learning Rate Hyperparameter Sweep

We trialled several hyperparameter settings when searching for the best learning rates and learning rate schedulers. We detail them in Table 5, alongside logging the number of epochs needed to achieve 90% loss reduction as a measure of convergence speed.

We report the aggregated scheduler metrics in Table 6.

D Time Series Inference Results

Synthetic data generation parameter sensitivity experiment outputs are shown in Figs. 5a and 5b.

Overall output metrics from our time-series inference comparison experiments are shown in Table 7.

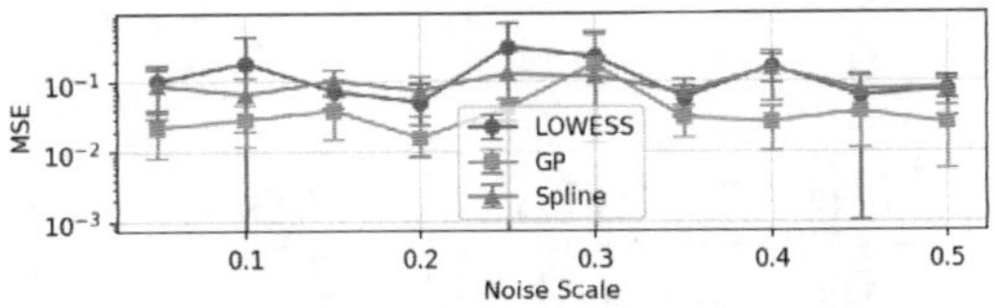

(a) Adjusting noise scale from 0.05 to 0.5.

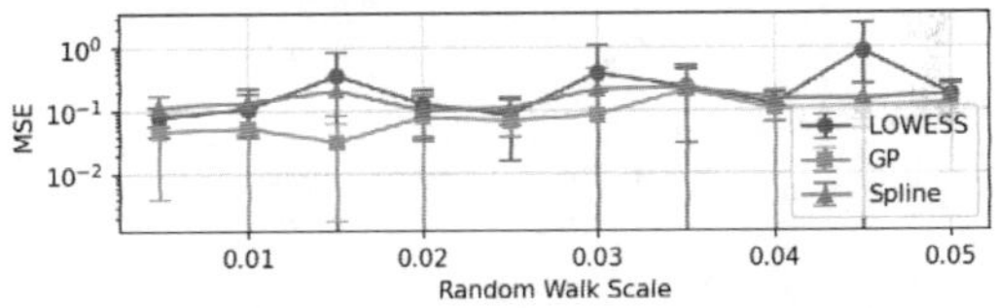

(b) Adjusting random walk scale from 0.005 to 0.05.

Figure 5: Mean MSE from 5 runs for each of 10 values of an adjusted synthetic data generation parameter, used to compare the GP, LOWESS, and spline models.

Scheduler	Min. Loss	Num Epochs Conv.
None	1.12	97
Cosine Warm Restarts	1.19	112
Cosine	1.19	73
Step	1.22	74
Exponential	1.22	87

Table 6: Evaluation of learning rate schedulers, using minimum loss achieved and number of epochs to 90% loss reduction as measures of efficacy and speed, respectively.

Method	MSE	Training Time
GP	0.069 ± 0.13	21.7 ± 7.2
LOWESS	0.197 ± 0.46	0.003 ± 0.001
Spline	0.130 ± 0.12	0.002 ± 0.007

Table 7: Comparison of time series inference methods. Numbers listed are mean $\pm$ standard deviation.

SHORTCHECK: Checkworthiness Detection of Multilingual Short-Form Videos

Henrik Vatndal
University of Stavanger
henrik@factiverse.ai

Vinay Setty
Factiverse AI and University of Stavanger
vsetty@acm.org

Abstract

Short-form video platforms like TikTok present unique challenges for misinformation detection due to their multimodal, dynamic, and noisy content. We present SHORTCHECK, a modular, inference-only pipeline with a user-friendly interface that automatically identifies checkworthy short-form videos to help human fact-checkers. The system integrates speech transcription, OCR, object and deepfake detection, video-to-text summarization, and claim verification. SHORTCHECK is validated by evaluating it on two manually annotated datasets with TikTok videos in a multilingual setting. The pipeline achieves promising results with F1-weighted score over 70%. The demo can be accessed live at http://shortcheck.factiverse.ai.

1 Introduction

The popularity of short-form video platforms such as *TikTok*, *YouTube Shorts* and *Instagram Reels* has transformed how information is produced, consumed, and spread. With billions of monthly active users, these platforms create fertile ground for the spread of misinformation on sensitive topics including politics, health, and social issues. Unlike traditional text or image-based content, these videos may include multiple modalities such as speech, text overlays, music, and visuals, often edited in ways that obscure meaning or context, though not all of these elements are always present; for example, some videos contain only on-screen text without audio, while others show just a speaker without any additional graphics or overlays. For example, Figure 1 shows a TikTok screenshot where the overlay text makes the claim, while the audio transcript (translated to "it's a shame") does not provide any useful information. The video summary notes an urban explosion, indicating potentially contentious content for fact-checkers.

The multimodal complexity of short videos makes automated fact-checking technically challenging and manual efforts are increasingly unsustainable, especially for under-resourced fact-checkers facing unprecedented content scale and funding cuts. In this demo, we present a prototype designed to automate the identification of potentially checkworthy videos, significantly reducing the time required by human fact-checkers. Our prototype is easy to use and can predict checkworthiness in over 30 major languages.[1]

Field	Value
overlay_text	Someone captured the | missile in the Beirut blast
transcript	عيبه اي اي منلو ارهى مريك عيبه
video_summary	The video captures footage of the 2020 Beirut blast, showing destruction and chaos in an urban area, with explosions visible throughout.
buzzword_detected	False
transcript_verdict	hostile
summary_verdict	contentious-issue
overlay_verdict	hostile
Checkworthiness	True

Figure 1: TikTok video with overlay text claiming "Someone captured the missile in the Beirut blast," and noisy Arabic audio and explosion visuals. Features below show why SHORTCHECK marked it *Checkworthy*.

Most existing misinformation detection systems are designed for structured, single-modality content such as news articles, social media posts, or deepfake detection, with a primary focus on either text, audio, transcriptions or visual modalities. We summarize the existing fact-checking systems and their modalities in Table 1. However, these approaches

[1]Intersection of languages supported by Meta Llama3 https://ai.meta.com/blog/meta-llama-3/ and OpenAI Whisper https://github.com/openai/whisper

Proceedings of The 14th International Joint Conference on Natural Language Processing and The 4th Conference of the Asia-Pacific Chapter of the Association for Computational Linguistics: System Demonstrations, pages 77–85

Table 1: Fact-checking systems categorized by input modality, granularity, multilinguality, and fact-checking support.

System	Text	Audio	Image	Video	Granularity	M.lingual	Full FC
BRENDA Botnevik et al. (2020)	✓	✗	✗	✗	Long Text	✗	✓
FLEEK (Bayat et al., 2023)	✓	✗	✗	✗	Single Claim	✗	✓
QACHECK (Pan and et al., 2023)	✓	✗	✗	✗	Single Claim	✗	✓
CLAIMLENS (Devasier et al., 2024)	✓	✗	✗	✗	Single Claim	✗	✗
TRUTHREADER (Li et al., 2024)	✓	✗	✗	✗	Long Text	✗	✓
OPENFACTCHECK (Iqbal et al., 2024)	✓	✗	✗	✗	Long Text	✗	✓
FACTCHECKEDITOR (Setty, 2024a)	✓	✗	✗	✗	Long Text	✓	✓
LOKI (Li et al., 2025)	✓	✗	✗	✗	Single Claim	✓	✓
AUDIOCWD (Ivanov et al., 2024)	✗	✓	✗	✗	Single Claim	✗	✗
LIVEFC (Venktesh and Setty, 2025)	✓	✓	✗	✗	Long Text	✗	✓
PODFC (Setty, 2025)	✓	✗	✓	✗	Long Text	✓	✓
FAUXTOGRAPHY (Zlatkova et al., 2019)	✓	✗	✓	✗	Single Claim	✗	✓
AVERIMATEC (Cao et al., 2025)	✓	✗	✓	✗	Single Claim	✗	✓
CER (Barone et al., 2025)	✓	✓	✓	✓	Single Claim	✗	✓
COVID-VTS (Liu et al., 2023a)	✓	✓	✓	✓	Single Claim	✗	✗
SHORTCHECK (ours)	✓	✓	✓	✓	Long Text	✓	✗

are not suited for short-form video content found on platforms like TikTok or YouTube Shorts due to the casual unstructured nature of the content.

Short-form videos pose unique challenges due to their *limited multimodal generalization*. They often blend speech, text, music, and visuals in non-linear, asynchronous ways that traditional unimodal models struggle to interpret (Alam et al., 2022; Yao et al., 2023; Guo et al., 2022; Singhal et al., 2019). These videos also exhibit *noisy or incomplete modality signals*: some lack audio, others feature distorted overlays or rapid cuts, making existing detectors brittle in real-world conditions (Jindal et al., 2020; Venktesh et al., 2024). Furthermore, most models offer *low interpretability*, returning binary predictions without justifications. This hinders adoption in professional workflows that require transparent, evidence-backed reasoning (Schlichtkrull et al., 2023; Guo et al., 2022; Alam et al., 2022; Venktesh and Setty, 2025).

While multimodal fact-checking is gaining traction, the gap between research prototypes and deployable, interpretable tools for short-form video remains substantial. Bridging this divide requires not only improved multimodal understanding but also system outputs that align with the needs of human fact-checkers in high-throughput environments.

Our Contributions. This paper introduces a demonstration system for detecting checkworthy TikTok videos. Our key contributions are:

- A **modular multimodal pipeline** that integrates OCR, transcription, video-to-text captioning, semantic classification, retrieval and fact-checking modules.
- Two **new multilingual annotated datasets** of TikTok videos labeled for checkworthiness.
- An **evaluation and error analysis** showing which modalities contribute most to reliable classification.
- A **demo interface** that allows fact-checkers to upload videos, inspect intermediate results, and link claims to existing fact-checks.

Together, these contributions provide a step toward bridging the gap between state-of-the-art research and practical tools for combating misinformation on emerging short-form video platforms.

2 Related work

Automated fact-checking has advanced through benchmark datasets such as FEVER (Thorne et al., 2018) and subsequent surveys (Thorne and Vlachos, 2018; Guo et al., 2022), along with real-world datasets like MULTIFC (Augenstein et al., 2019), AVERITEC (Schlichtkrull et al., 2023) and QUANTEMP (Venktesh et al., 2024). Within checkworthiness detection, early work introduced context-aware ranking (Gencheva et al., 2017) and systems such as CLAIMRANK (Jaradat et al., 2018) that support real-time prioritization of claims for journalists.

Multimodal research now combines text, audio and visual cues (Alam et al., 2022), enriched by datasets and models such as FAKINGRECIPE (Bu et al., 2024), SPOTFAKE (Singhal et al., 2019), NEWSBAG (Jindal et al., 2020) and end-to-end video fact-checking systems with explanation generation (Yao et al., 2023). Deepfake detection architectures like MESONET (Afchar et al., 2018a) further support authenticity analysis within video pipelines.

Practical systems such as BRENDA (Botnevik

et al., 2020), FACTCHECKEDITOR (Setty, 2024b), PODFC (Setty, 2025) and LIVEFC (Venktesh and Setty, 2025) have begun bridging research and real-world fact-checking needs, though they typically focus on single-modality inputs or long-form content. SHORTCHECK differs by targeting short-form video platforms and integrating text, audio, image and video signals within a modular and interpretable pipeline designed to support professional fact-checkers.

3 System Overview

Given that the checkworthiness of a TikTok video can be inherently subjective, we base our approach on established best practices followed by professional fact-checkers. In particular, we consulted the guidelines of Faktisk.no[2] This also aligns with the definition of fact-checkworthiness in the literature(Jaradat et al., 2018; Barrón-Cedeño et al., 2024)

Short videos up to ten minutes may contain multimodal claims, and are checkworthy only when they pose potential public harm in areas like politics, health or society. Content such as celebrity gossip, sports or advertisements is excluded.

We propose a modular, inference-only pipeline for detecting potentially misleading or checkworthy content in short-form videos, particularly those published on platforms like TikTok. The system assigns each video one of two categorical labels: `Checkworthy`, or `Not_Checkworthy`. Unlike prior work that builds monolithic or end-to-end models, our design emphasizes modularity, interpretability, and adaptability. Each component in the pipeline can be independently replaced, which makes the system robust to failures in specific modalities and easier to maintain in production settings.

3.1 Pipeline Components

The pipeline comprises feature extraction modules tailored to speech, text, visuals, and metadata, whose outputs are aggregated by a rule-based engine for final video classification. Additional modules, such as object detection for weapons, were tested but excluded due to limited contribution.

Optical Character Recognition (OCR): The first stage involves extracting visible on-screen text through Optical Character Recognition (OCR), using the EasyOCR library[3]. This module captures embedded captions or textual overlays, which are common in TikTok videos. However, OCR performance is often challenged by stylized fonts, rapid transitions, and visually noisy frames.

DeepFake Detection: To detect synthetic media, we incorporated a deepfake detection module into the pipeline. Since many methods rely on identity-specific data or high-quality frontal imagery, we evaluated their generalization to TikTok's unconstrained, user-generated content (Abbas and Taeihagh, 2024). We tested three zero-shot models: *MesoNet* (Afchar et al., 2018b), a mesoscopic CNN; *EfficientNet* (Bonettini et al., 2021; Dolhansky et al., 2020), an attention-based model from the DFDC challenge; and *Wvolf/ViT*[4] (Bonettini et al., 2020), selected for its plug-and-play accessibility. Their outputs contributed as signals in the rule-based decision logic.

Speech Transcription: Speech transcription is handled by OpenAI Whisper (Radford et al., 2022), which offers robust multilingual transcription and performs well in noisy audio environments. However, overlapping music or sound effects, which are prevalent in entertainment-oriented videos, can still degrade transcription quality.

Video Summarization: To obtain a visual semantic summary, video frames are sampled and passed through LLaVA (Liu et al., 2023b), a vision-language model that generates frame-level captions describing people, objects, and scenes. These captions are subsequently summarized and contextualized using Meta's LLaMA 3 model, which also performs high-level semantic classification. The model predicts whether a video is political, hostile, benign, or promotional in nature. All models are hosted via Ollama, a lightweight, local model serving platform that supports REST-based inference.[5]

Ideological Language Detection: In addition to these core modules, we incorporate a rule-based system for detecting ideological buzzwords and coded language, often referred to as dog whistles. This module operates on both OCR and transcript outputs, scanning for terms known to encode political or ideological meaning in subtle ways. The

[2] A Norwegian non-profit organization accredited by the International Fact-Checking Network (IFCN).

[3] `https://github.com/JaidedAI/EasyOCR`

[4] `https://huggingface.co/Wvolf/ViT_Deepfake_Detection`

[5] `ollama.com`

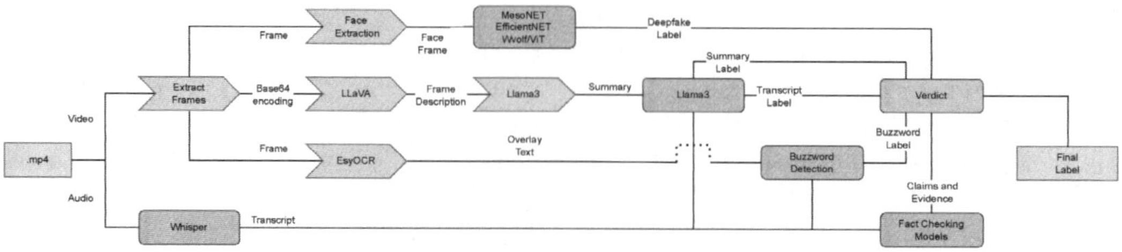

Figure 2: Modular pipeline for fact-checking TikTok videos.

detection rules are informed by prior literature on dog-whistle communication (Albertson, 2015) and curated datasets from organizations such as Faktisk.no.

Text-based fact-checking To further refine the decision-making process, we incorporate a claim detection and external fact-checking module. This component leverages fine-tuned transformer models for claim detection and natural language inference (NLI), applied to both the transcript and the visual summary of the video. Following the approach proposed by (Setty, 2024b), the module identifies declarative, factual statements and attempts to verify them against a fact-checking evidence database. While this does not fact-check the entire content of the video, it provides fact-checkers early signals indicating whether the video may contain verifiably false or misleading information.

Finally, the system aggregates the outputs from all modules using a rule-based logic engine. A scoring system considers multiple module outputs, including the presence of claims, ideological language, or political classification. If the cumulative score exceeds a threshold, the video is marked as `Checkworthy`. Advertisements are detected and filtered early in the pipeline and override all other scores. Videos that do not meet either criterion are labeled as `Not_Checkworthy`. This decision process is entirely transparent and configurable, enabling future refinement without retraining models.

3.2 Verdict Evaluation

Our system produces a final binary label using a lightweight rule-based scoring function that aggregates signals from multiple modules. Each module contributes a fixed weight to a cumulative *Checkworthiness score*.

The scoring scheme assigns concrete weights to each signal: detecting ideological buzzwords adds +2, and transcripts labelled as a contentious issue add +2 while other checkworthy transcript categories add +0.5. Summary and overlay-text classifiers contribute +1.5 for contentious-issue labels or +0.7 for other checkworthy labels. Evidence-supported claims add +0.5 when at least one such claim is present, with an additional +0.25 for each extra supported claim. The total score of over 2 is considered checkworthy otherwise not.

The weights and threshold were manually selected based on findings from the initial thesis work. At the current stage, no automated parameter optimization has been implemented.

3.3 Model Configuration and Deployment

All models used in the pipeline are inference-only and require no task-specific fine-tuning. We use prompt engineering to adapt general-purpose models to specific sub-tasks. The LLaMA 3 and LLaVA models are deployed using Ollama, which allows for lightweight, local hosting and fast prototyping. Custom prompts, temperature settings, stop sequences, and token limits are adjusted to ensure consistent outputs across modules.

3.4 Interpretability and Modularity

A key design goal of our approach is interpretability. Each module exposes intermediate outputs that are human-readable and can be inspected by fact-checkers. This transparency builds trust and enables feedback-driven improvement of the system. The modular design also ensures that any individual component, such as the OCR engine or the semantic classifier, can be replaced or updated without disrupting the entire pipeline. This is especially important for deployment in evolving information ecosystems where content formats and threat types change rapidly.

3.5 Overhead and Concurrency

The video-to-text module is consistently the dominant computational cost, requiring approximately 20 s or more per video regardless of length. Largely due to the amount of frames being fixed. The `fact_check` module also exhibited substantial variability, between 25.9 s and 1.2 s, depending on the amount of claims present. Audio transcription scaled more directly with video duration, typically accounting for 10–30% of the video length. Lighter modules such as OCR and deepfake detection contributed comparatively little overhead (approximately 2–4 s combined), while buzzword detection, advertisement detection, and final verdict evaluation added negligible cost.

It is important to note that the current prototype processes videos sequentially and does not employ modular concurrency.

4 Experimental Evaluation

4.1 Setup

All experiments were conducted on a local machine with an **NVIDIA A10 GPU (24GB VRAM)**. All models, including vision-language models and LLMs, were served locally via `Ollama` using REST-based endpoints. For full implementation see[6]

4.2 Datasets

We evaluate ShortCheck on two manually annotated dataset in their entirety. Summary of dataset statistics is shown in Table 3

Norwegian influencer data: This dataset includes 249 TikTok videos curated by Faktisk for an emotional analysis study on political trolling via buzzwords like "Stem FRP".[7] We manually annotated each video, with annotator(2) agreement of 96%, for checkworthiness using the guidelines in Section 3.

TikTok Videos from Fact-Checking Websites: This dataset, curated by (Bu et al., 2024), was compiled from fact-checking platforms including Snopes, PolitiFact, FactCheck.org, and Health Feedback. While the majority of content is in English, some posts and modalities appear in other languages. We annotated a sample of 254 videos from this collection, following the same guidelines described before.

4.3 Results

In this section, we present the overall results and ablation studies. In addition, we also present the effectiveness of some of the modules such as DeepFake detection. We plan to evaluate other modules in detail in future work.

Overall Results: The model performs well on both Norwegian and English TikTok videos, with notable differences in class-wise behavior. For Norwegian content, the system achieves strong recall for `Checkworthy` instances (0.91) and high overall accuracy (0.81), indicating robust performance in identifying relevant claims. In contrast, the English dataset shows higher precision for `Checkworthy` (0.82) but lower recall (0.58), suggesting the model is more conservative in flagging English videos as checkworthy. Combined macro-averaged scores are comparable across languages (F1: 0.73 for Norwegian, 0.74 for English), highlighting the pipeline's cross-lingual generalizability with slightly better balance in the Norwegian case.

4.4 Ablation Studies

The ablation study shown in Table 5 demonstrates that textual modules are the most influential components in determining checkworthiness. The removal of the *Transcript Verdict* and *Buzzword* modules resulted in the largest decreases in recall and F1-score, highlighting the critical role of spoken content and ideological language. In contrast, excluding modules such as *Weapon Detection*, *Fact Check*, or *Video-to-Text Verdict* had minimal impact, indicating their limited standalone contribution. Notably, the *Weapon Detection* module slightly reduced overall performance, likely because such content appears infrequently; as a result, it was omitted from the final pipeline. These findings reinforce the system's reliance on semantic and linguistic features rather than visual or metadata-based cues. Finally since removing individual modules does not show a huge drop in performance, the overall performance is attributed to contribution of modules.

DeepFake detection The models were evaluated in a zero-shot setting, without any fine-tuning on the target dataset. Among them, *EfficientNET* outperformed all others across evaluation metrics, achieving an accuracy of 0.612 and a remarkably high precision of 0.992, indicating highly reliable positive predictions. However, its recall of 0.573 suggests it still misses nearly half of actual deepfakes. *MesoNET* and *Wvolf/ViT* perform very poorly.

[6] `https://github.com/factiverse/shortcheck`

[7] `https://www.faktisk.no/artikkel/faktisk-analyse-av-tiktok-menn-mest-negative/109375`

Table 2: Results on TikTok videos in Norwegian and English. CW = Checkworthy, NCW = Not Checkworthy. Combined metrics are macro-averages. Metrics: Precision (P), Recall (R), Accuracy (Acc) and F1-weighted (F1-W)

Dataset	**CW**			**NCW**			**Combined (Macro)**			
	P	R	F1-W	P	R	F1-W	P	R	F1-W	Acc
Norwegian influencer	0.42	0.91	0.58	0.98	0.80	0.88	0.70	0.85	0.73	0.81
Fact-checking websites	0.82	0.58	0.68	0.72	0.90	0.80	0.77	0.74	0.74	0.76

Table 3: Dataset composition by language and checkworthiness class. CW: Checkworthy and NCW: Not Checkworthy.

Dataset	**CW**	**NCW**	**Total**
Norwegian influencer	33	204	237
Fact-checking websites	114	140	254
Total	147	344	491

Table 4: Evaluation scores of DeepFake detection models. Precision (P), Recall (R), Accuracy (A), and F1-weighted (F1-w)

Model	**A**	**P**	**R**	**F1-W**
MesoNET	0.114	0.808	0.019	0.038
Wvolf/ViT	0.100	0.000	0.000	0.000
EfficientNET	**0.612**	**0.992**	**0.573**	**0.727**

Table 5: Ablation study showing the performance change when individual modules are removed. Values represent the change from the full system (Baseline). Red indicates a drop in performance. Metrics: Precision (P), Recall (R), Accuracy (Acc) and F1-weighted (F1-W).

Removed	**P**	**R**	**Acc**	**F1-W**
Weapon detection	+0.005	+0.002	+0.004	+0.004
Video summary	+0.001	-0.008	0.000	-0.002
Transcript	+0.027	-0.076	0.000	-0.024
Buzzword	-0.024	-0.050	-0.021	-0.033
OCR	-0.005	-0.030	-0.003	-0.004
Fact Check	+0.013	-0.040	+0.004	-0.009
All modules	**0.737**	**0.727**	**0.884**	**0.720**

5 Demonstration

Our demo system integrates the pipeline into a web interface (Figure 3). The UI allows users to upload videos, inspect transcripts, OCR text, and visual captions, view the final classification with explanations, access linked fact-checks, and examine errors through confusion matrix visualizations.

6 Conclusion and Future Work

We presented SHORTCHECK, a modular, multilingual pipeline for detecting checkworthy content in short-form videos. The system integrates multiple modalities—text, audio, video, and image—and achieves strong performance on manually annotated TikTok datasets in both Norwegian and English.

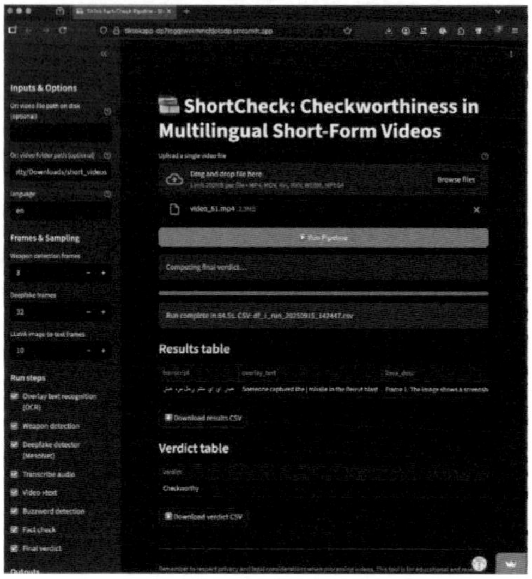

Figure 3: Demo interface for fact-checkers.

Through ablation studies, we showed that transcript features and ideological language signals contribute most strongly to checkworthiness, while visual features such as deepfake detection and object recognition provide limited standalone utility.

The system can be extended to broader fact-checking settings, tougher video and text conditions, learned fusion, and user-centered evaluation to improve robustness and interpretability. Replacing handcrafted weights with data-driven tuning would strengthen generalization across languages and domains. Expanding ideological language resources beyond Norwegian and English would support more accurate detection across diverse linguistic contexts.

7 Ethical Considerations

No personal information is stored, and all uploaded files are processed locally within the session. Files are not accessible to other users or administrators and are deleted after the session ends. The system focuses exclusively on automated analysis of user-submitted content and does not collect behavioral data, usage histories, or identifiers.

ShortCheck operates on short-form videos that may contain sensitive political, social, or ideological material. To reduce potential harm, the system is designed to support human fact-checkers rather than replace them. Its outputs are interpretable, allowing users to inspect intermediate signals and avoid unverified automation. The model does not attempt to generate verdicts beyond checkworthiness and avoids producing judgments that could misrepresent individuals or contexts.

As ShortCheck is multilingual, care is taken to avoid bias toward specific languages or cultural framing. However, disparities in transcription accuracy, OCR performance, or ideological language coverage may still introduce uneven behavior. Future work includes expanding lexical resources and conducting user studies with fact-checkers to identify unintended biases, failure modes, or misclassifications across diverse contexts.

References

Fakhar Abbas and Araz Taeihagh. 2024. Unmasking deepfakes: A systematic review of deepfake detection and generation techniques using artificial intelligence. *Expert Systems with Applications*, 252(Part B):124260.

Darius Afchar, Vincent Nozick, Junichi Yamagishi, and Isao Echizen. 2018a. Mesonet: a compact facial video forgery detection network. In *IEEE Workshop on Information Forensics and Security*, WIFS '18, pages 1–7.

Darius Afchar, Vincent Nozick, Junichi Yamagishi, and Isao Echizen. 2018b. Mesonet: a compact facial video forgery detection network. In *2018 IEEE International Workshop on Information Forensics and Security (WIFS)*, pages 1–7. IEEE.

Firoj Alam, Stefano Cresci, Tanmoy Chakraborty, Fabrizio Silvestri, Dimiter Dimitrov, Giovanni Da San Martino, Shaden Shaar, Hamed Firooz, and Preslav Nakov. 2022. A survey on multimodal disinformation detection. In *Proceedings of the 29th International Conference on Computational Linguistics*, COLING '22, pages 6625–6643.

Bethany Albertson. 2015. Dog-whistle politics: Multivocal communication and religious appeals. *Political Behavior*, 37(1):3–26.

Isabelle Augenstein, Christina Lioma, Dongsheng Wang, Lucas Chaves Lima, Casper Hansen, Christian Hansen, and Jakob Grue Simonsen. 2019. Multifc: A real-world multi-domain dataset for evidence-based fact checking of claims. In *Proceedings of the 2019 Conference on Empirical Methods in Natural Language Processing and the 9th International Joint Conference on Natural Language Processing*, EMNLP-IJCNLP '19, pages 4685–4697.

Mariano Barone, Antonio Romano, Giuseppe Riccio, Marco Postiglione, and Vincenzo Moscato. 2025. Cer: Combating biomedical misinformation through multi-modal claim detection and evidence-based verification. In *Proceedings of the 48th International ACM SIGIR Conference on Research and Development in Information Retrieval*, pages 4025–4029.

Alberto Barrón-Cedeño, Firoj Alam, Tanmoy Chakraborty, Tamer Elsayed, Preslav Nakov, Piotr Przybyła, Julia Maria Struß, Fatima Haouari, Maram Hasanain, Federico Ruggeri, et al. 2024. The clef-2024 checkthat! lab: Check-worthiness, subjectivity, persuasion, roles, authorities, and adversarial robustness. In *European Conference on Information Retrieval*, pages 449–458. Springer.

Pouya Bayat, Sahisnu Mazumder, Niket Tandon, Yash Kumar Lal, and Xiang Ren. 2023. Fleek: Factual error detection and correction with evidence retrieved from external knowledge. In *Proceedings of the 2023 Conference on Empirical Methods in Natural Language Processing: System Demonstrations*, pages 147–155.

Nicolò Bonettini, Edoardo Daniele Cannas, Sara Mandelli, Luca Bondi, Paolo Bestagini, and Stefano Tubaro. 2020. Video face manipulation detection through ensemble of cnns.

Nicolò Bonettini, Edoardo Daniele Cannas, Sara Mandelli, Luca Bondi, Paolo Bestagini, and Stefano Tubaro. 2021. Video face manipulation detection through ensemble of cnns. In *2020 25th International Conference on Pattern Recognition (ICPR)*, pages 5012–5019.

Bjarte Botnevik, Eirik Sakariassen, and Vinay Setty. 2020. Brenda: Browser extension for fake news detection. In *Proceedings of the 43rd International ACM SIGIR Conference on Research and Development in Information Retrieval*, SIGIR '20, pages 2117–2120.

Yuyan Bu, Qiang Sheng, Juan Cao, Peng Qi, Danding Wang, and Jintao Li. 2024. Fakingrecipe: Detecting fake news on short video platforms from the perspective of creative process. In *Proceedings of the 32nd ACM International Conference on Multimedia*, pages 1351–1360.

Rui Cao, Zifeng Ding, Zhijiang Guo, Michael Schlichtkrull, and Andreas Vlachos. 2025. Averimatec: A dataset for automatic verification of image-text claims with evidence from the web.

Jacob Devasier, Rishabh Mediratta, Phuong Le, David Huang, and Chengkai Li. 2024. Claimlens: Automated, explainable fact-checking on voting claims using frame-semantics. In *Proceedings of the 2024 Conference on Empirical Methods in Natural Language Processing: System Demonstrations*, pages 311–319.

Brian Dolhansky, Russ Bitton, Ben Pflaum, Juncheng Lu, Ryan Howes, Menglin Wang, Cristian Canton Ferrer, Michael Barajas, Wissam Essifi, Daniel McDuff, and et al. 2020. The deepfake detection challenge dataset.

Pepa Gencheva, Preslav Nakov, Lluís Màrquez, Alberto Barrón-Cedeño, and Ivan Koychev. 2017. A context-aware approach for detecting worth-checking claims in political debates. In *Proceedings of the International Conference on Recent Advances in Natural Language Processing*, RANLP '17, pages 267–276.

Zhijiang Guo, Michael Schlichtkrull, and Andreas Vlachos. 2022. A survey on automated fact-checking. *Transactions of the Association for Computational Linguistics*, 10(1):178–206.

Hasan Iqbal, Yuxia Wang, Minghan Wang, Georgi Georgiev, Jiahui Geng, Iryna Gurevych, and Preslav Nakov. 2024. Openfactcheck: A unified framework for factuality evaluation of llms. In *Proceedings of the 2024 Conference on Empirical Methods in Natural Language Processing: System Demonstrations*, pages 219–229.

Petar Ivanov, Ivan Koychev, Momchil Hardalov, and Preslav Nakov. 2024. Detecting check-worthy claims in political debates, speeches, and interviews using audio data. In *ICASSP 2024-2024 IEEE International Conference on Acoustics, Speech and Signal Processing (ICASSP)*, pages 12011–12015. IEEE.

Israa Jaradat, Pepa Gencheva, Alberto Barrón-Cedeño, Lluís Màrquez, and Preslav Nakov. 2018. Claimrank: Detecting check-worthy claims in arabic and english. In *Proceedings of the 2018 Conference of the North American Chapter of the Association for Computational Linguistics: Demonstrations*, NAACL '18, pages 26–30.

Sarthak Jindal, Raghav Sood, Richa Singh, Mayank Vatsa, and Tanmoy Chakraborty. 2020. Newsbag: A multimodal benchmark dataset for fake news detection. In *Proceedings of the SafeAI@AAAI 2020 Workshop on Artificial Intelligence Safety*, SafeAI@AAAI '20, pages 1–8.

Dongfang Li, Xinshuo Hu, Zetian Sun, Baotian Hu, Shaolin Ye, Zifei Shan, Qian Chen, and Min Zhang. 2024. Truthreader: Towards trustworthy document assistant chatbot with reliable attribution. In *Proceedings of the 2024 Conference on Empirical Methods in Natural Language Processing: System Demonstrations*, pages 89–100.

Haonan Li, Xudong Han, Hao Wang, Yuxia Wang, Minghan Wang, Rui Xing, Yilin Geng, Zenan Zhai, Preslav Nakov, and Timothy Baldwin. 2025. Loki: An open source tool for fact verification. In *Proceedings of the 31st International Conference on Computational Linguistics: System Demonstrations*, pages 28–36.

Fuxiao Liu, Yaser Yacoob, and Abhinav Shrivastava. 2023a. Covid-vts: Fact extraction and verification on short video platforms. In *Proceedings of the 17th Conference of the European Chapter of the Association for Computational Linguistics*, pages 178–188.

Haotian Liu, Pengcheng Lin, Chaoyi Wu, Xiangning Li, Kevin Lin, Ying Zhang, Jingren Du, and Jian Fang. 2023b. Llava: Visual instruction tuning. *arXiv preprint arXiv:2304.08485*.

Yuchen Pan and et al. 2023. Qacheck: A demonstration system for question-guided multi-hop fact-checking. In *Proceedings of the 2023 Conference on Empirical Methods in Natural Language Processing: System Demonstrations*, pages 137–146.

Alec Radford, Jong Wook Kim, Tao Xu, Greg Brockman, Christine McLeavey, and Ilya Sutskever. 2022. Whisper: Robust speech recognition via large-scale weak supervision. *arXiv preprint arXiv:2212.01234*.

Michael Schlichtkrull, Zhijiang Guo, and Andreas Vlachos. 2023. Averitec: A dataset for real-world claim verification with evidence from the web. In *Advances in Neural Information Processing Systems 36 (Datasets and Benchmarks Track)*, NeurIPS '23, page –.

Vinay Setty. 2024a. Factcheck editor: Multilingual text editor with end-to-end fact-checking. In *Proceedings of the 47th International ACM SIGIR Conference on Research and Development in Information Retrieval*, pages 2744–2748.

Vinay Setty. 2024b. Surprising efficacy of fine-tuned transformers for fact-checking over larger language models. In *Proceedings of the 47th International ACM SIGIR Conference on Research and Development in Information Retrieval*, pages 2842–2846.

Vinay Setty. 2025. Fact-checking multilingual podcasts. In *Proceedings of the 18th ACM International Conference on Web Search and Data Mining*, WSDM '25, pages 1100–1101.

Shivangi Singhal, Rajiv Ratn Shah, Tanmoy Chakraborty, Ponnurangam Kumaraguru, and Shin'ichi Satoh. 2019. Spotfake: A multi-modal framework for fake news detection. In *Proceedings of the IEEE International Conference on Multimedia Big Data*, BigMM '19, pages 39–47.

James Thorne and Andreas Vlachos. 2018. Automated fact checking: Task formulations, methods and future directions. In *Proceedings of the 27th International Conference on Computational Linguistics*, COLING '18, pages 3346–3359.

James Thorne, Andreas Vlachos, Christos Christodoulopoulos, and Arpit Mittal. 2018. Fever: A large-scale dataset for fact extraction and verification. In *Proceedings of the 2018 Conference of the North American Chapter of the Association for Computational Linguistics: Human Language Technologies*, NAACL '18, pages 809–819.

V. Venktesh, Abhijit Anand, Avishek Anand, and Vinay Setty. 2024. Quantemp: A real-world open-domain benchmark for fact-checking numerical claims. In *Proceedings of the 47th International ACM SIGIR Conference on Research and Development in Information Retrieval*, SIGIR '24, pages 650–660.

V. Venktesh and Vinay Setty. 2025. Livefc: A system for live fact-checking of audio streams. In *Proceedings of the 18th ACM International Conference on Web Search and Data Mining*, pages 4–7.

Barry Menglong Yao, Aditya Shah, Lichao Sun, Jin-Hee Cho, and Lifu Huang. 2023. End-to-end multimodal fact-checking and explanation generation: A challenging dataset and models. In *Proceedings of the 46th International ACM SIGIR Conference on Research and Development in Information Retrieval*, SIGIR '23, pages 248–258.

Dimitrina Zlatkova, Preslav Nakov, and Ivan Koychev. 2019. Fact-checking meets fauxtography: Verifying claims about images. In *Proceedings of the 2019 Conference on Empirical Methods in Natural Language Processing and the 9th International Joint Conference on Natural Language Processing (EMNLP-IJCNLP)*, pages 2099–2108.

`ChartEval`: LLM-Driven Chart Generation Evaluation Using Scene Graph Parsing

Kanika Goswami[1], Puneet Mathur[2], Ryan Rossi[2], Franck Dernoncourt[2], Vivek Gupta[3], Dinesh Manocha[4]

[1]IGDTUW, India

[2]Adobe Research, San Jose, USA

[3]Arizona State University, Tempe, USA

[4]University of Maryland, College Park, USA

Demo Video: `https://youtu.be/HcPuJaV004s` **Demo Link**: chartEval.ai

Abstract

Accurate assessment of generated chart quality is crucial for automated document creation and editing across diverse applications like finance, medicine, policy making, and education. Current evaluation approaches suffer from significant limitations: human evaluation is costly and difficult to scale, pixel-based metrics ignore data accuracy, while data-centric measures overlook design quality. Recent multimodal LLM evaluators show promise but exhibit concerning inconsistencies due to prompt sensitivity and subjective biases. Existing metrics fail to evaluate chart quality holistically across visual similarity, semantic alignment, and data fidelity, often producing misleading scores that unfairly penalize good charts while rewarding bad ones. We introduce **`ChartEval`**, a novel chart evaluation system that compares generated chart images with ground truth by leveraging scene graph parsing to decompose chart images into hierarchical scene graphs of chart objects, attributes, and relations. Subsequently, it applies graph-based similarity measures to compare candidate chart scene graphs against reference scene graphs for measuring chart quality. We demonstrate that our evaluation approach achieves significantly stronger correlation with human judgments compared to existing metrics like GPT-Score, SSIM, and SCRM using a comprehensive benchmark of 4K chart images paired with generation intents and human quality ratings. We demonstrate the utility of the `ChartEval` system as a reliable automatic chart quality metric on diverse tasks including *language-guided chart editing, chart reconstruction, and text-to-chart synthesis* using both open-source and API-based LLMs. **Demo Website & Video**: chartEval.ai

1 Introduction

Effective data visualization transforms vast amounts of information into actionable insights, playing a critical role across professional domains including financial reporting, scientific publishing, policy analysis, and clinical documentation. However, creating high-quality charts requires substantial technical expertise, driving growing demand for automated chart generation systems. While chart question-answering and captioning have been extensively studied, text-to-chart generation and chart editing have recently gained significant attention as Large Language Models (LLMs) enable users to create visualizations through natural language.

Despite these advances, evaluating chart quality presents significant challenges that existing metrics fail to address comprehensively. Human evaluation, while thorough, is costly and impractical for scaling across large datasets with diverse visualization types. Existing automated evaluation methods, though scalable, suffer from fundamental limitations that compromise their reliability. Data-centric approaches such as SCRM (Xia et al., 2023) extract underlying data tables from charts, but focus exclusively on data accuracy while ignoring visual design quality like mismatched color schemes, misleading labels, or cluttered layouts. Pixel-based metrics like SSIM perform direct image comparisons at the pixel level (Yan et al., 2024), but unfairly penalize semantically equivalent charts that exhibit minor visual differences due to different rendering libraries or styling choices. LLM-as-a-judge methods leverage multimodal LLM prompting to assess generated visualizations (Shi et al., 2025; Xia et al., 2024), offering better scalability but suffering from inconsistent outputs due to prompt sensitivity and subjective biases. These limitations result in evaluation systems that frequently mischaracterize chart quality, incorrectly penalizing well-designed charts while rewarding ones with poor visual communication.

We propose **`ChartEval`** (Fig.1) - a novel chart evaluation system that views chart images as visual scene graphs. In this representation, visual objects such as data marks and legends form nodes,

Proceedings of The 14th International Joint Conference on Natural Language Processing and The 4th Conference of the Asia-Pacific Chapter of the Association for Computational Linguistics: System Demonstrations, pages 86–93
December 20-24, 2025

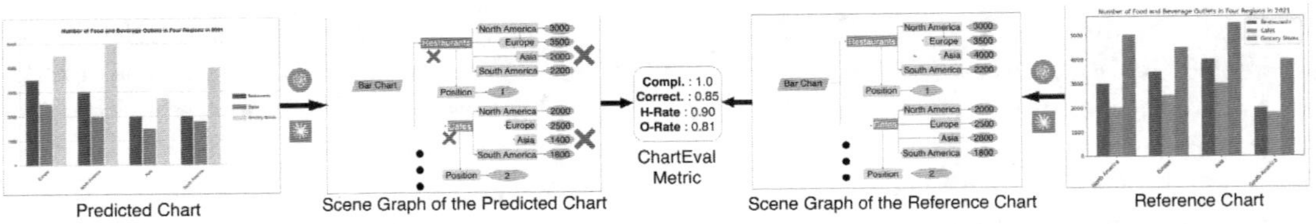

Figure 1: **ChartEval** evaluates chart quality by (1) decomposing predicted and reference charts into visual scene graphs via ChartSceneParse prompting using multimodal LLMs; (2) applying graph-based similarity measures: Graph-BERTScore for semantic correctness and completeness, Hallucination Rate for spurious content, and Omission Rate for missing information. Red crosses (×) highlight values in scene graph of candidate chart that do not match the ground truth chart.

with each object defined by attributes like colors, sizes, and positions, while edges capture relations such as spatial arrangements and data mappings between objects. Given a candidate chart image and its ground truth reference, `ChartEval` decomposes both charts into structured representations using standardized grammar formats (e.g., Vega JSON specifications) that captures overall chart semantics. To enable this decomposition, we introduce `ChartSceneParse`, a novel prompting technique that leverages Chain-of-Thought reasoning (Wei et al., 2022) to systematically extract scene graphs from chart images using multimodal LLMs. We compute graph similarity between the extracted scene graphs of predicted and ground truth charts using four complementary metrics to judge for semantic correctness, completeness, hallucination of spurious content, and omission of critical components. Users can utilize `ChartEval` to evaluate charts generated via multiple methods, including but not limited to SOTA open-source and API-based multimodal LLMs, considering their semantic similarity, visual alignment, and data fidelity.

Lastly, we propose a new benchmark - `ChartGen` comprising of 4K diverse reference chart images paired with their generation intents and human quality ratings across three diverse tasks: language-guided chart editing, chart reconstruction, and text-to-chart synthesis. This benchmark was assembled by integrating four open-source datasets - ChartCraft, ChartMimic, ChartX, and Text2Chart31. We validate the performance of `ChartEval` on `ChartGen` benchmark to demonstrate that `ChartEval` achieves significantly stronger correlation with human judgments compared to existing metrics across most scenarios, confirming its effectiveness as a reliable chart evaluation tool. Results show that participants find the `ChartEval` metric to be an accurate and reliable metric for fact checking generated charts.

Our **main technical contributions** are:

- **ChartSceneParse** prompting technique that leverages Chain-of-Thought reasoning to systematically extract hierarchical scene graphs from chart images using multimodal LLMs and Vega JSON grammar.
- **ChartEval** system that compares generated charts with ground truth by decomposing both into scene graphs and applying graph-based similarity measures (Graph-BERTScore, Hallucination Rate, Omission Rate) for comprehensive quality assessment.
- **ChartGen benchmark** of 4K diverse chart images with human quality ratings across chart editing, reconstruction, and text-to-chart synthesis tasks, achieving significantly stronger correlation with human judgments than existing metrics.

Our **main system-level contributions** are:
(1) Interpretability: `ChartEval` promotes interpretable chart evaluation by providing granular descriptions of visual, semantic, and data hallucinations/omissions through `ChartSceneParse`.
(2) Explainability: `ChartEval` provides logical rationales alongside metric scores to clarify the reasoning behind identified hallucinations and omissions. By transforming charts into hierarchical entity representations, it transcends simple visual similarity metrics and enables direct attribution to chart metadata.
(3) Reliability: `ChartEval` assists professionals across business, education, and finance domains by reducing time spent fact-checking generated charts, allowing users to focus on more productive tasks while enhancing overall evaluation reliability.

2 `ChartEval` - Target Audience

ChartEval's scene graph representation unlocks powerful reference-free applications by transforming charts into structured, analyzable formats: (1) **Automated Quality Control**: Analyze scene graph structure to detect missing legends, unlabeled axes, or inconsistent data encodings in document editing workflows. (2) **Enterprise Style Compliance**: Define corporate chart standards as scene graph templates to ensure all generated charts follow consistent color schemes, font choices, and layout patterns across reports. (3) **Cross-Chart Consistency**: Verify that multiple visualizations within documents use compatible scales, similar encoding principles, and coherent design languages. (4) **Data Integrity Validation**: Compare extracted scene graph data points against source datasets to automatically flag discrepancies, incorrect calculations, or missing information without requiring reference charts. (5) **Collaborative Quality Standards**: Enable teams to maintain quality standards by detecting when charts violate readability principles, accessibility guidelines, or domain-specific conventions. (6) **Template-Based Generation**: Allow users to define desired chart patterns as scene graphs, then automatically evaluate whether generated visualizations match these structural requirements. This structured representation transforms chart evaluation from purely comparative assessment to comprehensive quality analysis, enabling automated editorial assistance, style enforcement, and accuracy verification in production document workflows where reference charts don't exist.

3 `ChartEval` - System Architecture

`ChartEval` (Fig.1) evaluates the representational fidelity of a candidate chart against a ground truth chart in two stages. First, it employs `ChartSceneParse` prompting to decompose the chart images into a structured grammar representations (eg. Vega Json) with a standardized taxonomy to construct hierarchical scene graphs. Second, we compare the extracted chart scene graphs using three complementary evaluation metrics: GraphBERTScore for semantic similarity, Hallucination Rate for spurious content detection, and Omission Rate for missing information assessment.

3.1 Chart Scene Graph Parsing

`ChartEval` decomposes chart images into structured scene graphs in three steps:

(1) Chart Structure parsing describes data visualization designs into a declarative JSON specification language by leveraging the Vega visualization grammar[1] (Satyanarayan et al., 2016). Vega grammar represents charts as hierarchical compositions of primitive graphical properties such as view dimensions, data definitions, map scales, axes, legends, marks (like lines, points, bars), and symbols that encode the underlying data, neatly organized into nested groups with explicit coordinate systems and data bindings. By structuring the extraction process around these core Vega primitives, `ChartSceneParse` systematically converts visual chart elements into their corresponding declarative representations, enabling precise reconstruction and analysis of the original visualizations.

We employ `ChartSceneParse` prompting, an LLM-based Chain-of-Thought reasoning (Wei et al., 2022) technique to systematically extract chart elements as Vega structural primitives: (i) mark types (line, bar, point) and chart layout, (ii) titles and axis labels with exact transcriptions, (iii) axis components (domains, ticks, and grid lines), visual properties (stroke, fill, opacity), and (iv) data points with both visual coordinates and semantic values. We provide prompt instructions to use the identified axis domains and tick positions as spatial anchors for accurate coordinate mappings of data points, pairing pixel positions with actual data values. The extraction follows Vega's hierarchy—first identifying the root frame, then cataloging nested components (axes, marks, titles) with their functional roles. Each extracted element is mapped to Vega's declarative format where visual properties become explicit JSON attributes and spatial relationships are encoded through coordinate transformations. For charts with incomplete information, the system infers reasonable scales while flagging approximations. The LLM is prompted to provide exact textual transcriptions of all visible labels and numerical values to mitigate any hallucinations. Few-shot examples guide the LLM to enforce Vega grammar compliance such that it preserves the proper z-ordering and coordinate system relationships between chart annotations to maintain visual parity with the source image.

(2) Self-Reflection Prompting: LLM-based parsing may be prone to hallucinations which need to be mitigated to avoid spurious results. Hence, we utilize Altair API [2] to convert the intermediate Vega specification back into a chart image and its corresponding data table. The intermediate chart

[1] https://vega.github.io/vega/docs/
[2] https://altair-viz.github.io/

image, its data table, and the reference chart image are sent to GPT-5 to illicit a match score (0-10) and a comparative feedback via Reflexion (Shinn et al., 2023) to correct the generated Scene Graph in the next iteration. We continue this iterative process until match score > 8 or maximum of 3 rounds.

(3) Scene Graph Construction – The Vega grammar JSON is converted into a directed graph $G = (V, E)$ where vertices represent chart components and edges encode their relationships. **Node Creation**: The algorithm generates typed vertices $v_i \in V$ for each functional component—title nodes (v_{title}), chart-type nodes (v_{type}), axis nodes ($v_{\text{x-axis}}, v_{\text{y-axis}}$), and data-point nodes (v_{data_i}). Each node stores attributes extracted from corresponding Vega elements: data nodes contain both visual coordinates ($x_{\text{pixel}}, y_{\text{pixel}}$) and semantic values ($x_{\text{data}}, y_{\text{data}}$), while axis nodes store domain information and labels. **Edge Formation**: Directed edges $e_{ij} \in E$ establish semantic relationships — data-to-axis edges $(v_{\text{data}_i}, v_{\text{x-axis}})$ and $(v_{\text{data}_i}, v_{\text{y-axis}})$ encode which axes govern each data point's positioning, while sequential edges $(v_{\text{data}_i}, v_{\text{data}_{i+1}})$ connect consecutive points to preserve spatial ordering. **Graph Attributes**: Node and edge attributes capture multi-level abstractions — visual properties (colors, styling), semantic content (trends, statistical summaries), and structural metadata (chart type, dimensions). This graph representation G_{chart} standardizes heterogeneous visualizations into a unified format enabling systematic structural comparison while preserving both geometric layout and data semantics.

3.2 Graph-based Scoring

After obtaining scene graphs $G_{\text{gt}} = (V_{\text{gt}}, E_{\text{gt}})$ and $G_{\text{pred}} = (V_{\text{pred}}, E_{\text{pred}})$ from ground truth and predicted charts respectively, we employ Graph-BERTScore (G-BS) (Saha et al., 2021), a semantic-level metric which extends the BERTScore (Zhang et al., 2019) for graph matching. Each edge in the graph is considered as a sentence and BERTScore is used to calculate the score between a pair of predicted and ground-truth edges. Both graphs are decomposed into semantic statements $S = \{s_1, s_2, \ldots, s_k\}$ encoding chart components (e.g., "X-axis represents: Year", "Data trend: increasing from 2010 to 2020"). We use pre-trained BERT (Devlin et al., 2019) contextual embeddings $\mathbf{e}_i = \text{BERT}(s_i)$ and compute pairwise cosine similarities $M_{ij} = \frac{\mathbf{e}_i^{\text{gt}} \cdot \mathbf{e}_j^{\text{pred}}}{||\mathbf{e}_i^{\text{gt}}|| \cdot ||\mathbf{e}_j^{\text{pred}}||}$ between all statement pairs. Following recent work in graph evaluation (Ghanem and Cruz, 2024), we calculate:

Statistic	ChartCraft	ChartMimic	ChartX	Text2Chart31
# charts (test)	5550	500/500	6000	1423
# human rated	1000	1000	1000	1000
Task	Editing	Editing/Reconstruction	Reconstruction	Desc-to-Chart
Input Format	Image + NL	Image + NL	Image	Text
Eval Metric	SSIM	GPT-Score	SCRM & GPT-score	CodeBLEU
Source	Synthetic	Human	Synthetic	Synthetic

Table 1: Comparative data statistics

(i) Correctness: Average of the maximum similarity scores between each predicted statement in S_{pred} and all ground truth statements S_{gt}: $P = \frac{1}{|S_{\text{pred}}|} \sum_{j=1}^{|S_{\text{pred}}|} \max_i M_{ij}$, analogous to precision.

(ii) Completeness: Average of the maximum similarity scores between each ground truth statement in S_{gt} and all predicted statements S_{pred}: $R = \frac{1}{|S_{\text{gt}}|} \sum_{i=1}^{|S_{\text{gt}}|} \max_j M_{ij}$, analogous to recall.

We perform direct scene graph comparison via:

(iii) Hallucination Rate (Ghanem and Cruz, 2024) quantifies spurious information in predictions. Hallucinations are defined as the presence of an entity or relation in predicted graph that is not present in the gold graph. We extract structured element sets $\mathcal{E}_{\text{gt}}$ and $\mathcal{E}_{\text{pred}}$ from the ground truth and predicted graphs, encompassing data points (x_i, y_i), axis labels, chart metadata, and visual properties. Mathematically, $H_{\text{rate}} = \frac{|\mathcal{E}_{\text{pred}} - \mathcal{E}_{\text{gt}}|}{|\mathcal{E}_{\text{pred}}|}$. We employ fuzzy matching with ϵ-tolerance for numerical values to account for minor coordinate differences while preserving semantic accuracy.

(iv) Omission Rate (Ghanem and Cruz, 2024) accounts for critical missing elements that compromise chart completeness, such as absent data points, unlabeled axes, or missing titles. Omissions are defined as missing entities or relations in the predicted graph that are present in the gold graph. Mathematically, $O_{\text{rate}} = \frac{|\mathcal{E}_{\text{gt}} - \mathcal{E}_{\text{pred}}|}{|\mathcal{E}_{\text{gt}}|}$.

4 System Demonstration

Figure 2 shows the `ChartEval` demo app (chartEval.ai) which has been created using Gradio, and can use OpenAI GPT-4o or Claude Sonnet-3.7 for chart evaluation. The interface includes a panel to upload pairs of predicted/reference chart images and an alternative option to select from pre-uploaded examples. The user can choose which LLM to use for the evaluation from the UI and also reset the interface for new evaluations. `ChartEval` shows an evaluation report with scores for completeness, correction, Hallucination Rate, and Omission Rate, along with an explanation on

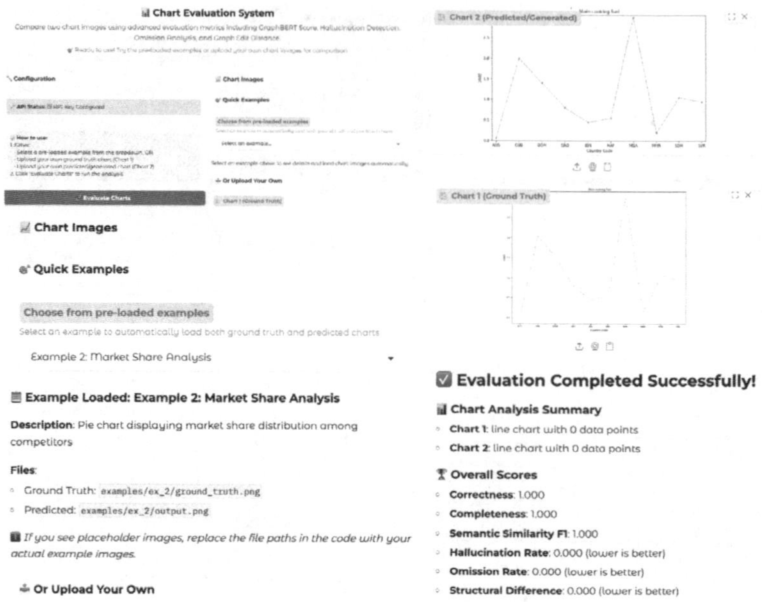

Figure 2: Demo App UI for ChartEval(chartEval.ai)

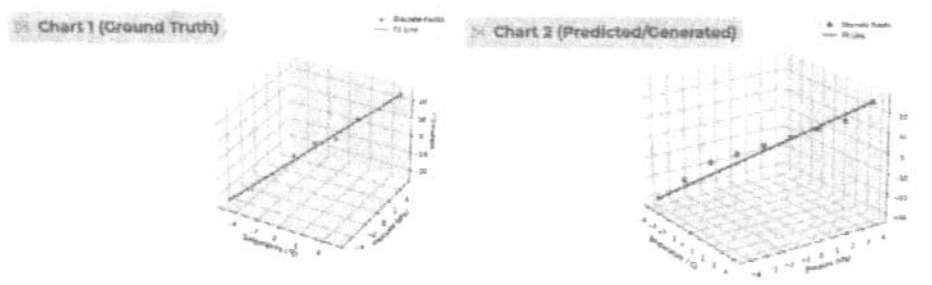

Metric	Score		
Model Used	Claude	Hallucination Rate	0.333
Correctness (Precision)	1.000	Hallucination Count	4
Completeness (Recall)	1.000	Omission Rate	0.000
F1 Score	1.000	Omission Count	0

Figure 3: ChartEval Example

the structural differences between compared charts.

System License: ChartEval is a proprietary system developed for research experimentation, and is not intended for any commercial purposes.

Usage Scenario Example: Figure 3 shows an example of our tool usage where a user can upload a chart image edited based on user request - "Add a data point (30,25,90) on the line chart" and evaluates it against the reference desired chart. user generated chart erroneously has added more than one data point which is accurately captured by ChartEval as part of H-rate. Further, axis rotation and deviation in rendering quality due to different software does not affect our evaluation system.

5 Experiments - User Study

Datasets: Table 1 summarizes our proposed ChartGen benchmark that comprises of four chart generation datasets spanning three real-world tasks: instruction-based chart image editing, chart re-drawing, and text-to-chart generation.

(1) ChartCraft (Yan et al., 2024) is a dataset of synthetically generated line and bar charts covering style, layout, format, and data-centric edits. We evaluate the language-based chart editing task to modify plot attributes based on user's intent while preserving the integrity of the original plot.

(2) ChartMimic (Shi et al., 2025) contains human-curated visualization from academic documents and scientific papers, covering 22 common chart types. ChartMimic evaluates two tasks: (a) Direct Mimic, where models generate code to reproduce a given chart, and (b) Customized Mimic, where models generate code incorporating new data while preserving the original chart's design.

(3) ChartX (Xia et al., 2024) contains synthetic chart images for re-drawing tasks, where models generate Python code and compare rendered outputs against ground-truth charts.

(4) Text2Chart31 (Pesaran Zadeh et al., 2024) provides chart data across 31 unique plot types, including 3D, volumetric, and gridded charts. We evaluate the description-to-chart task, where each input sample consists of an input textual description and corresponding reference chart.

Settings: We use GPT-4V and Claude-3.7 for ChartSceneParse prompting; GPT-4o, Claude Sonnet-3.5, and Qwen2.5-VL:32b for chart gen-

Metric	Model	ChartCraft						ChartMimic						ChartX						Text2Chart31					
		SSIM	SCRM	GPT-Sc	CB	O-G	O-C	SSIM	SCRM	GPT-Sc	CB	O-G	O-C	SSIM	SCRM	GPT-Sc	CB	O-G	O-C	SSIM	SCRM	GPT-Sc	CB	O-G	O-C
Correct.	GPT-4o	0.09	0.13	0.25	0.34	0.76*	0.69	0.11	0.15	0.27	0.29	0.79*	0.72	0.24	0.29	0.33	0.38	0.84	0.85*	0.18	0.19	0.25	0.25	0.76	0.78*
	Sonnet-3.5	0.10	0.15	0.23	0.33	0.75*	0.70	0.13	0.16	0.24	0.31	0.77*	0.73	0.25	0.27	0.31	0.37	0.86*	0.86	0.19	0.19	0.26	0.27	0.75	0.79*
	Qwen2.5-VL	0.15	0.18	0.28	0.36	0.79*	0.79	0.17	0.19	0.26	0.37	0.79	0.80*	0.28	0.29	0.33	0.39	0.88	0.89*	0.22	0.23	0.28	0.29	0.78	0.79*
Compl.	GPT-4o	0.10	0.14	0.23	0.31	0.74*	0.70	0.12	0.12	0.28	0.30	0.76*	0.71	0.22	0.26	0.31	0.35	0.81	0.82*	0.20	0.19	0.22	0.24	0.75	0.76*
	Sonnet-3.5	0.08	0.12	0.21	0.28	0.70	0.72*	0.10	0.15	0.21	0.29	0.75	0.77*	0.23	0.24	0.28	0.33	0.82	0.84*	0.21	0.22	0.23	0.35	0.67	0.72*
	Qwen2.5-VL	0.19	0.19	0.24	0.35	0.76	0.77*	0.18	0.20	0.23	0.34	0.73	0.75*	0.27	0.28	0.34	0.36	0.81	0.82*	0.24	0.25	0.28	0.28	0.76	0.78*
H-Rate	GPT-4o	0.07	0.11	0.15	0.18	0.45	0.48*	0.06	0.13	0.15	0.24	0.42	0.45*	0.05	0.13	0.20	0.24	0.50	0.52*	0.09	0.12	0.18	0.21	0.55	0.56*
	Sonnet-3.5	0.08	0.12	0.15	0.19	0.49	0.51*	0.08	0.17	0.19	0.28	0.48	0.52*	0.10	0.15	0.19	0.35	0.54	0.56*	0.11	0.14	0.20	0.24	0.59	0.60*
	Qwen2.5-VL	0.10	0.12	0.14	0.19	0.40	0.45*	0.09	0.14	0.19	0.27	0.45*	0.45	0.08	0.15	0.22	0.27	0.52	0.54*	0.08	0.14	0.13	0.23	0.53	0.57*
O-Rate	GPT-4o	0.13	0.15	0.19	0.22	0.51	0.54*	0.08	0.11	0.18	0.21	0.54	0.58*	0.12	0.14	0.23	0.28	0.48	0.51*	0.08	0.11	0.19	0.20	0.51	0.55*
	Sonnet-3.5	0.14	0.17	0.20	0.24	0.54	0.56*	0.10	0.13	0.21	0.23	0.55	0.59*	0.14	0.15	0.22	0.27	0.49	0.53*	0.12	0.14	0.18	0.22	0.54	0.56*
	Qwen2.5-VL	0.18	0.19	0.24	0.26	0.54	0.57*	0.16	0.18	0.23	0.25	0.57	0.61*	0.19	0.19	0.24	0.29	0.51	0.54*	0.17	0.18	0.19	0.23	0.55	0.58*

Table 2: Correlations of ChartEval and existing metrics with human ratings. Correct: Correctness, Compl: Completeness, H: Hallucination, O: Omission, CB: CodeBLEU, GPT-Sc: GPT-Score, O-C(G): Our proposed ChartEval with Claude Sonnet-3.5 (GPT-4) for ChartSceneParse prompting. * indicates statistical significance over GPT-Score ($p \leq 0.005$) under Wilcoxon's Signed Rank test.

eration tasks. More experiment settings in Sec. A.

Baselines Metrics: We compare ChartEval with **(1) GPT-Score** (Shi et al., 2025; Xia et al., 2024) uses GPT-4o to compare the candidate and ground truth chart images on a 0-100 scale (normalized to 0-1) based on prompt-based scoring criteria.

(2) SSIM (Wang et al., 2004; Yan et al., 2024) assesses the degree to which the candidate chart visually mirrors the expected outcome, capturing subtle and nuances in the pixel space.

(3) SCRM (Xia et al., 2023) evaluates extracted chart information by converting model-predicted linearized CSV tokens into triplet format, enabling transpose-invariant evaluation of chart data.

(4) CodeBlue (Ren et al., 2020) evaluates the similarity between the predicted and ground truth code for respective charts as in (Pesaran Zadeh et al., 2024). Note that code execution success rate is a standard metric for code generation tasks where unsuccessful executions are assigned a score of 0.

6 Results - User Evaluation

We collected human quality ratings for 4K test charts (1K per dataset) from three annotators, achieving high inter-annotator agreement ($\alpha = \{0.74, 0.82, 0.76, 0.85\}$) across all evaluation metrics. Table 2 presents Pearson correlations between various metrics and these human ratings across different dataset-model combinations. ChartEval consistently demonstrates stronger correlations with human judgments than existing metrics for both proprietary and open-source models across all four datasets. This superior performance indicates that our metric evaluates chart semantics more accurately than baseline approaches. Our analysis reveals several key advantages of ChartEval over existing approaches. Unlike SSIM, our metric avoids over-sensitivity to pixel-level perturbations while successfully capturing meaningful variations in visual attributes such as color schemes, text fonts, and sizing. Code-based metrics like CodeBLEU fail to evaluate spatial misalignment of chart components, which are typically under-specified in generated code. ChartEval offers a decisive advantage over SCRM, which exclusively evaluates underlying data accuracy while ignoring spatial layout and visual design features. Our approach surpasses GPT-Score by mitigating subjective biases inherent in prompt-based evaluation methods. ChartEval is the only metric that provides comprehensive evaluation across semantic, visual, and data dimensions simultaneously, establishing itself as a reliable chart quality assessment tool.

Qualitative Examples: Figures 4-6 illustrate ChartEval's performance across different scenarios. Figure 4 demonstrates accurate evaluation of a 2D area plot where ChartEval correctly identifies near-perfect similarity with zero hallucination rates, avoiding the over-penalization issues of pixel-based metrics. Figure 5 shows ChartEval successfully detects a hallucinated data point in the 3D surface plot, with the Correctness score (0.87) appropriately capturing both spatial inaccuracy and color scheme deviation. **Limitation**: Figure 6 reveals a key limitation that ChartEval struggles with low-resolution input images where the underlying LLM (GPT-4V) hallucinates during scene graph parsing, leading to inaccurate evaluation results. This limitation suggests that ChartEval performs optimally with high-quality images and may require preprocessing steps for low-resolution scenarios. Overall, these examples confirm ChartEval provides more nuanced assessment than existing metrics.

7 Conclusion

We introduced ChartEval, an evaluation system that converts chart images into visual scene graphs and compares their graph-based similarity with ground truth. Extensive experiments across chart reconstruction, text-to-chart synthesis, and editing tasks demonstrate the effectiveness of ChartEval as a reliable chart assessment tool. Future work will explore finetuning VLMs on low resolution chart images for better data extraction.

References

Anthropic. 2024. The claude 3 model family: Opus, sonnet, haiku. Technical Report.

Shuai Bai, Keqin Chen, Xuejing Liu, Jialin Wang, Wenbin Ge, Sibo Song, Kai Dang, Peng Wang, Shijie Wang, Jun Tang, and 1 others. 2025. Qwen2. 5-vl technical report. *arXiv preprint arXiv:2502.13923*.

Jacob Devlin, Ming-Wei Chang, Kenton Lee, and Kristina Toutanova. 2019. Bert: Pre-training of deep bidirectional transformers for language understanding. In *North American Chapter of the Association for Computational Linguistics*.

Hussam Ghanem and Christophe Cruz. 2024. Enhancing knowledge graph construction: Evaluating with emphasis on hallucination, omission, and graph similarity metrics. In *International Knowledge Graph and Semantic Web Conference*, pages 32–46. Springer.

Aaron Hurst, Adam Lerer, Adam P Goucher, Adam Perelman, Aditya Ramesh, Aidan Clark, AJ Ostrow, Akila Welihinda, Alan Hayes, Alec Radford, and 1 others. 2024. Gpt-4o system card. *arXiv preprint arXiv:2410.21276*.

Fatemeh Pesaran Zadeh, Juyeon Kim, Jin-Hwa Kim, and Gunhee Kim. 2024. Text2Chart31: Instruction tuning for chart generation with automatic feedback. In *Proceedings of the 2024 Conference on Empirical Methods in Natural Language Processing*, pages 11459–11480, Miami, Florida, USA. Association for Computational Linguistics.

Shuo Ren, Daya Guo, Shuai Lu, Long Zhou, Shujie Liu, Duyu Tang, M. Zhou, Ambrosio Blanco, and Shuai Ma. 2020. Codebleu: a method for automatic evaluation of code synthesis. *ArXiv*, abs/2009.10297.

Swarnadeep Saha, Prateek Yadav, Lisa Bauer, and Mohit Bansal. 2021. Explagraphs: An explanation graph generation task for structured commonsense reasoning. *arXiv preprint arXiv:2104.07644*.

Arvind Satyanarayan, Ryan Russell, Jane Hoffswell, and Jeffrey Heer. 2016. Reactive vega: A streaming dataflow architecture for declarative interactive visualization. *IEEE Trans. Visualization & Comp. Graphics (Proc. InfoVis)*.

Chufan Shi, Cheng Yang, Yaxin Liu, Bo Shui, Junjie Wang, Mohan Jing, Linran Xu, Xinyu Zhu, Siheng Li, Yuxiang Zhang, Gongye Liu, Xiaomei Nie, Deng Cai, and Yujiu Yang. 2025. Chartmimic: Evaluating lmm's cross-modal reasoning capability via chart-to-code generation. *International Conference on Learning Representations*.

Noah Shinn, Federico Cassano, Ashwin Gopinath, Karthik Narasimhan, and Shunyu Yao. 2023. Reflexion: Language agents with verbal reinforcement learning. *Advances in Neural Information Processing Systems*, 36:8634–8652.

Zhou Wang, Alan C Bovik, Hamid R Sheikh, and Eero P Simoncelli. 2004. Image quality assessment: from error visibility to structural similarity. *IEEE transactions on image processing*, 13(4):600–612.

Jason Wei, Xuezhi Wang, Dale Schuurmans, Maarten Bosma, Fei Xia, Ed Chi, Quoc V Le, Denny Zhou, and 1 others. 2022. Chain-of-thought prompting elicits reasoning in large language models. *Advances in neural information processing systems*, 35:24824–24837.

Renqiu Xia, Bo Zhang, Haoyang Peng, Hancheng Ye, Xiangchao Yan, Peng Ye, Botian Shi, Yu Qiao, and Junchi Yan. 2023. Structchart: Perception, structuring, reasoning for visual chart understanding. *arXiv preprint arXiv:2309.11268*.

Renqiu Xia, Bo Zhang, Hancheng Ye, Xiangchao Yan, Qi Liu, Hongbin Zhou, Zijun Chen, Peng Ye, Min Dou, Botian Shi, and 1 others. 2024. Chartx & chartvlm: A versatile benchmark and foundation model for complicated chart reasoning. *arXiv preprint arXiv:2402.12185*.

Pengyu Yan, Mahesh Bhosale, Jay Lal, Bikhyat Adhikari, and David Doermann. 2024. Chartreformer: Natural language-driven chart image editing. In *International Conference on Document Analysis and Recognition*, pages 453–469. Springer.

Tianyi Zhang, Varsha Kishore, Felix Wu, Kilian Q Weinberger, and Yoav Artzi. 2019. Bertscore: Evaluating text generation with bert. *arXiv preprint arXiv:1904.09675*.

A Settings

We conduct experiments using GPT-4o (Hurst et al., 2024), Claude Sonnet-3.5 (Anthropic, 2024), and Qwen2.5-VL:32b (Bai et al., 2025) for chart generation/editing. We render the chart code generated by these models and compare the resulting visualizations against ground truth charts. We use NVIDIA A100 GPUs for Qwen2.5, and APIs for rest. We experiment with GPT-4V and Claude-3.7 for `ChartSceneParse` prompting.

B Qualitative Examples

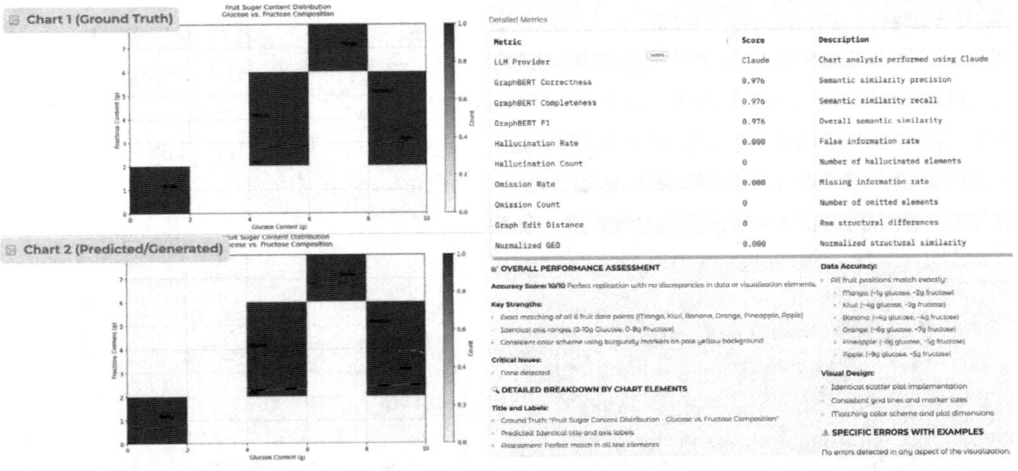

Figure 4: Example of 2D area plot generated by GPT-4o. ChartEval correctly identifies near-perfect chart similarity with zero hallucination or omission rates, demonstrating accurate evaluation of high-quality generated charts.

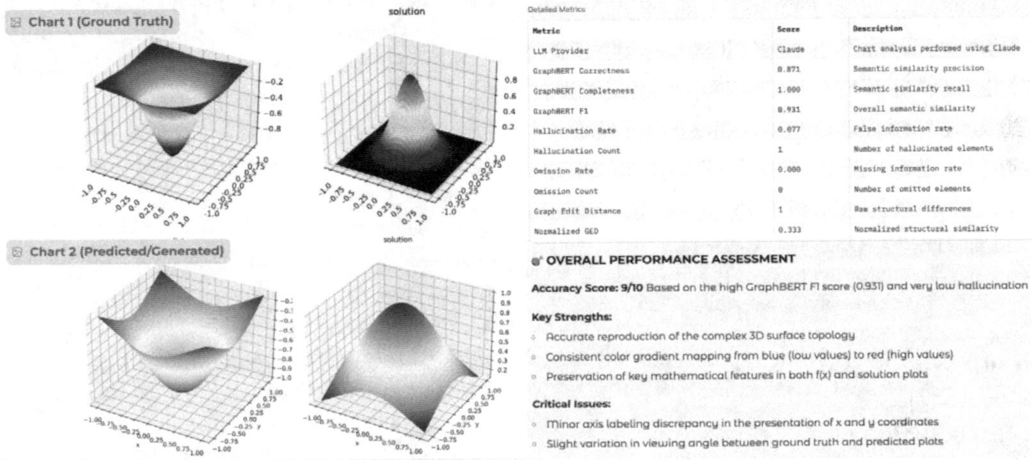

Figure 5: Example of 3D surface plot where ChartEval successfully identifies a hallucinated data point causing curvature distortion. Graph-BERTScore Correctness also accurately detects deviation in the color scheme (Correctness score = 0.87).

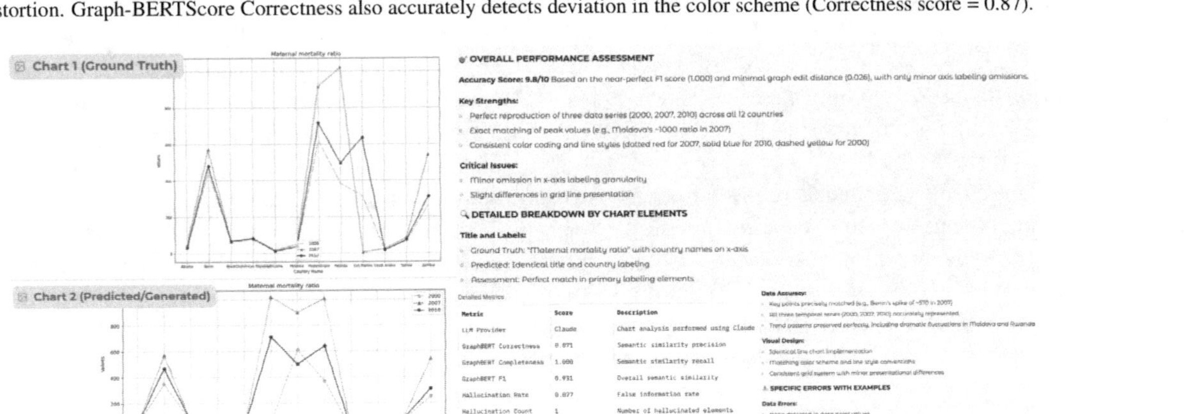

Figure 6: Example of ChartEval limitation on low-resolution images. The predicted chart contains significant data hallucinations and omissions that ChartEval fails to detect due to image quality constraints. Low-resolution inputs cause the underlying LLM (GPT-4V) to hallucinate during scene graph parsing, leading to inaccurate evaluation results.

SPORTSQL: An Interactive System for Real-Time Sports Reasoning and Visualization

Sebastian Martinez **Naman Ahuja** **Fenil Bardoliya** **Suparno Roy Chowdhury**
Chris Bryan **Vivek Gupta**
Arizona State University
{sjmart28, nahuja11, fbardoli, srchowd3, cbryan16, vgupt140}@asu.edu

Abstract

We present a modular, interactive system SPORTSQL for natural language querying and visualization of dynamic sports data, with a focus on the English Premier League (EPL). The system translates user questions into executable SQL over a live, temporally indexed database constructed from real-time Fantasy Premier League (FPL) data. It supports both tabular and visual outputs, leveraging symbolic reasoning capabilities of Large Language Models (LLMs) for query parsing, schema linking, and visualization selection. To evaluate system performance, we introduce the **D**ynamic **S**port **Q**uestion **A**nswering benchmark (DSQABENCH), comprising 1,700+ queries annotated with SQL programs, gold answers, and database snapshots. Our demo highlights how non-expert users can seamlessly explore evolving sports statistics through a natural, conversational interface.

1 Introduction

What if a soccer fan could ask, *"How did Mohamed Salah's scoring performance trend over the last five seasons?"* or *"Which midfielders in the Premier League are the most creative this season?"* and instantly receive not only a precise answer but also a dynamic visualization, grounded in up-to-date, real-world data?

Large language models (LLMs) have shown remarkable progress in translating natural language into executable programs, such as SQL. However, most existing systems are designed for static, domain-specific datasets. In contrast, domains like sports are inherently dynamic and structurally complex: match outcomes, player statistics, team formations, and injury reports evolve daily across multiple interlinked and semi-structured tables. Querying such data effectively requires compositional, temporal, and relational reasoning, along with the ability to operate over continuously changing schemas and distributed sources.

We introduce SPORTSQL, a fully automated system for Dynamic Sports Question Answering (DSQA), enabling users to pose rich natural language queries over live sports data and receive grounded, executable, and often visual responses. SPORTSQL operates through a modular pipeline: it begins by scraping and normalizing dynamic data and transforming it into a unified, temporally indexed relational database. Given a user question, the system uses only the schema (not the data itself) to prompt an LLM to generate symbolic SQL queries, making the approach scalable and robust to changes in content (Kulkarni et al., 2025). When appropriate, SPORTSQL also generates visualization code (in matplotlib, seaborn) to produce bar charts, timelines, or other graphical responses.

For instance, a user might ask, *"Compare Arsenal's goals scored in home vs away matches"* or *"List forwards with at least ten goals and five assists."* SPORTSQL retrieves accurate answers by executing SQL over the latest data, rather than relying on potentially outdated or hallucinated information from pretrained language models (Kulkarni and Srikumar, 2025). To evaluate the effectiveness of the system, we introduce Dynamic Sports Question Answering Benchmark (DSQABENCH), a new benchmark containing over 1700 questions that span various soccer metrics, reasoning types, and output formats. Each question is paired with its corresponding SQL program, gold answer, and the database snapshot at the time of execution. We further provide a type-aware evaluation framework that supports multiple answer formats, schema-only SQL generation, and fine-grained error analysis to assess system performance under dynamic conditions. Our contributions are threefold:

- We introduce the task of Dynamic Sports Question Answering and present SPORTSQL, a modular and interpretable system that enables real-time, schema-driven symbolic rea-

Proceedings of The 14th International Joint Conference on Natural Language Processing and The 4th Conference of the Asia-Pacific Chapter of the Association for Computational Linguistics: System Demonstrations, pages 94–101
December 20-24, 2025

soning and dynamic visualization over evolving sports databases.

- We construct and release DSQABENCH, the first benchmark of executable sports queries paired with live data, supporting multiple answer modalities.
- We develop a type-aware evaluation framework with support for diverse answer formats (textual, numeric, tabular, visual), schema-only SQL generation, and fine-grained error analysis to assess symbolic QA systems over dynamic content.

We invite the readers to explore SportsSQL's functionalities at the following links:

- Code & Data: `https://github.com/coral-lab-asu/SportSQL`
- Main Demo Video: `https://youtu.be/xqUyiA-R6aI`
- Try it out: `https://coral-lab-asu.github.io/SportsSQL`

Although SPORTSQL is designed for sports, its architecture is general and can extend to other dynamic, structured domains such as finance, healthcare, or elections, where users seek timely, accurate insights from evolving data.

2 SPORTSQL Architecture

SPORTSQL translates free-form user queries into executable answers via a tightly integrated, multistage pipeline. The system operates over a live, dynamically updated EPL database, refreshed periodically via cronjobs and at runtime based on query requirements. Upon receiving a natural language query, the system first performs entity grounding by executing SQL lookups against curated reference tables (e.g., teams, players), mapping surface forms to canonical entities. Conditioned on this context and the database schema, it generates an executable SQL query, which is run on the live database to produce a structured result. If the query involves visual reasoning (e.g., comparisons, trends, rankings), the output is forwarded to a visualization agent, which selects an appropriate chart type and returns self-contained Python code (Matplotlib + Seaborn) to render the plot. The full workflow is outlined below.

1. Database Streaming Our system ingests data from the public *Fantasy Premier League* (FPL) API,[1] which offers structured, frequently updated endpoints covering players, teams, fixtures, and per-match statistics. After normalization and deduplication, the data is stored in a MariaDB backend.

Hybrid Storage Strategy Storing full historical data for every player would require ~2,400 tables per season (3 per player × 800 players), resulting in a bloated schema and largely idle data. To balance granularity with efficiency, we adopt a two-tiered storage design:

- **Query-agnostic tables**: Core relations (`players`, `teams`, `fixtures`) that evolve predictably week-by-week. These are updated nightly via cronjob to maintain freshness.
- **Query-dependent tables**: Fine-grained views (e.g., "past 5 games", "next 3 fixtures") fetched on demand from the FPL API. These are materialized in memory for the duration of a query and discarded after use.

This hybrid architecture ensures (i) *freshness* via automated updates, (ii) *coverage* through just-in-time API access, and (iii) *efficiency* by limiting persistent storage. Figure 1 illustrates the relational schema and data flow.

2. Entity Recognition User queries often contain abbreviations, nicknames, or informal spellings (e.g., *"CR7"* for *Cristiano Ronaldo*, *"Donatello"* for *Kylian Mbappé*), making exact string matching unreliable. Additionally, the LLM operates only over the database schema and lacks direct access to cell-level values. To resolve entity mentions, we employ a prompt-guided procedure. The prompt instructs the LLM to: (i) use domain knowledge to infer canonical player or team names, and (ii) generate a case-insensitive wildcard SQL query over reference tables. The database returns a filtered set of candidate rows with unique IDs, which are retained as the resolved entity identifiers.

3. SQL Generation and Execution Given the resolved entity identifiers, we prompt a large language model to generate an executable SQL query. The model is provided with: (i) the user question, (ii) the set of resolved primary keys, and (iii) the database schema, along with targeted instructions to mitigate common pitfalls:

- **Table hints**: e.g., `players` is preferred for individual statistics

[1] `https://fantasy.premierleague.com/`

players	
player_id	int (PK)
web_name	varchar
player_position	varchar
team_id	int
goals_scored	int
assists	int
minutes	int

teams	
team_id	int (PK)
team_name	varchar
position	int
played	int
win	int
draw	int
loss	int

fixtures	
game_id	int (PK)
gw	int
finished	boolean
team_h_name	varchar
team_a_name	varchar
kickoff_time	varchar

player_history	
season_name	varchar (PK)
goals_scored	int
assists	int
minutes	int
yellow_cards	int
red_cards	int
saves	int

player_past	
player_id	int
event	int (PK)
goals_scored	int
assists	int
minutes	int
yellow_cards	int
red_cards	int

player_future	
event	int (PK)
event_name	varchar
team_h_name	varchar
team_a_name	varchar
is_home	boolean
difficulty	int
kickoff_time	varchar

Figure 1: DB schema, all tables shown, not all columns. Here, PK represent primary key.

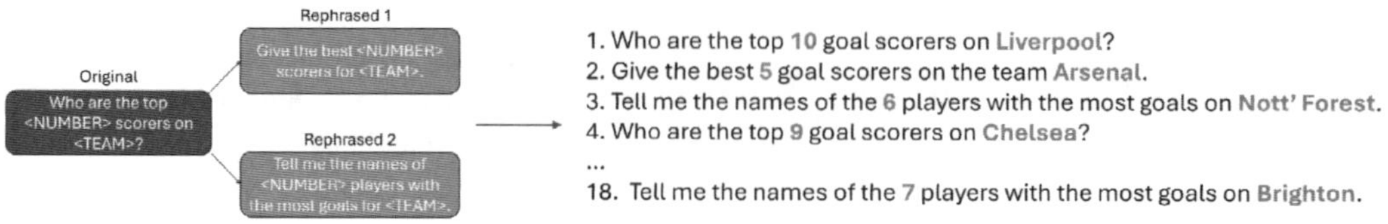

Figure 2: Sample Question Creation Expansion

- **Synonym mappings**: e.g., "team position" $\leftrightarrow$ `league_rank`
- **Column cautions**: e.g., penalty saves are almost always non-zero for goalkeepers only
- **Derived-field formulas**: e.g., `form` is the 30-day average of match points
- **Scale explanations**: e.g., `strength` ranges from 1 (weakest) to 5 (strongest)

These prompt elements help ensure syntactic correctness and reduce semantic errors arising from natural language variability.

SQL Execution. The generated SQL is parsed and executed against the dynamic MariaDB store. If the query references a non-materialized *query-dependent* table (e.g., a player's upcoming fixtures), the system issues a just-in-time API call to fetch the necessary data, loads it into an in-memory buffer, and re-executes the query. The temporary table is discarded post-aggregation, ensuring the persistent database remains lightweight.

4. Visual Output Generation Some information needs are better served through visualizations than text. To support this, the system automatically generates plots when either: (i) the user explicitly requests a "plot," "graph," or "trend," or (ii) the output dataframe exhibits structures—such as multi-season time series or long categorical rankings—that benefit from visual interpretation. For example, the query *"Plot a line graph of Kylian Mbappé's goal totals over the past five seasons"* produces a line chart with seasons on the x-axis and goals on the y-axis, revealing temporal trends. Similarly, the query *"Which five teams recorded the highest average possession in the 2024–25 campaign?"*—though not explicitly visual—triggers a horizontal bar chart ranking clubs by possession.

When comparative or temporal reasoning is detected, the result and original query are passed to a secondary code-generating LLM, which returns self-contained `Matplotlib` code (e.g., line plots for trends, bar charts for rankings). A validation layer ensures the dataframe referenced in the code matches the SQL output byte-for-byte; any mismatch triggers automatic re-querying.

This architecture enables near real-time visual responses, maintains the persistent database under 5GB, and supports fine-grained, player-level analytics without compromising freshness or correctness. Figure 3 presents an overview of the full system pipeline.

3 DSQABENCH Benchmark

To evaluate the SPORTSQL system, we introduce the **D**ynamic **S**port **Q**uestion **A**nswering benchmark (DSQABENCH), designed to assess natural language interfaces over dynamic, multi-relational sports data.

Query Creation. We construct a diverse set of natural language questions targeting various schema elements and reasoning skills. The process begins with manually written question templates, each rephrased to capture linguistic variation. Templates contain placeholders (e.g., team names, numerical thresholds), which are instantiated using real-world entities and context-appropriate values. This approach balances lexical diversity with semantic control. Additionally, we include a set of manually crafted, challenging questions to probe complex and multi-hop reasoning. An illustration of this process is shown in Figure 2.

Answer Annotation. Each question is paired with a manually authored SQL query, serving as the gold standard. These queries are executed against the underlying MariaDB-based *"Fut-*

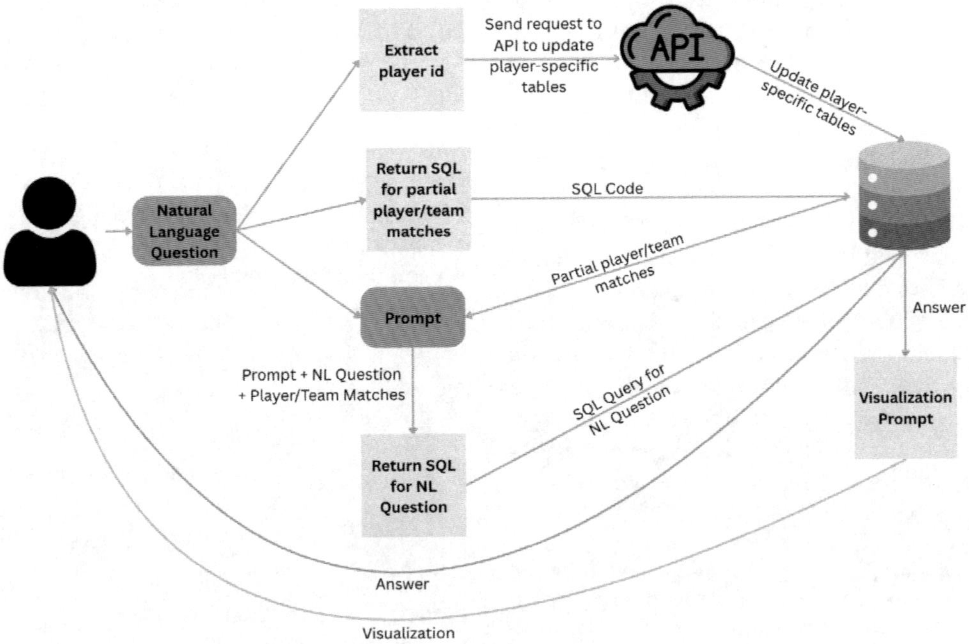

Figure 3: SportSQL Architecture and Workflow

SQL_FPL" database to verify correctness. This ensures high-quality supervision for evaluating both SQL generation and execution accuracy.

Dataset Statistics. DSQABENCH contains 1,793 questions derived from 180 base templates, each rephrased in three distinct ways and instantiated with real-world values. Among these:

- 1,395 questions yield scalar answers (e.g., strings, numbers); 398 require tabular outputs.
- 396 questions involve dynamic queries to player-specific tables via just-in-time API access:
  - `player_past`: 270 queries
  - `player_history`: 72 queries
  - `player_future`: 54 queries
- All questions are paired with manually validated SQL programs executable on the database.

DSQABENCH provides a rich and realistic benchmark for studying compositional generalization, schema coverage, and executable reasoning in sports QA systems.

4 Experiments and Analysis

Models. We evaluate two state-of-the-art LLMs: GPT-4O and GEMINI-2.0 FLASH. GEMINI-2.0-FLASH is selected for its balance of performance, latency, and cost, making it suitable for scalable deployment. GPT-4O is used to assess generalization. Both models use a temperature of 0.1 (for deterministic outputs) and a maximum token limit of 2048 (for reduced latency).

Evaluation Metrics. As the system produces both string and tabular outputs, we employ a type-aware evaluation. **String Answers**: Evaluated using exact match. We also employ LLMs as judges and prompt frontier models with the NL query, ground truth SQL, and system-generated SQL, and their SQL outputs, which models classify as equivalent/not equivalent. We use 3 frontier models: GPT-4o, GEMINI-2.5, and QWEN3-235b-A22B-INSTRUCT-2507, and take majority voting. **Table Answers**: Assessed using TABEVAL (Ramu et al., 2024), which converts tables into atomic natural language statements and computes pairwise entailment via ROBERTA-MNLI, yielding precision (Correctness), recall (Completeness), and F1 (Overall) scores.

4.1 Results and Analysis

Table 1 reports performance on both string and table-structured questions. The system achieves up to 80% exact-match accuracy and 0.75 macro-F1, indicating strong performance on structured

QA. GPT-4o consistently outperforms Gemini-2.0 Flash, with gains of 4.2 points in exact match and 0.05 in macro-F1. Completeness scores exceed correctness for both models, suggesting that relevant columns are more reliably identified than specific rows, a reflection of the higher complexity of row selection driven by SQL predicates. Moreover, we observe that the LLM-as-judge (majority voting) shows significantly higher accuracy than EM. This follows findings from previous works (Chandak et al., 2025) where deterministic evaluations over-penalize semantically coherent outputs. We observe multiple such cases, especially for more complex queries, where selecting extra/different columns in the output can lead to mis-evaluation. Hence, we use LLM as a Judge as our primary metric for further analysis.

Table 1: Model performance comparison on string and tables answered. Here, EM represents an Exact Match. Corr stands for Correctness, Comp stands for Completeness.

Model	String		Table (TabEval)		
	EM	LLM as Judge	Corr	Comp	Overall
Gemini-2.0	76.23	92.39	0.64	0.76	0.69
GPT-4o	80.48	93.82	0.70	0.81	0.75

4.2 Primitive-Based Analysis

To systematically assess performance across SQL query types, we annotate each ground-truth SQL template with a set of six reasoning primitives:

- **Calculate**: Arithmetic operations (`SUM`, `COUNT`, `AVG`, etc.)
- **Compare**: Value comparisons
- **Filter**: Conditional constraints (`WHERE`)
- **Order**: Sorting (`ORDER BY ASC/DESC`)
- **Manipulate**: Data transformations (`JOIN`, `UNION`, `MERGE`)
- **Retrieve**: Direct lookups of values (e.g., entity or attribute selection)

Clause Combinations and Their Impact. The system performs perfectly on single-primitive queries such as *Retrieve* (*"Show all EPL goalkeepers"*, 100%) and *Order* (*"Rank Premier League clubs by points"*, 97.6%). It also handles *Calculate + Compare* well (*"Did Haaland score more goals than Salah last season?"*, 96.3%). However, performance drops sharply with added complexity: *Retrieve + Filter + Calculate* (*"What's the average pass accuracy for midfielders under 23?"*) yields 69.3%, and *Calculate + Order* reaches 50.0%. Other challenging cases involve *Manipulate* operations (e.g., table joins) scoring 75%, and four-way compositions (e.g., *Compare + Manipulate + Order + Calculate*) showing similar results.

Impact of Query Complexity. We examine how performance varies with the number of reasoning primitives in a query. Figure 4 plots accuracy against the number of primitives (k), with 95% Wilson confidence intervals.

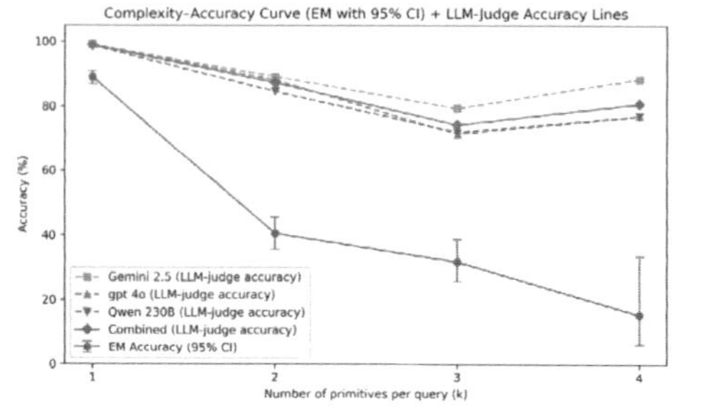

Figure 4: Accuracy Trend over Number of Clauses with LLM as Judge scores

LLM-as-a-judge accuracy is high for retrieval-based queries (99%) but drops to 91.2% with two primitives. This further drops for 3 primitives and slightly improves for queries having 4 or more clauses, possibly due to the scarcity of such complex queries generated from user questions. This trend highlights the importance of robust evaluation metrics as we see divergent trends with EM and LLM as a judge, especially for complex queries showcasing capabilities of frontier models like gemini/gpt to interpret NL questions into executable programs. It also suggests that future benchmarks should include more 3 and 4-primitive questions to better probe system limitations.

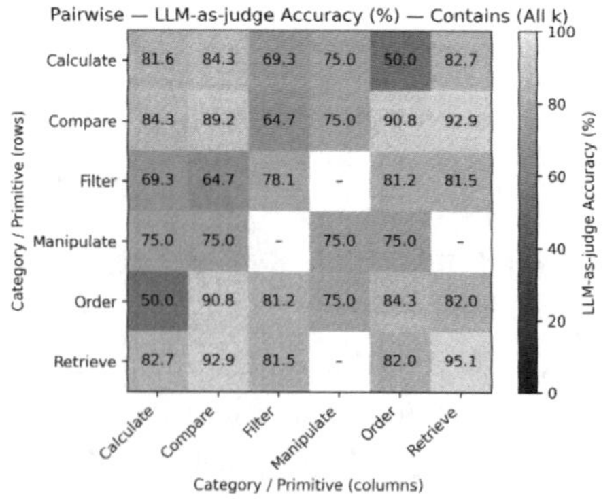

Figure 5: Pairwise Primitive Accuracy with LLM as Judge

Bottleneck Clause Pairs. Figure 5 shows accuracy for all pairs of reasoning primitives. *Retrieve +*

Compare performs well (≥92%), indicating strong compatibility between basic operations. In contrast, any pair involving *Manipulate* or *Calculate* drops sharply, even when combined with otherwise reliable primitives like *Filter*. These patterns align with the decline in Figure 4, where queries involving aggregation or table restructuring introduce significant error.

5 Related Works

Text-to-SQL. Text-to-SQL research has primarily framed the task as cross-domain semantic parsing over static relational schemas. Benchmarks like Spider (Yu et al., 2018b) and its extensions (Li et al., 2023; Zhang et al., 2024; Pourreza and Rafiei, 2023) focus on generalization to unseen databases, yet operate over fixed snapshots with limited domain dynamics. SyntaxSQLNet (Yu et al., 2018a) introduced syntax-tree decoders for nested queries, while recent advances (Zhang et al., 2023; Xie et al., 2024) improve compositional reasoning and execution accuracy.

However, these methods assume immutable schemas, overlook temporal drift in cell values, and sidestep challenges like domain-specific entity resolution (e.g., player aliases) that arise in continuously evolving datasets.

Sports QA. Prior work in sports question answering has largely centered on unstructured text or multiple-choice formats. LiveQA (Liu et al., 2020) explores NBA commentary, using timeline-based MCQs grounded in broadcast text. AskSport (Stoisser et al., 2025) retrieves top-k passages via BM25+RoBERTa, but lacks symbolic execution and numerical guarantees. These systems do not support natural language aggregation (e.g., "average points in last 5 matches") or multi-table joins—capabilities native to SQL.

Our work bridges Text-to-SQL and SportsQA by introducing SPORTSQL, a pipeline tailored to dynamic sports data, and DSQABENCH, the first benchmark pairing natural language queries with executable SQL over temporally indexed, continuously refreshed soccer statistics.

6 Conclusion and Future Work

SPORTSQL demonstrates how natural language interfaces can make complex, evolving sports data accessible to everyday users without technical expertise. The release of DSQABENCH provides a valuable resource for benchmarking and advancing research in dynamic, temporally grounded question answering.

In future work, we plan to (1) support more advanced query types, including comparative and multi-turn analyses across players, teams, and seasons (see Appendix (8)) and (2) generalize the framework to additional structured domains such as finance, healthcare, and other sports like basketball or American soccer. We also plan to perform comprehensive user studies (3) that showcase the effectiveness and applicability of this system for real-time analytics. This work lays the groundwork for scalable, domain-agnostic natural language access to complex, real-world databases.

7 Limitations

While our system performs well on natural language to SQL translation over dynamic sports data, several limitations remain. First, ranked queries using `LIMIT` (e.g., "top 5 goal scorers") may omit tied results due to default lexicographic ordering, yielding incomplete answers. Second, the system supports only English input, limiting accessibility for multilingual users. Third, context length constraints restrict the ability to encode real-time metadata such as recent transfers or lineup changes.

Moreover, the current system is tailored to the English Premier League and does not readily generalize to other sports or leagues without domain-specific adaptation. Expanding to new domains would require schema remapping and possible model fine-tuning. Future work may incorporate multilingual LLMs, retrieval-augmented generation, and adaptive components to improve robustness across languages, domains, and evolving contexts.

References

Nikhil Chandak, Shashwat Goel, Ameya Prabhu, Moritz Hardt, and Jonas Geiping. 2025. Answer matching outperforms multiple choice for language model evaluation. *arXiv preprint arXiv:2507.02856*.

Atharv Kulkarni, Kushagra Dixit, Vivek Srikumar, Dan Roth, and Vivek Gupta. 2025. LLM-symbolic integration for robust temporal tabular reasoning. In *Findings of the Association for Computational Linguistics: ACL 2025*, pages 19914–19940, Vienna, Austria. Association for Computational Linguistics.

Atharv Kulkarni and Vivek Srikumar. 2025. Reinforcing code generation: Improving text-to-sql with execution-based learning. *arXiv preprint arXiv:2506.06093*.

Jinyang Li, Binyuan Hui, Ge Qu, Jiaxi Yang, Binhua Li, Bowen Li, Bailin Wang, Bowen Qin, Ruiying Geng, Nan Huo, and 1 others. 2023. Can llm already serve as a database interface? a big bench for large-scale database grounded text-to-sqls. *Advances in Neural Information Processing Systems*, 36:42330–42357.

Qianying Liu, Sicong Jiang, Yizhong Wang, and Sujian Li. 2020. LiveQA: A question answering dataset over sports live. In *Proceedings of the 19th Chinese National Conference on Computational Linguistics*, pages 1057–1067, Haikou, China. Chinese Information Processing Society of China.

Mohammadreza Pourreza and Davood Rafiei. 2023. Evaluating cross-domain text-to-SQL models and benchmarks. In *Proceedings of the 2023 Conference on Empirical Methods in Natural Language Processing*, pages 1601–1611, Singapore. Association for Computational Linguistics.

Pritika Ramu, Aparna Garimella, and Sambaran Bandyopadhyay. 2024. Is this a bad table? a closer look at the evaluation of table generation from text. In *Proceedings of the 2024 Conference on Empirical Methods in Natural Language Processing*, pages 22206–22216, Miami, Florida, USA. Association for Computational Linguistics.

Josefa Lia Stoisser, Marc Boubnovski Martell, and Julien Fauqueur. 2025. Sparks of tabular reasoning via text2sql reinforcement learning. *arXiv preprint arXiv:2505.00016*.

Yuanzhen Xie, Xinzhou Jin, Tao Xie, Matrixmxlin Matrixmxlin, Liang Chen, Chenyun Yu, Cheng Lei, Chengxiang Zhuo, Bo Hu, and Zang Li. 2024. Decomposition for enhancing attention: Improving LLM-based text-to-SQL through workflow paradigm. In *Findings of the Association for Computational Linguistics: ACL 2024*, pages 10796–10816, Bangkok, Thailand. Association for Computational Linguistics.

Tao Yu, Michihiro Yasunaga, Kai Yang, Rui Zhang, Dongxu Wang, Zifan Li, and Dragomir Radev. 2018a. SyntaxSQLNet: Syntax tree networks for complex and cross-domain text-to-SQL task. In *Proceedings of the 2018 Conference on Empirical Methods in Natural Language Processing*, pages 1653–1663, Brussels, Belgium. Association for Computational Linguistics.

Tao Yu, Rui Zhang, Kai Yang, Michihiro Yasunaga, Dongxu Wang, Zifan Li, James Ma, Irene Li, Qingning Yao, Shanelle Roman, Zilin Zhang, and Dragomir Radev. 2018b. Spider: A large-scale human-labeled dataset for complex and cross-domain semantic parsing and text-to-SQL task. In *Proceedings of the 2018 Conference on Empirical Methods in Natural Language Processing*, pages 3911–3921, Brussels, Belgium. Association for Computational Linguistics.

Bin Zhang, Yuxiao Ye, Guoqing Du, Xiaoru Hu, Zhishuai Li, Sun Yang, Chi Harold Liu, Rui Zhao, Ziyue Li, and Hangyu Mao. 2024. Benchmarking the text-to-sql capability of large language models: A comprehensive evaluation. *arXiv preprint arXiv:2403.02951*.

Hanchong Zhang, Ruisheng Cao, Lu Chen, Hongshen Xu, and Kai Yu. 2023. ACT-SQL: In-context learning for text-to-SQL with automatically-generated chain-of-thought. In *Findings of the Association for Computational Linguistics: EMNLP 2023*, pages 3501–3532, Singapore. Association for Computational Linguistics.

8 Appendix

8.1 Qualitative Examples

Query 1: *Show me the top 10 goal scorers and their goal count.*

Generated SQL 1:

```
SELECT web_name, goals_scored
    FROM players
    ORDER BY goals_scored DESC
    LIMIT 10;
```

Generated Table 1:

web_name	goals_scored
M.Salah	27
Haaland	21
Isak	20
Wood	18
Mbeumo	16
Watkins	14
Wissa	14
Palmer	14
Cunha	14
Mateta	13

Generated Visual 1:

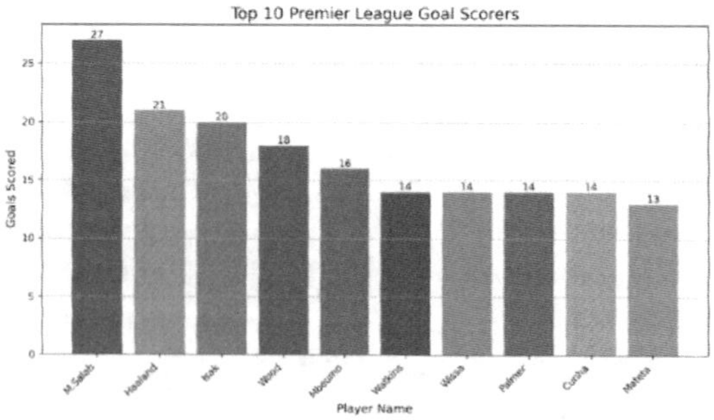

Query 2: *Give me the player history table for James Milner.*

Generated SQL 2:

```
SELECT * FROM player_history;
```

Generated Table 2:

season name	total points	minutes	goals scored	assists	clean sheet
2006/07	114	2675	3	7	0
2007/08	84	2227	2	2	0
2008/09	128	3060	3	9	0
2009/10	184	3172	7	12	0
2010/11	97	2134	1	7	11
2011/12	86	1586	3	5	6
2012/13	96	1724	4	4	11
2013/14	67	1373	1	6	5
2014/15	107	1749	5	8	7
2015/16	123	2409	5	11	8
2016/17	139	3154	7	4	12
2017/18	77	1759	0	3	6
2018/19	101	1778	5	5	9
2019/20	49	924	2	2	4
2020/21	44	1056	0	2	4
2021/22	38	844	0	1	4
2022/23	42	889	0	1	3
2023/24	28	770	0	2	4

Figure 6: Visualization Output Query 1.

Query 3: *Show me the team names, positions, points, and strength in a color scatterplot.*

Generated SQL 3:

```
SELECT team_name, position, points, strength
FROM teams;
```

Generated Table 3:

team_name	position	points	strength
Liverpool	1	76	5
Arsenal	2	63	4
Nott'm Forest	3	57	4
Newcastle	4	56	4
Man City	5	55	4
Chelsea	6	54	4
Aston Villa	7	54	3
Bournemouth	8	48	4
Fulham	9	48	3
Brighton	10	48	3
Brentford	11	43	3
Crystal Palace	12	43	3
Everton	13	38	3
Man Utd	14	38	3
Spurs	15	37	3
Wolves	16	35	3
West Ham	17	35	3
Ipswich	18	21	3
Leicester	19	18	3
Southampton	20	10	2

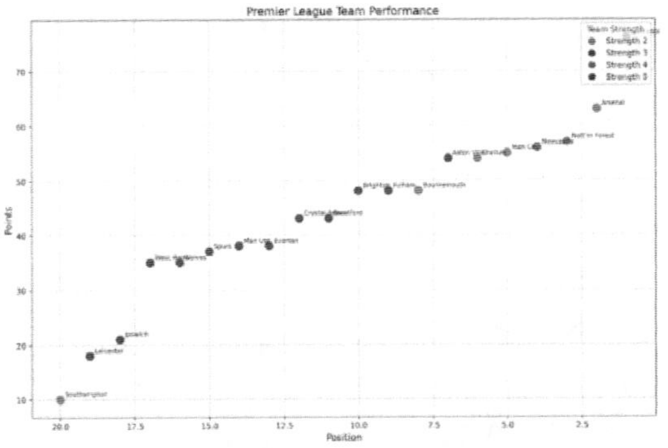

Figure 7: Visualization Output Query 3.

8.2 Deep-Analysis Mode: Multi-Step Reasoning Architecture

To address the limitations of single-shot natural language to SQL translation for complex analytical queries, we introduce a deep-analysis mode that implements a hierarchical decomposition strategy. This mode is specifically designed to handle subjective user questions requiring comprehensive insights that span multiple data dimensions, temporal ranges, and comparative analyses.

- **Stage 1: Entity Extraction and Resolution** The system first extracts entities using the same workflow as described in section 2.1.
- **Stage 2: Hierarchical Query Decomposition** After entity extraction, the system uses a planning module to break the query into focused sub-questions. The system analyzes the query's intent (player insight, team comparison, multi-season analysis) and generates 3-10 prioritized sub-questions that address the user's needs. Each sub-question targets a specific data retrieval requirement, with table hints and priority rankings to guide execution.
- **Stage 3: Parallel SQL Compilation and Execution** Each sub-question is compiled into SQL using a prompt-based translation mechanism, with added context for overall intent. Queries are executed in parallel where possible, and the results are aggregated into a comprehensive response, preserving the semantic relationships across dimensions.

We further plan to extend this feature by adding an insight generation module, extending the utility of this work to support real-time sports analytics at scale. To use this feature, toggle to deep analytics on the platform.

Author Index